D0952997

FOREWORD BY JAMES P. GORMAN, PRESIDENT, GLOBAL PRIVATE CLIENT, MERRILL LYNCH

THE WINNER'S CIRCLE® IV

WEALTH MANAGEMENT INSIGHTS FROM AMERICA'S BEST FINANCIAL ADVISORS

R.J. SHOOK

WITH AN INTRODUCTION BY PETER D. JONES, PRESIDENT, FRANKLIN TEMPLETON DISTRIBUTORS, INC.

This publication is designed to provide accurate and authoritative information in regard to the subject matter covered. It is sold with the understanding that neither the publisher nor the author is engaged in rendering legal, accounting, or other professional services. If legal advice or other expert assistance is required, the services of a competent professional person should be sought.

From a Declaration of Principles
Jointly Adopted by
a Committee of the American Bar Association
and a Committee of Publishers and Associations

ISBN 0-9721622-1-6

Published by

HORIZON
Horizon Publishers Group
Printed in the United States

10 9 8 7 6 5 4 3 2 1

To my beautiful Elisabeth

Contents

LIST OF TABLES

ACKNOWLEDGMENTS

HUNDREDS OF PEOPLE CONTRIBUTED TO THE CREATION OF *The Winner's Circle,* and I appreciate all their hard work, dedication, and passion for our mission of promoting best practices in the industry and the value of advice to investors. The *Winner's Circle* simply wouldn't exist without the tremendous support from the entire industry, ranging from the industry leaders who serve on my advisory board and home office support, to the *Winner's Circle* financial advisors who are dedicated to giving back to our industry.

To remain completely independent and objective, The Winner's Circle Organization and Shookbook, LLC do not accept money from financial advisors or their firms for our research and rankings. Instead, we rely on book royalties and support from the one firm that is deeply committed and dedicated to our missions of promoting best practices in the industry and the value of advice to investors. That firm is Franklin Templeton. The list of professionals at Franklin Templeton who have been supportive are—unfortunately—too long to list in this section. But I do want to recognize the firm's leadership, which has created an impressive culture of professionalism and integrity: Dan O'Lear, Bob Geppner, Phil Edelstein, Kent Strazza, John Greer. Of course I extend a special thank you to Peter Jones for writing an introduction to my book—and for our friendship. Peter stands out as a true leader in the world of asset management as one who truly cares about supporting the industry and investors in providing the highest standards possible with high moral code.

I would like to express how honored I am that James Gorman wrote my foreword. Wall Street and investors around the world have benefited greatly from his innovations and foresight. His vision, leadership, and high ethical code will continue to mold our industry far into the future. I am also appreciative of our friendship, which has developed as a result of our both sharing deep passions for our industry.

Special gratitude is also due to all members of The Winner's Circle Organization—including the Women's Winner's Circle advisor and the *Winner's Circle* Top 100—all of whom I have come to admire and respect. I deeply value the friendships that have developed along the way. These financial advisors need not seek publicity. Their dedication to clients keep them busy enough. However, two great characteristics of *Winner's Circle* advisors is that they are passionate about the industry and serving their clients, and they are dedicated to giving back to the industry to help raise standards.

Augie Cenname of Merrill Lynch (profiled in *The Winner's Circle III, Horizon Publishers Group, 2002*) once posed it this way: "Why not do something positive for the industry, and share our knowledge? It's our way of helping to promote best practices."

Along those lines, Joe Montgomery at Wachovia Securities said, "It's important to give back to the industry."

Other industry professionals have contributed countless hours to the *Winner's Circle:* Andrea Slattery, Erica Platt, Robin Ritenour, Ronice Barlow, Russell Sherman, Hilary (Roberts) Desrosiers, Dan Rhyasen, Alexandra Weber, Amie Tyler, Julie Conway, Jeff Edgar, Jan (Young) Marshall, Darla Lonergan, Todd Stewart, Dan Grip, Jim Escobedo, John McGee, Philip Bensen, Dan Reinhold, Joe Epstein, Margie Blue, Jim Clauss, Carol Wright, Joan Youngwirth, Armand Mastantuono, Heather Abbott, Laura Lange, Kandis Bates, Erik Hendrickson, Terez Hanhan, Bob Peters, Debra Herndon, Janet Matthews, Branden Happel, Tom Howe, Karen Morstad, Deb Hansen, Peter Casey, Katrina Clay, Kimberly Atwater, Susan Thompson, Tony Mattera, Brad Zucker, Bob Reyen, Brad Hanson, Tom Wright, Michael Wasz, Per Furmark, Craig Maxwell, Debra B. Fisherman, Eric Daley, Kevin Carevic, David Gullison, Barry Dyche, Dan Almuti, Mike Anders, Ray Bertrand, Bill Bishop, Jay Caruso, Adrian Jackson, Chris Jenkins, Angie Walsh Bradshaw, Phillip Haning, Darren Doughty, Joe McLean, Judy Spanos, John Tagliaferri, Roger Michaud, Chuck D'Amico, Bernie Buckley, Eric Momsen, John Laudadio, Joe Clancy, Andy Cyr, Gary LoDuca, Philip Loftus, Michael Mahoney, Susan Tallarico, Matt Cost, Sean Cullinane, Tom Peterson, Jeff Robinson, Robert Gauthier, Sherman Goodrich, John Nesnay, Dan Peterson, John Somers, Diane Tallarico, Richard Wriedt, Ken Jones, John Kelly, Bill Kerns, Jeffery Rose, Shane Davis, Brian Brenneman, Kevin Russell, Dennis Shannon, Paul Silva, Damian Eckstein, Chris Marek, Kristian Kjolberg, Allen Kuhn, David Lachina, John Martin, Dave McLaughlin, Sri Vemuri, Bob Whiting, Bobby Wilmath, Christopher Quinson, Rob Richardson, Mark Meyer, Darren Kinney, Scott Rogers, Alan Simeon, Tom Temeyer, Robert Thompson, Ian Valentine, Jennifer (Keltner) Nelson, Peter Black, Dan Bone. And a special thank you to Jim Wiggins for his endless wisdom and advice.

Like the advisors in this book, I rely on a world-class team to help with the editorial, writing, and administration. This includes Rebecca McReynolds, Ellen Uzelac, Debbie Watts, Ellen Coleman, Ruth Mills, Debra Thompson, Dom Del Prete, Eric Johnston. Thank you to my photographer Kenneth Applebaum for my cover photo and Brian Boucher for cover design. And, importantly, my world-class agent Al Zuckerman and the team of professionals at Horizon Publishers Group.

FOREWORD

By James P. Gorman
President, Global Private Client
Merrill Lynch & Co., Inc.

TODAY'S NEWLY REDISCOVERED RESPECT FOR THE VALUE OF A GOOD financial advisor is a direct result of the dot.com market bubble, which destroyed, if temporarily, $8 trillion in equity market capitalization and proved that do-it-yourself investing could indeed be hazardous to your financial health.

That this was the outcome of the "roaring 1990s" is all too clear with the gift of hindsight. That America's capital markets are history's greatest engines of broad-based wealth creation is beyond debate. Yet as effective as they have been over a long period, the financial markets can be both irrational and destructive at any single point in time.

The stock market, as great as it is, is driven by "animal spirits." Symbolized by the bull and the bear, these spirits run to extremes in eternal, cyclical conflict. On the individual level, two of the most powerful emotions, greed and fear, drive the market to unprecedented highs and, inevitably, to unthinkable lows. The cycle then begins anew.

At its core, this is a book about excellence and passion: excellence in mastering the extraordinarily complex art and science of wealth management, and passion in delivering this expertise for the greater good of each individual client.

While each of the financial advisors in this book may differ in his or her particular style or approach, they each follow a wealth management process that can be both replicated and customized to the unique needs of every client. Some might still call them "stockbrokers," but this description is archaic and inadequate. Yes, they know stocks and the critical role equities play in any comprehensive wealth management plan. But their expertise extends far beyond that to all asset classes and to the liability side of the balance sheet. Managing such things as borrowing, cash flow, and business financing is also within the new scope of duty. Tax management, generational wealth transfer, and philanthropic considerations also come into play. Indeed, for clients with the most complex needs, today's financial advisor is the equivalent of a personal CFO.

Many of the professionals you will read about in these pages function as leaders of teams. The industry is still well-served by some highly effective single practitioners, but, given the growing complexity of the activities they are engaged in, they are increasingly exceptions to the rule. Professional practices in law, medicine, and architecture have long recognized that they are strongest when organized as teams since no single individual can possibly master all the specialized knowledge of the profession.

The body of specialized knowledge in personal financial management is expanding constantly. This is why the advisors of *The Winners' Circle* exhibit a passion for self-improvement through continuing education. Many have sought and achieved advanced professional certifications. And many of the firms they work for are making this kind of professional development a core requirement.

The financial services industry has suffered a number of challenges to its reputation in recent years. The bad acts of a few have obscured the professionalism and dedication of the many. This book helps to reestablish a balance. It highlights people who raise the standards of their profession and who always place their clients' interests first. People who help make dreams come true by protecting those dreams from the intense emotions that drive the financial markets. I find their stories incredibly inspiring.

ABOUT JAMES P. GORMAN

James P. Gorman is executive vice president of Merrill Lynch & Co., Inc. and president of the company's Global Private Client group, which provides investment, insurance, banking, and retirement services for individuals and businesses. The largest business of its kind in the world, in 2003 it generated $8.9 billion in revenue and $1.6 billion in pretax profits, overseeing more than $1.2 trillion in client assets.

Mr. Gorman has been instrumental in creating and implementing a strategy that is revolutionizing wealth management. Key elements of the strategy include client segmentation through a multichanneled service delivery system, revenue diversification, and use of technology to ensure a consistent, high-quality experience for each client.

Before joining Merrill Lynch, Mr. Gorman served as a senior partner of McKinsey & Company, where he was a member of the financial services practice. During his career at McKinsey, he had a long working relationship with Merrill Lynch.

Mr. Gorman is a passionate advocate of fair and open financial markets and high professional standards within the industry. He serves as a director of the Securities Industry Association, the industry's leading trade association, and chair's the board's Public Trust and Confidence Committee. A native of Melbourne, Australia, he now resides in New York City.

INTRODUCTION

By Peter D. Jones
President
Franklin Templeton Distributors, Inc.

YOU'RE ABOUT TO READ SOME OF THE MOST MOTIVATING STORIES you'll ever find concerning the financial services industry. Why? Because they're all true. R.J. Shook has created a niche with his *Winner's Circle* series by interviewing the best of the best in our profession and sharing their best practices. This is his latest collection of these advisors' personalized approaches to identifying, prospecting for, then providing the highest forms of advice and service. In addition, he shares how these advisors are able to accomplish these approaches with the highest levels of professionalism and integrity.

These aren't your garden-variety "how-to" articles. They're compilations of no-holds-barred stories about advisors who have learned through trial and error how to be effective in their careers. While it may appear on the surface that a *Winner's Circle* advisor may have had it easy, these advisors are the first to admit they've made numerous mistakes while seeking excellence.

If you're a financial advisor, I encourage you to examine these paths to greatness, while avoiding the pitfalls and tribulations that have already been encountered.

If you're an investor, I encourage you to measure your advisor against the best practices of these advisors to ensure you're truly in caring hands.

If you're a do-it-yourselfer simply looking to build your own financial strategy, I highly encourage you to learn from these masters, but not without a word of caution: These advisors have masterfully built their expertise over the course of decades. It is my opinion that some aspects of our health, whether personal or financial, are best left in the hands of capable and trusted professionals.

To an industry professional or casual reader, these are great human interest stories. It's always fascinating to read about success stories like the ones profiled in this book because nothing was given to them on a silver platter. You're going to notice patterns among these *Winner's Circle* advisors because successful people tend to share many of the same characteristics. But since no two of us are alike, each story is unique.

For industry professionals, I encourage you to pick and choose from these advisors those ideas that are right for you and your practice.

As a financial advisor, you are a special breed of professional. I remember an investment forum we hosted during my early days with the Templeton organization, when Sir John Templeton told a group of advisors, "You are missionaries in the ministry of prosperity." While Sir John hasn't been affiliated with Franklin Templeton since his retirement and full-time devotion to the community, the mutual funds that bear his name still follow the philosophy and tenets he established more than 50 years ago.

Franklin Templeton Investments holds the entire financial advisor community in that same high regard. We are proud to be associated with all professionals, not just the *Winner's Circle* advisors, who are dedicated to helping people learn and practice the habit of thrift.

On behalf of the entire industry, I'd like to offer appreciation to all *Winner's Circle* advisors who are dedicated to sharing best practices to help better serve all investors. Next, to R.J. for his diligence and independence when seeking exceptional advisors throughout the country to compose the *Winner's Circle* lists. And finally, to all financial advisors who have made the commitment to be better at your business tomorrow than you are today.

Now, let R.J. introduce you to these exceptional *Winner's Circle* advisors. By incorporating their techniques into your own practice, you too can be a missionary in the ministry of prosperity.

Then everyone will be a winner.

Peter D. Jones
President
Franklin Templeton Distributors, Inc.

PREFACE

My Own Story

In the 1980s when I started in the business with a major wirehouse, I was on my own. Located in a small branch office, I had to figure it out on my own. My father once told me that, if you want to be the best, you have to learn from the best. I started calling top brokers at the firm and asked them questions about how they were able to develop their businesses and build relationships. They would give me a token amount of time, then get back to their own work. That's when I became determined to learn best practices from the best in the business—and I wanted to spend hours, not minutes, learning from the best.

Then one day it dawned on me to write a book. I figured there must be scores of other advisors who shared my desire to learn from the best. I called senior leadership at the major securities firms and asked them who they wanted to represent their firms in my book, based on my quantitative and qualitative criteria that would one day become the basis of all the *Winner's Circle* lists that I compose. These industry leaders were supportive of my quest and provided nominations. Then I determined, based on my criteria, which advisors would best represent the entire industry in my book. I then spent an entire day with each advisor, learning best practices. That's when the first of many *Winner's Circle* books was published.

More than a decade and three *Winner's Circle* books later, these same industry leaders encouraged me to build the circle into a formal organization of outstanding advisors from all firms to promote the missions of best practices and the highest code of ethics, integrity, and professionalism in the industry—and the value of advice to investors. I remember Jim Brinkley, now Chairman of Legg Mason Wood Walker, telling me, "R.J., we have the opportunity to do something wonderful for our industry." These industry leaders became some of my 16 advisory board members. They help to formulate the criteria and are open to discussing a myriad of issues as they surface. Additionally, all firms that are represented on our lists fully stand behind each of their advisors, with written and verbal recommendations from the highest ranks in their firms.

This is the beginning of the qualitative process, which starts with a survey of about 100 firms that employ advisors compensated by fees and/or commissions and have access to an open platform (i.e., advisors can objectively offer their clients nonproprietary products, like mutual funds from providers outside the securities firm). Each advisor is vetted through his or her firm's compliance area, then by my team, where we scour each advisor's U4 record, which collects all complaints, whether justifiable or falsely created. When an advisor has a complaint on his or her U4, I have researched the incident and, with a letter from senior management, determined the complaint was either unjustified or not due to the advisor (e.g., complaints can be logged against an advisor's assistant that hasn't been with the team in a decade, but still appears on the record). Also, in some instances a client complaint might be justified but not the fault of the advisor (for example, in the late 1980s, many firms were recommending that advisors' clients invest in limited partnerships, only to see many of these investments implode).

More qualitative checks include customer satisfaction reports, a minimum length of service of seven years, discussions with varying levels of management and peers and even with clients. Because a successful advisor has the numbers to prove it, we consider revenue and total (custodied and noncustodied) assets. A qualitative element is placed on assets (e.g., a lesser weighting is assigned toward institutional assets). The most rigorous diligence involves telephone interviews with each candidate and a half- to full-day interview session with the advisors.

The result is a list of America's finest wealth advisors who are setting new standards for all financial professionals. As I like to say to these individuals, "Congratulations for second place!" (Their clients always come first.)

WHY READ THIS BOOK?

Wealth management is a burgeoning field that is rapidly evolving. One thing is for sure: There is no one right approach. Just as there are many types of investors—ranging from a multitude of demographics to complex situations—there are myriad approaches. Who's to say which approach is correct? The answer lies in each investor's ability to reach his or her needs, goals, objectives, and dreams.

The Winner's Circle is designed to document the best practices of the industry's most outstanding wealth advisors. They all have developed their own techniques that they have fine-tuned for their clients. Because these advisors tend to focus on the "right" clients—that is, the investors to whom their practice caters—they have developed their team of specialists, systems, and investment strategies to tailor to their particular client types.

From this book, industry professionals will gain valuable insight into the most successful wealth management teams in the industry. For these professionals, I recommend picking and choosing the techniques that are right for you and your practice. You'll also benefit from learning best practices from the best in the business, from prospecting different demographics and building a referral system among a clientele to building a world-class team and offering superior advice and service.

Investors have the opportunity to learn wealth management techniques that are typically reserved for elite investors. If you are working with a wealth advisor, compare the levels of advice and service the team is providing you with these outstanding advisors, and obtain valuable ideas that you can share with the team that is serving you.

Each of the wealth advisors in this book is a dedicated professional who is well qualified to serve as a role model to others in the investment field. I hope that many existing and future advisors will pattern themselves after one or more of the people profiled in this book. If so, my writing will have made a valuable contribution to the investment community around the world.

CHAPTER 1: JOHN F. ERDMANN III (JEFF)

Family Man

Merrill Lynch & Co, Inc.
Greenwich, Connecticut

Photo by: Christopher Semmes,
Greenwich, Connecticut

THERE'S ONE PHRASE THAT BEST DESCRIBES JEFF ERDMANN: family man.

On the night of our interview, Jeff took his wife Barbara and two sons to a baseball game; the next morning they were working at a homeless shelter. Even his professional team is part of his family: "We care about each other," Jeff says. "If someone on the team has a problem, whether personal, financial, or whatever, I am always there for them." Each team member shares ownership of the practice and everyone is treated as an equal. "We've developed a culture that is based on trust and respect, whether it's for each other or our clients. Between our team and clients, we're really one big family."

His family includes 100 wealthy families, entrusting him with over $2 billion in assets as of this writing. As his family of clients grows and evolves, Jeff and team are relentlessly seeking ways to offer them more value and a higher level of service. "We're constantly asking ourselves, how can we provide more value for our families," Jeff insists.

Jeff has always planned his business around his rule: "Always invest in changes and in your beliefs." This philosophy has resulted in a world-class infrastructure that provides extraordinary advice and service for each part of the family.

When Jeff first joined Merrill in 1985, he knew he had to invest significant time, always the first to arrive in the office and the last to leave. He also had to invest money in his business and build a team to properly service his clients. "My first investment was an intern, which was a really big deal to me because it meant sacrificing a good portion of my compensation," he recalls. "But I needed to spend more time with my clients to build a business, and less time doing administrative work," he says of his long hours split between servicing his clients, cold calling, and giving seminars.

When Jeff got married, he told his wife, "We're not going to be able to do what we wanted in the housing market this year because I need to hire some administrative help, and it's going to require a percentage of my income to do that." Jeff says his wife's support during these trying times was critical to his success. Looking back, he says, "I paid a very high price to get the business to the service model that I wanted. In hindsight I made the right decisions and was able to raise my service model to higher levels."

From the beginning of his career, Jeff always posed the question: "How can I add more value for my clients?" This has required Jeff to constantly enhance his business to better anticipate his clients' changing needs. In fact, every year he updates his business plan. "If you look at any successful model, the model is always changing; nothing is right for everyone all the time."

While the model may be tweaked every year, certain constants never change. For example, Jeff firmly believes that his business can't revolve around elements he can't control. "You see so many people in our business whose model revolves around a specific investing strategy or market; I never thought I was smart enough to figure out how to make that work consistently. Instead, we focus on the elements we can control, such as balancing the portfolios, servicing the clients, and maintaining a high level of integrity. All the elements that are first and foremost to a relationship." He adds that he has never lost a client (his client-loss ratio is miniscule) because he underperformed the markets, and he has never relied on winning clients solely because of past investment performance. "We'll never be off the charts for clients, so they won't say, 'Hey, you should hire Erdmann, he was up sixty percent last year.' It isn't going to happen. I call myself a wimp when it comes to taking risks, but I think most people appreciate that. Essentially, we don't lose clients because we'll never make big bets with their money. Our clients don't hire us to make them rich. Typically they have created wealth through risks they have already taken in their careers. It is our job to manage that wealth responsibly and creatively and make sure that it grows consistently."

In the mid-1990s Jeff made his greatest investment to date. To build a team of specialists that will provide the ultimate infrastructure for serving his wealthy families. His objective was to compartmentalize roles, where specific tasks are assigned to specialists, with distinct processes that cover all elements of the service model. He also believed that each individual on the team must feel and act like an owner, sharing pain with clients and enjoying the benefits of the upside. "We're all equals, a real family environment. The team approach is essential in order to give a family the type of coverage they deserve." According to Jeff, having the right infrastructure is critical to this family approach. "The best teams that I've seen in the industry are run by people that really care about people. You can't be selfish and be successful in this business. You have to surround yourself with people that care like you do."

"While there is no single perfect model, for me a vertical team makes the most sense; every team must adopt the right model that's best for their clients. I've found that in order to cover a hundred very wealthy families, I need to have pure partners on my team who care in what I do."

Though each individual shares ownership of the practice, Jeff is the lead financial advisor for most of the relationships and works personally with each family. Rob Giannetti and Mario Forlini are also primary advisors on many of the relationships and like with all the families, they work together on each account. After the initial meeting, Jeff leaves the team to spend three weeks putting the financial plan together and reviewing it with appropriate advisors, from estate attorneys to CPAs.

Another integral partner, Susan Christy, is head of administration for the business and is directly responsible for 30 families. Jeff describes Susan's role as "hands-down the most important component on the team." He tells the story of a $30 million referral the team received from a client. After the prospect became a client, the referring client told Jeff: "Susan gets the credit because she has done such an amazing job managing our family. When it comes bonus time make sure she is taken care of." Jeff mentions that while she did get the credit, like all new business everyone shares in team successes. In addition to the team's trader, they use a mortgage and technology specialist to ensure efficient communications between the team and the families. He spends time in family's homes setting up their computers, connecting them to Merrill's online resources, and resolves technology issues on the telephone and through e-mail." Ken Doyle is at each client's beck and call to make sure they're linked into us electronically and to solve any transaction- or technology-related concern. We have probably had five to ten referrals over the last couple of years where the first thing they say is: 'Is it really true you have someone come out to our house and help us with our computer? And link into Merrill's bill payment system?' Our clients love it." Several months ago a referral called Jeff. His opening line was, "Come on, will you really do that?" After Jeff met with him and presented the team's model and investment philosophy, the prospect hired the Erdmann Group and transferred a $15 million account to Merrill.

"In addition to Susan and Ken, the team is complemented by two terrific administrative team members who help cater to our clients' needs," Jeff continues. "Carey Wunsch, who is also pursuing her MBA, and Margaret Denver, who has fifteen years of experience working with wealthy families, also work closely with Susan and Ken to provide the best possible service."

Jeff firmly believes in working side by side with clients in selecting money managers and never wants to be fired by a client for an element out of his control, such as poor stock selection. Jeff correctly anticipated that, though he is the advisor, his clients wanted to have some say in a portion of their investments. In 2000 Jeff hired an equity portfolio manager, Rob Giannetti, formerly of Bank of New York. "Rob runs a core equity portfolio of twenty companies that currently yield about three percent, and in this market, it's very comforting for us to hold great, solid companies that we feel comfortable owning over the next decade that are generating cash dividends of three to four times money market rates. This is a nice complement to a passive index fund or even a very aggressive money manager." Jeff feels his clients are more at ease knowing that there are portfolio managers with long-term proven track records overseeing their entire portfolios, customizing portfolios for their own needs, and always available for a discussion.

"We guessed correctly that many wealthy families wanted to be directly involved with at least a portion of their investments," Jeff says. "Additionally, we can offer these investment services at lower fees than traditional money managers, while complementing the managers' work. This was a big investment on our part to recruit Rob and it has clearly paid off for us."

In the spirit of change and trying to develop their team, in the spring of 2004 Jeff recruited a new team member with very specific duties. Mark Brookfield is coordinator of business development and also acts as a fixed-income specialist and investment assistant to Jeff and Rob. Because of the inflow of referrals to their practice, Jeff felt it necessary to have a dedicated person ready to manage new business.

"During an ongoing analysis of our practice, we found that over seventy percent of our top clients came from referrals, and our consultants suggested that our next team enhancement should be to create an advisory board to the Erdmann Group." The advisory board consists of ten clients, five outside lawyers and accountants and two very senior executives at Merrill Lynch. "We ask our board to take a half hour twice per year to look under the hood of our business and tell us what we can improve and make better. We also ask our board members to think of people like themselves with similar financial needs who may need our services. This is a new endeavor for us and our board has been very helpful and supportive of our team."

To provide truly exceptional service, Jeff partners with Merrill financial advisors who are located geographically close to the families. Jeff seeks partners and shares the revenue with the financial advisor in exchange for a local presence near one of Jeff's clients. Additionally, many Merrill financial advisors who don't have the infrastructure to provide highly specialized services for wealthy families approach Jeff as a prospective partner. "Situational teaming is a real win for the client—they benefit from a local presence and a team that caters specifically to their unique needs," Jeff says. "And the financial advisor doesn't have to start from scratch to build a team to support a particular client." Recently, Jeff asked a financial advisor in Dallas to partner with him for two clients for whom Jeff felt a local presence was necessary.

The night prior to our second interview in Greenwich, Jeff received a call from a Merrill advisor in Darien, Connecticut. The advisor, Dan Anderson, arranged a meeting with a $5.5 million prospect. The prospective couple was already in the second round of interviewing potential advisors. Jeff and Dan met with the couple for an hour. "We were able to give the couple a wonderful situation where they would work closely with the Darien advisor they have known for years while realizing the maximum benefit from my team, which specializes in their unique needs," Jeff says. Administratively, the account resides in the Darien office, and that advisor oversees it. Jeff's fixed-income manager makes recommendations and manages the portfolio with the advisor. "With all of our teaming, we work side by side as partners for life." Jeff has joined with over 25 such financial advisors throughout the country. "It's rare that I've ever approached a prospective client with a potential partner and we didn't get hired. The fact is wealthy clients appreciate that a special team has been formed to address their complex situation. Merrill financial advisors from many parts of the country come to us with prospective clients in their geographic area and take comfort in telling the prospect that the firm is committed to providing them with the best resources both locally and globally."

In this situation, the couple was impressed with Jeff's in-house fixed-income portfolio. At the end of the meeting, the man said, "This is exactly what we are looking for." The wife agreed, but said, "We're supposed to have a second meeting with another advisor at one o'clock." The couple looked at each other, then said almost simultaneously, "We've made up our minds. We want to go with you."

Jeff's team makes a point to meet each family, whether it's their sole client or the result of a partnership. These meetings can occur quarterly, semiannually, or even more frequently, depending on each client's preferences. Each family is assigned an assistant who is responsible for related administrative work. "Every year we're trying to build and mold a team that revolves around how we can provide the best value for the client. This is all a part of growing with our families."

Jeff has grown with his clients at least as much as he has helped them grow. He earned his first client as a result of a cold call in the early 1980s. It was his third month in the business, and he was hired to handle the client's $2,500 IRA rollover. Over the years, as the relationship developed, the client built a thriving distribution business, just as Jeff's business had evolved to provide specialized services for wealthy families. In 1998 Jeff took the client out for lunch to celebrate his fiftieth birthday. During lunch, Jeff asked the client if he'd ever consider selling the business. The client replied, "Funny you should ask me. Two Wall Street firms have visited me and valued my company at thirty million dollars." Jeff was shocked to learn that the client hadn't immediately thought of him for advice, because he always considered the relationship close. "My accountant set up the meetings," the client admitted, then looked Jeff in the eyes: "Is Merrill in that business?"

"Of course we are," Jeff replied. "We have great experience and a track record for selling private companies." Jeff then arranged a meeting with two Merrill bankers. The meeting was held on January 1999. Five months later Merrill sold the company for about $100 million. "Never in his wildest dreams did he realize he would receive a valuation of that magnitude," Jeff says with pride.

With the team in place, a comprehensive plan was proposed for the newly minted centimillionaire and implemented over time. Multiple trusts were established for his children. Half the money was placed in a managed tax-free portfolio of bonds. Several equity managers and hedge fund managers were engaged for the portfolio, and the assets were properly allocated. Additionally, Jeff helped the client put together some real estate ventures, and provided advice when the client bought a private jet and yacht. "He is a great client, but, importantly, he is a dear friend," Jeff says sincerely. "He lives out of state but has visited my family. I've been to all his family's events, from birthdays to bar mitzvahs and we enjoy fishing and traveling together. In addition to having a lifelong friend, it is rewarding because we've helped him in so many ways. This was all the result of a simple cold call I made twenty years ago from a Dunn & Bradstreet lead."

When discussing his wealth advisory process, Jeff recalls a mistake he made early in his career. "When I started in the business I made the process more complex than it needed to be, from explaining solutions to wanting to show how knowledgeable I was.

Secondly, I thought it was my job to make our clients rich," Jeff says. "It didn't take me long to figure out that it's our job to help them grow their wealth at a responsible rate. For clients who have already created their wealth, it's our job to help them maintain it. Most of all, wealthy people are interested in simplifying their lives, preserving what they have, and they're definitely not coming to us to lose it for them."

"I have a very simple process, which evolves around what's in the best interests of the client, and how to create value for them," Jeff explains. "My processes are the same for everyone." Jeff's four-step methodology to providing an extraordinary experience for clients begins with financial planning.

The financial planning process starts during the first meeting with a prospect. Jeff asks a lot of open-ended questions at the outset of the meeting to fully understand the potential client and to ensure that he is the right advisor for the prospect's needs. Jeff always lets the prospect or client do most of the talking. "Give them time to discuss what's on their mind," Jeff says, "whether it's about their job, bad experiences with previous advisors, their families, or their interests. Whatever the subject, it's my opportunity to learn more about them and how I can improve and enhance their specific planning and investment situation. Also, it gives them a chance to open up." When it's Jeff's turn to discuss business, he'll often begin with his elevator pitch: "Let me take thirty seconds to tell you what we do. I run a unique team within the Merrill Lynch Private Banking and Investment Group. We work with a select group of corporate executives and wealthy families, helping them plan and manage all aspects of their finances and investments. This includes everything from our clients' bill payment system, their mortgage, liabilities, investment managers, and their sophisticated financial plans." Then he'll add, "'Tell me exactly how your relationships with your current advisors are going now.' I always like to learn what may be wrong with their current relationship, and what they're looking for in a new one. Then I ask them questions to profile and understand what the family's needs are. For instance, the first thing a wealthy family wants to know is 'Can I maintain my lifestyle?' or 'Can I enhance my lifestyle?' I ask open-ended questions to let them talk." He emphasizes that, no matter the client, it is crucial to be a thoroughly good listener. "I take in all the information. Too many financial advisors spend way too much time talking about themselves, their processes. Then they miss out on the clients' needs, and the opportunity to build a relationship."

Jeff then takes them through six or seven scenarios "so we can answer those two words every client asks: 'What if?' 'What if I retire tomorrow?' 'What if I sell my company?' 'What if I gift eleven thousand dollars a year to each of my grandchildren, how will my retirement lifestyle be impacted?' 'What if I set up a charitable remainder trust, put my stock into it, and deplete my net worth by three million dollars. How does that affect me?' "

"We proceed through those scenarios, then run a cash flow analysis using a Monte Carlo simulation (an analytic technique that approximates the probability for solving a problem by generating a considerable number of simulations, or trial runs). Then we can say to a client, 'Here's how it will affect you. You can live on *X* amount per month until you're one hundred and ten years old under the following scenario. Or you can live on *Y* amount until you're seventy-two under this scenario.' We like to do this up front so we can set realistic expectations for the client."

"The growth rates and depletion rates I use are conservative. I'll tell them: 'Our goal is for you never to draw more than four percent of your portfolio as a living expense. We'll plan more than four percent on your investments, but history has shown us, as well as other pension consultants, that a balanced portfolio under our scenarios will carry you through extended bear markets without eating away at your portfolio for a prolonged period of time.'

"What shocks us is when we get new clients and look at the plans their previous advisors have created with analyses of eight percent or even twelve percent withdrawal rates. You run those numbers over fifteen or fifty years, and it looks imprudent at best! So we really try to underpromise the performance using Merrill's standard cash flow analysis, and I leverage Merrill's family office department to run the scenarios for us.'"

"Since so many of our clients are senior-level executives or founders of companies, they tend to have low basis stock, and typically have worked at the company for a long time," Jeff explains. "So we spend a lot of time on the planning side to determine how to best handle concentrated stock positions. We produce innovative strategies to create diversification for these positions in a tax-efficient manner. This can include collars, prepaid forwards, charitable remainder trusts, forward sales, and other strategies that allow them to hedge their positions and diversify the positions for the greatest tax advantage. While we've been very disciplined in offering these solutions, too many people learned the hard way in the 1980s and 1990s that you shouldn't have all your eggs in one basket. No matter how strong the company is, there must be diversification. One reason our business is up so much is because of the referrals, many from executives who hedged reluctantly during the market peak, and now show their appreciation with referrals."

"Once we work as a team to develop a financial plan we believe in, we'll recommend and implement everything from private banking and portfolio management, to liability management, estate planning and wealth transfer," Jeff says. "One of the biggest problems our clients have is how do they convey the philosophies of wealth to their children? Not only with regard to how they transfer it, but also how they should teach their children to respect wealth and handle it appropriately. We set up a lot of family foundations and charitable trusts, and one suggestion we make is to make the beneficiary of the family trust their family foundation. This can give their family many generations of philanthropic involvement. This happens to be one of my more fun and satisfying aspects of the job: working with clients on that level, not just the parents, but building relationships with the children and grandchildren. This is how our relationships grow."

"Importantly, I make the financial planning process simple," Jeff says. "Too many people in this business overcomplicate this process. While I don't want to oversimplify it, it is important that the client or prospect fully comprehend what I'm talking about. After all, how else would you know if you're moving in the right direction?"

"With the financial plan created, we meet to describe the course of action in simple terms, and make sure they're on board with the decisions. Once approved, we immediately get involved with their advisors, attorneys, accountants, trustees, and other family advisors. We play the active role of managing the whole process, which could take several months or even years to fully implement. Over the last four or five years we'd give a client their equity level of fifty-five or sixty percent, but in very few cases have we gotten to that level because of a very conservative approach to putting money to work in the equity markets. We choose alternative investments as additional choices to some of our long-term equity."

When advising a client on the right course of action, Jeff stresses simplicity. "The wealthiest and most successful people are decision makers," he begins. "They're used to hiring decision makers. I don't recall ever meeting with the chairman or CEO of a company and seeing paperwork or files on their desks. That's because there are a tremendous number of smart people behind the executive; these executives are decision makers, they want expert opinion from people they can trust and rely on. They count on us to sort through the details for them."

"Could you imagine going to a heart surgeon because you have palpitations and he says, 'Well, we could do this, or we could do that'? I'm looking for a doctor that does his homework on me, knows everything about my body, and says you need to do the following for the following reasons. If a mechanic says, "Well, we could replace the carburetor, or maybe just fix it, or how about putting on a band-aid so you can run it for a while?' I want that mechanic to look me in the eye and say, 'You have a problem. If you don't fix it, it could break at any time. Think about your wife driving late at night with your two sons and then it breaks down and leaves them on the side of a road.' I want the type of professional that is credible, someone whom I can trust, and they give me good sound advice. When I started in the business, I didn't have that realization. I remember giving clients choices, 'You can do it this way, this way or this way.' Families come to us for expert guidance."

"When we meet to present the financial plan to the families, they rarely last over one and a half or two hours. I know other financial advisors will open their computer for modeling, show complex charts, and give a complicated presentation. We've been doing that for weeks before the meeting in the background. We'll say, 'Here are the three scenarios of your retirement. If we get *X* and *Y* returns, here's how you should allocate your assets to take the right amount of risk. Here's how you should title the securities, the amount you should put in the charitable remainder trust, the amount of stock you should exercise and sell, here's the amount you should collar, and here are the central reasons why. The credibility is built in. They've met our team beforehand and they know its decisions are made by a team and everything is part of a well thought-out plan developed by a group of professionals. We develop a plan, tell them the course of action, then we execute the strategy."

Jeff sums up the importance of the financial planning process with a quote he borrows from his dentist: "He always tells me to 'floss the teeth I want to keep.' I perform a comprehensive financial plan for every client. If they don't do it with me, they'll do it somewhere else and I'll lose that client," he says of his first of four steps. "This is the easiest and best way to add value for a client. I always come away with five or six major action steps that will help that family go to the next level, addressing everything from portfolio management and liability management, to estate plans and wealth transfers, to private banking."

The second step: Jeff purports to be each family's private banker. "Wealthy people truly appreciate this type of service," Jeff says.

"One group of professionals to handle all of their banking needs. We'll help them with their bill payment system, consolidated tax reporting system. We are one group of professionals for all their banking needs. This is the best way to add immediate value and to simplify their lives.

In the mid-1990s, Jeff called the chairman of a large corporation. For five years Jeff kept in periodic contact with the prospect, calling him and sending him information. The prospect repeatedly told Jeff there was no way he was going to invest with anyone but his advisor, who was his best friend and college roommate. One day the prospect told Jeff that he respected his persistence; a Wall Street firm was visiting him to discuss after-tax equity returns. "Like I told them," the prospect said candidly, "you won't get my business, but you are welcome to give me your presentation." Jeff arranged to meet with him in his town at a local Merrill office, and requested that his wife join them. The prospect replied, "I'm afraid it will be a waste of your time."

Jeff began the meeting listening to the couple, asking open-ended questions to build a rapport and to understand their needs. Among the series of questions was, "Who is your private banker? What institution helps you manage and coordinate all your finances and provides you with a bill payment system?" The wife leaned forward and spoke up: "I'm the one who pays the bills. Every month it's such a pain." Jeff discussed his business and specialties, including the private banking services he provides, such as sending over a member of the team to set up their computer system and to connect them to Merrill's online services, such as bill payment. "We will even input your vendors," he said. "You decide who to pay, how much, and when." She replied, "That's great." "Tell me about your frequent-flyer program," Jeff asked the couple, then paused to look at me, and said: "People look at me funny when I ask them that question because they may be worth ten or twenty million dollars and it may sound petty."

Jeff continued with the story: "The woman asked, 'Why?'" Jeff told her, "For our wealthy families we have one of the best frequent flyer programs in the industry, in fact there are no blackout dates. For clients who have over certain asset levels you get upgrades to first class." The couple clearly was very intrigued. "Then I talked about our open architecture, which we're very proud of at Merrill. We work with hundreds of the top investment advisors in the world. So when we review a portfolio and put a financial plan together, we're able to expose you to some of the top talent in the world." Overall, the meeting lasted an hour, and they never even discussed after-tax equity returns.

At 8 o'clock the next morning, Jeff received his first phone call of the day. It was the prospect: "How much do I have to wire to Merrill to have someone help us with our computer and online bill payment?" Jeff answered: $10 million. Within a day the money was wired to his new Merrill account. A month later, the chairman retired, receiving $55 million. That money was transferred to Merrill as well. Within two years the client closed his other relationship and transferred all assets to Merrill.

Jeff has since earned two referrals from the client, both over $25 million in assets, and they became strong clients. Jeff simplifies his process: "Wealthy people and senior executives are yearning for people they like and can trust and who provide great service. This client's assets have performed to our expectations—he has a large municipal bonds allocation, we hired outside managers in our open architecture, he loves our service, and he's been real happy to refer business to us. In fact, he refers to us as his family office. That's our niche for clients we're going after. On average, people with five to fifty million dollars won't typically set up their own family office. But they are typically very successful, busy, and looking for someone they like and can trust who has the infrastructure in place to manage the whole process for them. As 'a mini private bank,' or outsourced private office, we are involved in, and coordinate, each family's finances, and we become very close with each family."

"Our business is very high-touch, high-service. When you get as close as we are with our clients, you become involved in all aspects of their financial and personal lives," Jeff says, leading into his third methodology, "We're really more of a family advisor than a financial advisor," he says. "We're more than stocks, bonds, and mutual funds. We deal with intimate decisions, such as helping a client decide if a nursing home is the right decision for a parent, issues with children or spouses, and, of course, any financial issue that may arise. We get involved because we truly care about each other."

When the appropriate time comes, Jeff requests that additional family members join the meetings. "Clients in their thirties and forties may not feel a need to bring their spouse into the meetings," Jeff says. "By the third meeting I'll request it, saying it's a good idea to get spouses involved early, so we can form a relationship. This is important not only from the standpoint of learning more about their needs, but just in case—God forbid—there's a tragedy. I want them to feel comfortable knowing that we are always here to support them, and that all financial information is documented."

"This is what gets us so excited about our business. We have wonderful clients that are great people. They're successful, they're interesting, and like anyone else they're yearning to have a relationship with someone they can trust and grow old with."

Jeff always seems to be helping others plan their future. As a board member of the Fairchester National Federation for Teaching Entrepreneurship, since the early 2000s, every six weeks he's been visiting low-income high schools, speaking about building business, and mentoring students. "This is one of the most important and challenging things I do," he says emphatically. He likes to begin by making fun of himself, pointing out his mistakes in life and business. Jeff helps the students build a business plan, and the winner is presented an award. Jeff also challenges them: "If anyone of you call me in the office for help, whether getting a job, starting a business or even a personal issue, I will do whatever I can to help you." Recently, a boy with a speaking disability approached Jeff to express the incredible influence of Jeff's lecture, and promised to follow his advice and stay in school and start a business.

Jeff also receives several emails and calls per week from financial advisors asking for his advice and guidance. Jeff prides himself at always making time to give back and help the advisors. Jeff also spent the past eight years as a trustee of his children's school, while also serving as chairman of his Alumni Board.

"As with anything in life, balance is extremely important," he says thoughtfully. "I always tell my kids, 'we have to give back to people that don't have the advantages we have.' It's extremely satisfying to help young adults get a break, and pursue a dream."

"It seems that every night I drive home I feel like I need to pinch myself—I feel so fortunate that I can make a positive difference in people's lives. I go home every night and feel so good about my business, and that my team and clients are lifelong friends, family members. We're really like one big family."

CHAPTER 2: NIALL GANNON

High Touch

Smith Barney
St. Louis, Missouri

SEVERAL YEARS AGO, A PROSPECTIVE CLIENT OFFERED NIALL GANNON a check for $50 million to invest. Niall's immediate reaction: "No thank you."

At peak, the prospect's net worth was about half a billion dollars. "It was going to be an account where I would manage the money as a margin loan off one hundred million dollars' worth of restricted stock," says Niall. "When I said no, he asked why and I said because that would be taking your family backward, not forward."

Niall was right. Today, the company has gone under. "We don't think it can happen—that all of it can be taken away. However, as we have seen, the paradigm shifts and all of a sudden, everything that you've done up until that point is all that you've got. You've either planned for it or you haven't."

PERSONAL QUALITIES

The personal qualities Niall brings to his practice—discipline, diligence, and enormous empathy—are rooted in a family saga that unfolds like a classic American tale. It starts with Niall's parents, who emigrated from Ireland to St. Louis in 1967 with just $20 and two suitcases. Niall was born six months later.

"My mom said we would come for one year and try out this America thing," says Niall, whose father, a psychiatrist, worked for the State Hospital of Missouri. "And he promised her we would just do it for one year. Then Americana kissed them and they decided to stay."

To keep in touch with their homeland, Niall's parents taught Irish music to thousands of people in the St. Louis region. Niall himself still plays the violin, which he took up at age five. Later, Niall taught music, and a parent of one of his students, Pat Kearns, a manager for Shearson Lehman Brothers (which later became a part of Smith Barney), introduced him to the industry with an internship—and eventually, a spot in the firm's training program.

As a youth, however, it wasn't finance, but the U.S. military that attracted Niall's interest. Niall graduated in 1990 with a business degree from The Citadel in South Carolina "with the objective of earning my commission as a U.S. Army officer and doing my duty."

But events intervened.

A week before he was to have been commissioned with his graduating class—just before Iraq's invasion of Kuwait—Niall was diagnosed with mononucleosis. A one-year medical discharge from the Army followed. Niall would have to painfully watch as his classmates went into battle. A career path so interrupted would have devastated many people. Not Niall. While he was in "limbo," as he puts it, he began taking finance courses at the University of Missouri and working odd jobs, including the music-teaching job that introduced him to a branch manager at Shearson Lehman Brothers.

A TRUE CALLING

The manager recognized Niall's perseverance and determination to return to the Army the following year to earn his commission. To pass the time, Niall was working any job he could muster to earn a living: "I was a meat cutter. I was a bartender and a music teacher. I did whatever I had to do to make money, learn about things," Niall says. The manager recognized a unique talent that Niall possessed. "He knew that I liked interacting with people and solving problems," notes Niall. "I think that's why he said, 'I think you might want to look at this business.' "

Niall began his internship with Shearson in late 1991. It was an eye-opening experience—cold calling for senior brokers, working with the operations area, opening mail. "We did everything," he says. "We saw people's successes and failures. We saw the divorces. We saw the good, the bad. We were in there on Saturdays and we saw that some people worked and some people's offices were dark. There were four of us, all about the same age, twenty-two or so, and we got the opportunity to view the business in a way that I don't think many people do. The recipe was right there: You had to work harder and smarter than anybody else to be successful."

After a six-month break the following year to attend the M1 tank platoon commander course at Fort Knox, Kentucky, Niall got his Series 7 license and began Shearson's full-blown training program in Southern California. It was 1992 and Niall was hooked on becoming a financial advisor.

"I remember there was a group of fifty of us and we were all really excited. When it was time to get our broker numbers, some of us asked if we could make cold calls from the pay phone in the lobby. We were just ready to go," recalls Niall. "We felt like the world was our oyster and we hit the ground running when we came home."

BUILDING A TARGETED CLIENTELE

During his first five years with Shearson, Niall estimates that he made 150,000 cold calls. With a goal of ten quality contacts a day, he mined the Missouri and Illinois manufacturer's directories, screening out companies with fewer than 25 employees. His sights were lofty—no one other than the president of a firm was targeted.

It was during this period in the early 1990s that this St. Louis-based financial advisor, now with Smith Barney, began developing a client list in a way that was forward thinking at the time. For starters, he put people above product—presenting himself as both partner and problem solver. "What we are trying to do is establish a partnership," he says. "We are trying to create something through this [process] that doesn't exist without this work." Today, he credits two clients in particular, a doctor and a pharmaceutical company CEO, with teaching him about what matters most in the advisory relationship. Niall calls them his mentors. Here's what he says they taught him.

THE DOCTOR

At 8:30 one night, Niall cold called a doctor, clearly interrupting him. He pitched the doctor anyway, but the prospect cut him short with a proposition that would forever transform Niall's practice.

"I just want to stop you for a second," the doctor told Niall. "I have hundreds of thousands of dollars in no-load funds. I'm trying to do it myself and I am scared. I think I'm hurting myself. I need to find someone. I paid ten thousand dollars [to a competing firm] and spent two days in a hotel with their wealth management people. [The event] was co-run by the American Medical Association, trying to teach doctors how to run their finances. At the end of those two days, I received a solicitation from the same firm for a muni bond, just like you are doing to me right now. I am just trying to find that [right] person to help me reach my goals."

Niall's response? "Doctor, what time do you get in? He replied: 'Seven-thirty.' I'll see you in the morning." The next day, Niall visited the prospect. "There was an Irish flag in his office, which was a good thing," he recalls. Over the next few hours, Niall talked to the man about what he wanted in life. The conversation seemed to stun the doctor. "He just told me, 'No one has ever sat down and talked to me like you are talking to me now. No one has ever asked me for my wife's opinion,'" notes Niall.

As it turned out, Niall says, the doctor had an agenda: He wanted to retire within a year, move to Florida and buy a house for cash. As Niall puts it, "He wanted to put his career behind him and start doing that thing that he sees in the brokerage firm commercials that too seldom happens."

For the next four to five months, Niall worked with the doctor and his wife—both to get to know them better and to begin structuring their finances to help them meet their goals.

"I was clearly no expert in finance then, but the fact that I listened about the things that were important to them mattered. It worked. I remember the day I went to sign the papers and we wound up doing managed accounts. It struck me that he had just signed all the papers, a huge stack of papers," Niall says. "And he said, 'Tell me again what we are going to do with the money and what the fee is.' I said we are going to manage your money in a format that will be guided by the parameters we have set together. We are doing this all fee-based, which is a percentage of your assets. He said, 'That's great. That's what I want.' "

Driving home, Niall, then just 23, realized he had learned something that's not taught in any training program. "It made me realize that on these cold calls, I don't have to argue with people like I would hear the other brokers doing. That there were people that were actually waiting for my phone call that were without help and that I could actually change their lives for the better," adds Niall. "The fee was not an issue. Performance was not an issue. If someone would take their concerns and somehow make them their own, that was the value proposition. It was a huge revelation."

Today, Niall describes the doctor and his wife as "one of the forks in the road" that profoundly affected the path he forged as he began to build his practice. "The immediate change to my approach became: How can I help you? I used to tell my colleagues, 'This sounds crazy but there are people that are actually not mad when we call them,' " says Niall.

"Again, I was twenty-three years old. What could I possibly offer to people? Yet we found something and moved forward. They are down in Florida now. They are living the dream. And I'm happy about that," he adds. "But that phone call changed things for me because from then on I was no longer a salesman. I had a mandate to make something happen on behalf of these families who had entrusted their livelihood to me."

THE CEO

In the mid-1990s, Niall spent a year and a half prospecting the CEO of a major pharmaceutical company. As Niall recalls, "He was sitting on a huge concentrated stock position—he had never sold a single share—which was almost his entire net worth." Finally, the CEO participated in a secondary offering and sold a large block of stock.

Niall called the CEO for a congratulatory chat that had something of a surprise ending. "The CEO said, 'I've got you down for a million.' I'm happy that I earned some of his business. But then again, he just cashed in over five times that amount in stock. The disappointing news was: What's going on with the rest of the money?"

A lot of advisors would have been satisfied with the million-dollar investment, at the least viewing it as an opening. That wasn't the case with Niall; for him, he can't offer solutions if he doesn't have the serious money. "At the end of the day, I'm better off if the client is better off first." Niall demanded a meeting with the CEO the next morning. There, the CEO called Niall "tenacious," going so far as to say Niall reminded him of himself as a younger man.

"I said, 'I just want to ask you one question. This is a huge fork in the road for you because you've never taken any liquidity out of the company for yourself and your family. You've never smelled the roses. You've never gotten a payday from what's been built over the last fifteen years,'" Niall recalls saying. "'What are you going to do with the rest of your money?'"

The CEO then told Niall that he had four other advisors with whom he was working and that they were each going to get $1 million as well. Now Niall understood.

"At the risk of losing a huge opportunity in my career, I would rather compete for all of it and that I am going to be a big boy and walk away if I don't make the cut," Niall told the executive. "But, I think you could be making a mistake with this approach. Instead, I said: 'Take your time. Find the [right] person, whether it's me or someone else. I'd like to see you do what's in your best interests."

Later, the CEO asked him to come back with one proposal for $5 million and another for $1 million. Niall returned with a single proposal—for $5 million.

"He said, 'Where's the proposal for $1 million?' I said I didn't bring it. 'This is the proposal. This is what you should do. I am interviewing for a job to be your chief of staff. If I am not selected that's fine. But this is how you should execute.'"

The proposal, to the CEO's surprise, didn't involve stock recommendations but discussed the need for cash flow and income. "At that time he didn't know when he was going to retire. But he had mentioned that he and his wife were going to be gone one week a month from here on out. So that was my first entree into the fact that this guy might want to start living the life off of his investments—and that a little income wouldn't be bad," recalls Niall.

After reading the proposal, the CEO asked Niall for one more thing: a night to think about it. "I know the way you are trained and I know you don't want to hear when I say this," he told Niall. "But I sleep on every big decision in my life. You'll know in the morning." Niall agreed, "It's a big decision, so take your time and solicit other opinions, from your wife, accountant, lawyer, and others." Shortly after Niall walked into his office the next morning, the CEO's funds were wired to Shearson for Niall to manage.

In the years since, Niall has helped the CEO with much more than just money. As he puts it, "This was clearly not a person who had ever been properly advised about his wealth. He did not have a trusted advisor who could bring new ideas about wealth protection, legacy building, other issues for a family like his. He needed someone to do that thinking for him and to make suggestions. So I guess I proved myself by being direct and willing to ask a lot of questions to better understand him and his family. Then I could offer solutions. Every once in a while I might strike a nerve, but it always seems to tighten our relationship."

If there is an overarching theme to Niall's practice, it is his empathy for his clients—as evidenced by the doctor and the CEO. About the latter, he says, "He had everything. And he let me in. He gave me a chance. And then I gave him something that he hadn't gotten before. And that was a different look. A new and comprehensive perspective."

Niall says his clients have taught him "when the time comes you don't get to rewind the tape and fix what you missed. I get to know my clients so well that it's highly unlikely we'll miss a detail."

BUILDING A NICHE

From those early relationships, a niche was born. "There are a lot of corporate executives who have been devoted to—and have taken care of—their employees and shareholders and [who have] never leaned the needle toward family or self. When I find them at that point—where they are just starting to say 'my family has taken a backseat to my shareholders and to my employees because I've been there for my employees and my shareholders, but I have missed the births of my children. I've missed the birthday parties.' When I find someone who has the wealth but doesn't know how to make that transition, that's where I offer my full value proposition. And that's where I am today.

When Niall started in the business, he envisioned building a high-touch practice that provides extraordinary advice and service to a limited selection of families. Now in his second decade, Niall has reached that pinnacle: His clientele includes a handful of ultrahigh net worth families, each with a net worth of $25 million to over $1 billion.

Today, Niall has assembled a team of financial professionals, consisting of three specialists who exemplify Niall's commitment to unbiased advice. Matt Rogers, a certified financial analyst, is responsible for coordinating and operating both research and trading. Cindy Feaster is the team's sales assistant, and she helps to coordinate cash flow, as well as to interact with attorneys and CPAs. In addition, she manages the payroll and financial operations for household staff, yacht crews, pilots, etc. Barbara Stuart is the administrative assistant for the group and coordinates internal initiatives.

Their mission: To manage wealth for CEOs, retiring entrepreneurs, and their families. "Our goal is to actively assist our clients to live their lives free of financial concerns," Niall states with conviction.

PORTFOLIO MANAGEMENT

With a strong track record managing portfolios, Niall is often asked, "Why not focus solely on managing portfolios since it can be far more lucrative?" Niall shrugs off the remuneration aspect, instead focusing on the real rewards: "In my opinion, portfolio managers that don't have the ongoing client contact are missing out. They don't get to see the faces of the kids they're helping put through college, the individuals whose dreams you're helping to attain. I feel most rewarded by helping clients."

Niall continues: "Our investment performance is homemade, not store bought—it is fresh and never frozen. As a result of this, we take ownership of our results. We believe that decades from now we will be judged by what we did or failed to do. To accomplish this successfully, we must be humble and open-minded. We must constantly test and refine our strategy to make sure we are prepared to do the job ahead of us."

Niall's time is divided equally among deepening relationships with clients and managing money. "We spend an equal amount of time researching securities markets and strategy as we do the people whose lives are affected by those decisions," he says. "Half my time is investment due diligence and the other half is client due diligence."

Most of the investing time is spent researching companies. His equity portfolio consists of approximately 35 companies. He participates in many annual meetings and conference calls, whether in person or via web casts. In a typical year, he'll personally attend as many as ten annual meetings. Recently, at a Pfizer annual meeting, out of 300 attendees, Niall was one of the few, if not the only, financial advisor in attendance.

"The benefits of this personal time brings us closer to the answers to the tough questions. For us to own a stock in a company we must understand it and its management team. Since we believe that stock prices are driven by the fundamentals of companies, we must put effort into understanding how those fundamentals work. Most every scandal that has racked the investment industry would have been avoided if investors simply took a practical approach to their investments instead of chasing indexes and fads. This is not to say performance and profit are not important—they are both very important. However, one must ask if their advisors are performing for the benefit of themselves or their client. If you are true to yourself, willing to admit when you are wrong—and take ownership of your results—then everyone wins."

Niall speaks with high conviction when discussing his investment philosophy. "We believe that we have a truly unique investment strategy. We begin with the premise that our strategy is built for private investors who have reached the pinnacle of entrepreneurial success. Most of the asset allocation advice on Wall Street today is driven toward institutions and nontaxable pools of money. The basic goal for our clients is to live debt-free, own a portfolio of high-quality tax-free bonds for income, and a diversified high-quality equity portfolio which will build wealth for future generations."

Niall remembered when he began shifting his focus toward municipal bonds near the end of 1999 and 2000. "Back then we were buying triple-A rated tax-free bonds with taxable-equivalent yields north of nine percent in some cases. High yields on conservative investments seemed worth consideration for taxable investors, especially when the price-earning multiple of the S&P 500 was at record levels. Despite this, the investing public sold bonds and continued to pour money into stocks as the market was peaking. This is where the practicality came in: Bonds were yielding more than double the earnings yield of stocks, yet very few people understood what was happening. A private investor survey in that year found that the average ultrahigh net worth investor had only seven percent of their portfolio invested in municipal bonds."

One of the topics with which Niall takes issue in the investment industry is what he calls "equity market bias," in reference to numerous studies that show stocks outperform bonds over the long term. He also says, "The returns of the next fifty years will be similar to the previous fifty years." He argues that stocks have risen over recent decades because their earnings have grown in a declining interest rate environment. Failing to understand this phenomenon of the past 20 years could cause investors' expectations to rise to unsustainable levels. He insists that enthusiasm from past performance should be adjusted to reflect *today's* economic environment. "Investment professionals have a responsibility to their clients to make sure they constantly stress-test their strategy in order to prevent complacency," he says.

Niall believes that, to grasp the profit potential of a stock, he must first understand the business, assume reasonable growth expectations, and be firm on the multiple he is willing to pay. Niall maintains that you won't find a single family on the Forbes 400 who built their wealth by indexing, shorting stocks, market timing, or following investment newsletters. "What you will find is that the majority of them were owners of high-quality businesses who grew their earnings over time. Too often investors admire these wealth creators for what they have built, then completely ignore their example of how they went about building it."

WAR, TERRORISM, AND DOWN MARKETS

Niall has recognized a change among his clients over the past five to ten years. Long an advocate of wealth preservation strategies for his clients, his insistence on exposure to bonds for retired clients seemed too conservative for some as the tech-heavy NASDAQ surged through the first quarter of 2000. On the other hand, when the market downturn hit, under Niall's guidance and investing discipline, clients' portfolios were well positioned for the storm that followed. Niall remembers sending Matt to the library in the last week of December of 1999 to obtain copies of *The Wall Street Journal* from the days and weeks before the Great Stock Market Crash of 1929. What they found in those 71-year-old newspapers seemed "eerie," Niall explains. "Headlines with quotes from the Fed to the large Wall Street brokerage firms seemed to imply that everything was going to be fine and that investors should not worry." It was very disturbing to me how similar the mood of the country in the late 1920s was to that of the late 1990s. This experience solidified Niall's belief that, if he was going to advise clients through good times and bad, he had better not rely on outsiders to form his investment philosophy. He had better do the job himself. He had better understand history and learn its lessons.

As a financial advisor, Niall also focuses on his clients' "other" wealth, such as time, family, and doing the things they enjoy doing. "The spectacular creation of wealth which occurred from 1982 to present is highly unlikely to be duplicated for the current generation of company founders and CEOs," Niall says. "One of the biggest risks facing this group is that they could stay at the table too long—perhaps missing out on an abundance of quality years of enjoying time with their families. I want to tell this story as often as I can. The current environment is the perfect storm of opportunity."

"I am encouraging my clients to enjoy their wealth," he explains. "Once we properly positioned our clients to weather the storm of the early 2000s, we became convinced that the best new investments were in 'human capital.' Examples of this would include making meaningful gifts to children now versus waiting until death, and making a large-scale philanthropic impact today rather than trickling out small amounts over fifty years."

As an example, he says: "For a lot of my clients I ask, 'Is it going to really impact your kids' lives if you pass away at the ripe, old age of ninety-two and your kids become multimillionaires in their late sixties? If they're taking Geritol, all that money to do things may not be worth it. It's thinking through things. I don't think many people really look at how the dollars are going to wind up impacting people's lives. We'll leave this life, and those dollars will go somewhere. If we don't plan for it, investment success can be a terrible thing. We either have the money and do it right—to enrich lives—or we just give it all away now. But don't wing it."

In many respects, Niall says, it's "the everyday things" that are important when it comes to measuring the contents of a life—and creating a financial plan to accommodate it. For so long, he says, the profession "didn't spend much time on the people. And now we realize we have to spend a lot of time on the people. If we are going to prescribe medicine, we've got to know the patient."

ENRICHING LIVES

Niall thanks his clients for building his business model. "I was guided by each relationship," he says. "In pursuing what's right for my clients, I built an infrastructure that caters to each individual. I'd like to say it was a grandiose plan that I cooked up in my head. But it wasn't. It was the people. It's always about the people. They created me. That's the truth."

In building his relationships with clients, Niall says everything counts. As for the doctor and the CEO, he adds: "Nothing is superficial. Nothing is mundane. I was talking about very real things with these people. And as it's turned out, all of these clients are mentors to me—not only because they gave me a chance but because I've watched their decisions in life and I've listened to every single thing that's ever happened to them since childhood. I've gotten the benefit of their life experiences."

It has worked in reverse, too, with Niall's clients benefiting from his life experience because this is a man who has never forgotten his immigrant parents, the $20, and the two suitcases.

"With the clients I am dealing with now I often tell them that the way we want to approach their wealth shouldn't be influenced by the number of zeroes behind them because you have to deal with where you are today. I think that's so often overlooked," he says. "You could have told my parents: Here's what's happened to other immigrants when they came over. But it's your own starting point and individual situation that makes the difference."

Niall has made a difference, and in the process he's carved out a niche helping families enjoy fuller lives.

"That was going to be my value proposition. And that's where I am today," he says. "It was no grandiose plan that I cooked up in my head. It was just these people guiding me. My business model was guided by each of those relationships and all the others. They're each very special to me."

Niall pauses, then looks up: "My job is to enrich people's lives."

CHAPTER 3: CHARLES ZHANG

A Foundation for Success

American Express Financial Advisors
Portage, Michigan

Charles Zhang is an unlikely success story. When he became a financial planner in the early 1990s, he had a hard time attracting clients, and almost lost his job as a result. Since none of his family members or personal friends had ever worked in financial services, he couldn't turn to anyone close to him for trusted advice on how to solve his dilemma.

But Charles had other characteristics in his favor, most notably a strong work ethic and an unrelenting desire to achieve professional excellence. "There was nothing more that I wanted than to be successful in this industry," he recalls.

Today, Charles can reflect on the first 13 years in this business and feel satisfied that his efforts have exceeded even his wildest expectations. That's because Charles Zhang is not only among the top financial planners at his firm, he is one of America's very best—and has been for several years. His commitment to providing extraordinary advice and service is evidenced by the ongoing referrals he receives from clients, as well as a client retention rate of more than 99 percent. Basically, when Charles earns business, clients are with him for life.

"The key to my success has been my desire to improve myself every day," he says flatly. (His credentials include CFP®, ChFC, CLU, CMFC, and CFS. He also has an MBA from Kellogg School of Management, Northwestern University and has been through Executive Education at Harvard Business School.) "Personal goals are very important to me. I also put the time in the long hours, probably twelve hours every day. What's more, I have a lot of respect for my clients. Once I make a commitment to an investor, I try to provide the best service for the life of the relationship."

CHARLES' BEGINNING

Born in China and educated in the United States, Charles Zhang is a Certified Financial Planner with American Express in Kalamazoo, Michigan. While he provides a broad spectrum of services, he specializes in serving the diverse investment, estate, and financial planning needs of high net worth investors.

Charles attended Western Michigan University (WMU) on a scholarship after he came to the United States. Influenced by his parents, both of whom have spent their careers in education, Charles excelled in graduate school, just as he did during his scholastic years growing up in Shanghai.

After Charles earned a master's degree in economics from Western Michigan, he had two choices. He could complete the Ph.D. program and pursue a teaching career or he could start his professional career. Charles and his wife, Lynn, a Certified Public Accountant at the time, thought about the long-term potential of a career in teaching. "Together," he recalls, "we decided that becoming a Certified Financial Planner offered greater income potential and more freedom while giving me the opportunity to help others. Becoming a positive impact on people's lives is important to me."

Charles began sending his resume to brokerage houses, banks, and other financial institutions. Given his educational background, he received job offers from a number of major companies before deciding to join American Express. "I chose American Express because of its heavy emphasis on the financial planning process. While other firms still looked at their representatives as salespeople or stockbrokers, American Express called them personal financial advisors or business financial advisors. I wanted to be part of this culture."

After meeting with division vice president Dave Kreiger, who was one of the top division vice presidents at American Express, Charles decided that he wanted the opportunity to become part of the team. He was given that opportunity in the autumn of 1991. Charles was happy, but not long after he began his career, that happiness quickly faded.

A TOUGH START

Having known nothing but success in the classroom, Charles figured that his formula of hard work and commitment to service and perseverance would enable him to thrive in the business world. But Charles soon discovered that the road to riches on Wall Street would be a far more difficult one.

A challenging market environment was partly to blame for his struggle. Charles entered the business soon after the Gulf War, a period punctuated by economic uncertainty and increasing nervousness among investors. In addition, his Chinese accent hindered his ability to conduct business. "I was afraid people wouldn't understand me very well," he concedes.

To say his first few months in the business were tough is a colossal understatement. "I couldn't convince people to buy a financial plan from me, no matter how hard I tried," he recalls. "After a few months, I was beginning to believe that perhaps I couldn't do this job. At one point, the firm even told me I didn't have to come back."

But Charles Zhang never stopped coming back. Unfortunately, he kept facing disappointment—even from the people who he thought he could count on for business. He called professors at his alma mater, but most didn't need a financial advisor. He tried contacting prospects in the Chinese community, believing his heritage would give him an edge over his competition, but there were fewer than 50 families in the area, and most of them either didn't have much money to invest or were not in the market for financial advice.

Struggling and earning just a nominal amount of money at the time, Charles decided to begin buying what he believed were high-quality leads at $7.50 apiece. "These were the names of individuals who had supposedly requested information from a financial institution, but sometimes when I called them, I discovered that they never requested information. "I was frustrated but I kept telling myself quitters never win, and winners never quit. Quite frankly, I didn't want to be a loser. It would have been easy to throw up my hands in disgust because things were so tough. I could have blamed it on the uncertainty in the market. I could have blamed it on the fact that I was new to the area and had no people who could help me get on track. But I decided to keep trying."

With each passing day Charles' struggle seemed more frustrating than the one before. Fortunately, his wife Lynn holds a master's degree in accountancy and found a job with PriceWaterhouseCoopers as a tax consultant. She told Charles not to worry about the finance because she would be able to support the family. "Just focus on your business; in fact, don't even be concerned about making money the first year. I think this career is right for you," she told Charles.

Finally, after three months in the business, Charles started to attract some quality clients. One was a retired police officer, whose name he had gotten from one of the seemingly dead leads. "When I completed a financial plan for him, he said to me, 'I just want you to know, the reason that I am doing business with you is not because of anyone else in the firm—it's because I trust you.' Those words were very inspirational. At that moment I began to realize if you really try hard, you *can* make it happen."

And for Charles it did. Over the next few weeks, investors he had tirelessly prospected began sending business his way. Charles kept pursuing new prospects, and within a few weeks they turned into clients. Within 12 months, he was the top first-year advisor in the nation out of almost 1,000 new advisors. This brush with success was not to be short-lived. In fact, it proved to be the foundation for the incredible success that was yet to come.

A RAPID ASCENSION

In his second year, Charles Zhang became the number one second-year advisor in the nation and began the process of building a team. In his third year, he was among the firm's elite planners, becoming a member of the President Advisor Counsel, which includes the top 1 percent of American Express financial advisors in the nation.

Charles made a significant change to his business that enabled him to become one of the firm's top producers. By now, Charles wasn't just making prospecting calls. He was conducting seminars on financial planning, education planning, and retirement planning. What's more, he was no longer trying to latch onto every piece of business he could find.

"When I started, if someone wanted to invest just two thousand dollars in an IRA," he says, "I would be happy to get the business. But I finally realized that I would never maximize my potential with this approach because I would have too many clients. I don't think it is right that I invest two thousand dollars in an IRA for a client and don't have time to service his account. So I decided to begin working with high net worth clients who had a minimum amount of money to invest."

"At first, I focused on investors with as little as fifty-thousand dollars," he recalls. "For investors outside Michigan, my range was between a quarter million and half million. As the practice became more successful, I began to ratchet up those numbers and began focusing solely on investors with higher net worth. By 1996, I was doing business only with clients who agreed to have a financial plan and had a minimum of one hundred thousand to invest or an average net worth of a million dollars. For investors outside Michigan, my minimum is half a million in investable assets."

His approach proved rewarding. By the sixth year of operation Charles was the number one advisor in the country with a strong team in place to help support his efforts.

Today, Charles has three paraplanners (licensed advisors) on his team. They handle much of the in-house work that needs to be done to help facilitate a client's overall plan. He has one office manager and, at any given time, three or four planning assistants.

Seeing that she, too, could make a significant contribution to her husband's business, Lynn left a management position at Kellogg

Company to join her husband's team in the winter of 1997. She earned the Certified Financial Planner designation and became an important asset to Charles' practice. In addition to helping Charles on the financial planning side of the practice, she helped him develop a budding employee stock options business. Lynn is a Certified Employee Stock Option Specialist and a recognized national expert in this field.

"We market our employee stock options business by inviting employees to learn how they can save thousands of dollars every year with stock options," Charles says. "Most individuals who receive stock options want to defer as much money as possible. We explain that we have a way to help them maximize this potential, which really does create interest."

In fact, Charles and Lynn have created so much interest in their ability to help employees manage their stock options, they are now doing consulting work for executives with a broad range of corporations, as well as several Fortune 500 companies. "As a result, we have people with CPA designations, controllers, even vice presidents of finance coming to us," says Charles. "Recently, senior management in the finance department of one of the Fortune 500 companies asked us to conduct a seminar at the firm on this topic for the company's executives."

MARKETING

Given the size of his practice, one might assume that Charles does a good deal of marketing to keep his business growing strong. But he only advertises periodically in a local newspaper and occasionally will create an advertisement that runs on television. Two-thirds of his business, he says, comes from referrals. "We typically don't prospect for the sake of prospecting," he says. "Instead, we tell our existing clients to ask their parents, brothers, or sisters, friends, coworkers to call us if we can help. We also say, 'If you know of any person who is in a similar situation that needs financial guidance, please let me know.' That's really the extent of our prospecting efforts." Charles says he takes a passive approach for two reasons: "I want prospective investors to see us as a prestigious firm, and I want to keep a manageable client base," he explains. "While I receive anywhere three hundred to five hundred calls from prospective clients each year, I typically only take on no more than a hundred clients a year."

Many of his clients come from outside Michigan, and they are willing to travel far and wide to see him. He has one client, an executive with a Fortune 500 company, who drives six hours to meet with him every six months. "The client came to me as a referral from one of his close friends who was happy with our service. He told him, if you are looking for a financial planner, you have to see Charles. And he does."

A SOUND APPROACH TO FINANCIAL PLANNING

Over the years, Charles has created a financial planning approach that has resonated with all types of high net worth investors. After receiving a phone call from a prospect, Charles' office sends the prospective client a package. The package contains information on Charles, his practice, and American Express Financial Advisors. Prospective clients are expected to review the information before they arrive for the initial consultation. The process begins with a one-hour free initial consultation to see if both parties feel comfortable enough to work together. After the first meeting, the client is given "homework." "Essentially, we ask investors to go through the personal papers related to finance and return to the next meeting with all pertinent financial documents that will give us a good overview of his or her total financial picture," Charles says. "Generally, this information includes investment statements, tax returns, trust documents, a will, cash flow analysis, and insurance policies. When the client comes back for the next meeting, we look at this information carefully to determine his strengths and weakness."

The second meeting is for data gathering. Charles and one of his para planners are involved in the meeting to gather all the relevant information for developing a plan. Following that second meeting, Charles points out that his team will analyze this information, which usually involves ten hours or more, depending on the complexity of the case. Charles and his team perform financial planning analysis through sophisticated probability modeling. They use a unique financial planning tool, Apex Select, which utilizes the Monte Carlo Simulation and does 6,750 simulations with over 40 years of historical data to help their clients make more realistic decisions. Simulation is based on statistical probabilities using thousands of calculations.

"At the third meeting we review the plan and offer specific recommendations. After giving our suggestions, we help people implement their plan and conduct reviews of their accounts once or twice a year."

During this interaction, Charles and the paraplanner might also discuss the flexibility that they have in managing client assets. For example, he may point out that the team not only has the ability to access a client's asset allocation and investments at the tap of a few keys on the computer, but also detailed information such as the portfolio's beta as well.

Charles and the paraplanner may even address the team's investment flexibility. "We can invest in four thousand different mutual funds, plus ten thousand different stocks and bonds," Charles points out. "This kind of broad investment flexibility gives clients the confidence they need to know we have all of the necessary financial vehicles available at our disposal."

The risks of investing are not overlooked. "We like to emphasize the risks as well as the rewards because investors need to know the full picture," Charles says. "This can turn off a client, and we have even lost some business by taking this approach, but it is good policy, I believe."

After the financial plan has been implemented, Charles meets his clients at least annually to review their accounts and the progress made toward achieving their goals. During those annual or semiannual meetings, Charles provides clients with a comprehensive breakdown of the assets under his management. "For example, we show them how much money they have invested, how much they have redeemed, and how much they currently have to work with," he points out.

Charles says showing clients how much money they redeemed over a given period is important. "Some people withdraw money during the course of the year and forget they did, then wonder why their portfolio is less than it was at a particular point in the past," he says.

At these meetings, which usually last around 30 minutes or so, Charles also shows clients how their portfolios are performing over different time periods and asset allocation analysis.

EXCEEDING EXPECTATIONS

Charles is well aware that neither he nor any financial planner can determine which way the financial markets will move from year to year, let alone one day to the next. So in his ongoing effort to keep clients happy, he focuses on those parts of his business that he can control and tries to exceed expectations in those areas.

One way is by remaining true to his word at all times. "When I quote a price, whether for a financial plan or advisory fees, I try to estimate the time we would need to spend on the case. In many cases we would spend more time than what I have estimated and I have to write off the hours. But I will never charge clients more than what I have quoted them. This is important because when you deliver what you promise at or below a specified price, you build trust and give clients an impetus to give you referrals. I truly believe that I receive so many referrals because I am true to my word, and people respect that."

"For example, a few weeks ago a contractor gave me a quote to do some work on my house. He told me the cost would be four thousand dollars. He proceeded to do a great job, and I was very happy with his work. When I received the final bill, however, I saw that he charged me more than his original estimate [$4,800]. He said it took him more time than he estimated. After he completed the work, he asked me for a referral. Even though I was happy with his work, there was no way I would give him one."

Charles is always looking for ways to make a client feel important. For example, when it's time for a client to meet with him for a periodic review he will send a notice. Before the day of the meeting, a member of his team calls to confirm the appointment. He also sends clients personal notes and birthday cards. Clients who have been with him for a while and know his family well receive a Christmas card with his family portrait.

If that's not enough, Charles likes to give clients financial advice when it doesn't benefit him at all. Case in point: "I had a client who, several years ago, needed long-term care insurance, but because she had previous medical problems, she was not qualified to purchase the long-term care insurance. So I recommended that she look to an assisted living home."

"The one I had in mind requires an upfront payment and a monthly fee thereafter, but once you could no longer afford to pay, you still are able to live there. At the time, she had approximately a hundred and fifty thousand dollars, so we took some money out to get her into the assisted living facility. That was ten years ago."

"She is eighty-five years old now, and no longer has money, but because of our advice, she now has a very nice place to live. They waive the monthly fee, and she has food on table, a nurse taking care of her, and best of all, she's happy. We do work for her, and because she has no money, we do the work for free. We will continue to work for her as long as she lives."

LEARNING FROM MISTAKES

Another reason for Charles' success has been his ability to recognize mistakes and make the appropriate adjustments to help ensure he wouldn't make the same ones in the future. When asked for an example, Charles recalls how he once wished he had been more forceful in getting a client to take his advice.

"I have a client who had five million dollars' worth of stock options after working with a major technology company. Lynn did a complete stock option analysis—some fifty pages—for him. He realized he needed to diversify but insisted that he wanted to wait until the stock got up to ninety before exercising it. At the time it was in the nineties. I said you should diversify at least half, if you want to play it safe. He said, no. He wanted to wait until the stock hit ninety."

"Well, this was during the tech bubble, when it seemed every company affiliated with the high-tech sector would keep going up. But I didn't press him on the issue. Of course, you know what happened to the stock. Now his stock option is worth less than half a million, though it has come back somewhat thanks to the rise in tech stocks in 2003 and 2004. The only mistake I made is that I wish I had been a little more firm in my assertion about the importance of diversification."

When he meets with a client, instead of talking about returns, Charles emphasizes the importance of managing risk. "I bring this up when I first meet a client, which can be a turnoff to some," he admits. "In fact, sometimes I lose people for that. They'll say something like, 'Well another financial advisor told me he can guarantee fifteen percent.' "

"But that doesn't phase me," he continues. "I want them to know that their portfolio, with a moderately aggressive approach, could be down twenty percent in any given year, and as often as three out of the next ten years. It's not pleasant to hear this, but people respect me for being that honest. And I have found that when you are open and frank, people tend to trust you, which is the basis for any winning relationship."

TIRELESS AMBITION

In addition to running a booming practice, Charles still finds time spend personal time with Lynn and their two children. Despite all his success, Charles places a high value on growing his education and training. He recently completed his Executive MBA at Kellogg School of Management, Northwestern University, one of the top business schools in the world. "The school requires two thousand hours a year," he says. "I took four courses quarterly. It's almost like a full-time job. But I don't mind. Education is very important to me."

Charles has been teaching financial planning as an adjunct professor at Western Michigan University since 1998. While teaching, he tape recorded the conversations in his classroom and used the information as the foundation to write a book. The book, *Make Yourself a Millionaire,* coauthored by Charles and Lynn, was published by McGraw-Hill in March of 2003. Charles says he enjoys teaching because it helps him keep his skills sharp, but he also likes it because it gives him the opportunity to give something back. "I feel I owe the university," he says. "When I didn't have the money, they gave me a scholarship. I never forgot that. I want to share my experience to help the school build on its already impressive reputation."

Charles' love for Western Michigan University is deep. He makes significant financial contributions to the university regularly. In fact, he is the youngest member of the school's McKee Society, which permanently recognizes those who have most generously supported the university. In addition, he is a trustee member of the WMU Foundation. He is a board member of the business school finance department, and has set up a scholarship for the finance department as well as a travel fund for the professors of the department of economics. Charles regularly helps nonprofit organizations such as Miller Auditorium. He has sponsored shows and concerts for artists, including Michael Bolton, Kenny Rogers, and Randy Travis.

When Charles was struggling in the early 1990s, he could never have imagined how his life would turn out. And while he is extremely thankful for his good fortune, he believes the best is yet to come. "I still put in almost as many hours outside the office as I do in it," he says. "And when you keep working, even through the tough times, I believe success is sure to follow."

CHAPTER 4: HANK McLARTY

Above and Beyond

Morgan Stanley
Atlanta, Georgia

THEY WILL FLY OUT TO DELIVER A TIMELY DOCUMENT TO A CLIENT. AT *a moment's notice, they'll be at a client's side anywhere in the country and help coordinate all aspects of a client's financial life—still devoting the time to giving back to their community. Hank McLarty has built a unique team that provides a high-end, high-touch service.*

Caring for the well-being of others is central to everything Hank does. The team's mission statement for their business gets right to the point: "Our clients have empowered us to do what is right for them and, in turn, it is our job to always exceed their expectations," Hank says with conviction. But that is more than a feel-good plaque hanging in the office. It's become a daily mantra that guides every decision they make. "Everyone on this team cares about our clients. We are constantly looking for opportunities to demonstrate our desire to be their personal Financial Advisor."

"I tell the team on regular basis that we have to differentiate ourselves and show the clients that they get much more from us than just financial advice," says Hank.

That commitment is what separates the great financial advisor from many others just looking for the next sale. In fact, Hank has taken it so far that he does not worry about making a sale. His team offers solutions for the client regardless of whether or not they get paid for it. "Clients always come first," he says. "It is important that they understand our goal is to provide solutions for their needs and we will go to whatever lengths are necessary to give them choices that make sense for them."

WHATEVER IT TAKES

Clients might be surprised by the integrity and tenacity that Hank brings into every relationship, but no one who knows this *Winner's Circle* financial advisor would expect anything less. His work today reflects the same commitment and mental toughness he showed when he decided he wanted to be a starter on the football team at Roswell High School in Atlanta. He made the team, but spent most of his sophomore year sitting on the bench.

"If you don't start when you are a sophomore, you don't have much of chance at playing division I football," he says.

But Hank wasn't taking "no" for an answer. He spent his Saturdays and Sundays on the field with his father taking him through footwork drills. When he wasn't on the gridiron, he was eating and lifting weights, doing everything he could to bulk up. By his junior year he was a starting linebacker on the team, and by the time he graduated from Roswell, he was entertaining scholarship offers from football powerhouses Georgia, Tennessee, Auburn, and Alabama. He chose Auburn University. While there he earned a reputation as one of the hardest working players on the team.

"I was one of those guys that got to Auburn one hundred percent on effort and not on athletic ability," he says. "But in the off season, I always got most improved or most dedicated. I would lift twice as many days as were required, or do whatever it took."

Hank enjoyed some great years at Auburn. They beat Alabama, Auburn's archrival, every year he was there. They won the South Eastern Conference three years in a row and he played in two Sugar Bowls.

Despite all his hard work on and off the field, though, Hank knew that he would never have the size or natural ability to make it in the pros, so on his father's advice he majored in finance—carrying straight A's through his last two years of school.

He wasn't sure of his career path yet, but he knew two things. A degree in finance would expose him to a broad range of business options, and since he knew he was willing to outwork anyone else on the field, he wanted a career that would pay him for his efforts, not just put him on the same management track as everyone else.

A college friend had joined the training program of a national brokerage firm, and Hank liked what he saw—an opportunity to put the life lessons he learned on the gridiron to work in a job that would reward his efforts.

"I wouldn't be a tenth of what I am today if I hadn't played college football," he says. "I got a heck of a lot more out of that than I have any other experience in life. I learned that when you feel like you are going to drop you can go a little further. You can run one more hill or take on one more fullback, even when you feel like you have no strength left. I would never have felt that or known it had I not played ball. It develops, maybe not a business-oriented confidence, but confidence in yourself."

That's exactly what he needed to survive the grinding struggle of the bullpen. While many fellow rookies sat around complaining about the tedium of cold calling and the relentless sting of rejections, Hank knew all he needed to do was work harder.

"A lot of people go into this business knowing that this is what they want to do," he says. "They've learned about it. They've pursued it. The training to be a financial advisor was a whole new world for me. One of the few things I was sure of was what it took to be successful in this business. I've seen the smartest people in all the areas of the market fail because they didn't want to work."

Of course, Hank didn't make it easy on himself. Between his father and grandfather's business associates and friends, he had plenty of prospects that he could hit up for a quick sale. But he refused to call any of them.

"Everybody knew me as a linebacker from college that trained hard as hell but probably didn't have a whole lot of confidence in my knowledge of the market," he says. "And neither did I."

COLD WALKING HIS WAY TO SUCCESS

In the same way that he always went the extra mile in football, as soon as Hank got his license, he started going the extra mile for his clients—literally. After putting in his hours on the phone making cold calls, he hit the pavement, knocking on doors and introducing himself.

"I thought the biggest challenge of this job was cold walks," he says. "In the beginning, so many days are spent working with little success to show for it. I would feel good at the end of the day, because even if I didn't get one client out of it, at least I knew I had gone out and challenged myself."

He didn't have to worry about not getting anything out of it, though. He landed his first high net worth client on one of those early cold walks. In fact, the prospect was so impressed with Hank's perseverance, that he wanted to hire him. He settled for just doing business with him.

He had spent the morning cold calling a list of businesses that wound around the industrial route that Hank had targeted for his cold-walking sojourns. The president of the company answered his own phone, so Hank got him in the first call.

"This man wasn't exactly happy to hear from me," Hank remembers. "After about forty-five seconds of verbal abuse from the business owner, he ended the call before I could really say anything." The call came during an already frustrating morning and prompted Hank to confront the prospect. He jumped into the car and drove to the prospect's door.

When Hank knocked on the door, the prospect said, "Yeah, what do you want." Hank said, "I am the [expletive omitted] you just cussed out on over the phone ... I wanted to see what I could do to earn your business."

"We sat down and talked for about four hours," Hank says.

It turns out that the prospect was interested in expanding his business. They had a strong product, a solid market, and a debt-free balance sheet. Still, the owner wasn't interested in going public. Hank was stumped; he admitted he didn't have the answers, but would speak to the right people. He tapped a senior broker for guidance, and together they put together a solution.

"He ended up getting tens of millions of dollars from the venture capital firm. He called me up and told me to come get it, and open the account." Hank says. "It was a great feeling."

It was more than a great kick-start for his career. That experience validated everything Hank's gut was telling him about how to succeed in this business. His instincts kept telling him that the real value came when he listened to what his clients needed. Anyone could sell product. Hank believes in providing solutions.

BUILDING FINANCIAL FOUNDATIONS

That early experience convinced Hank that full-service, comprehensive financial planning was the right way to do business—and the only way he wanted to do business. Hank kept his eyes focused on the long-term goal of providing every client with solutions.

What one major client wanted was a piece of the syndication market that was white-hot in 1995. Hank was still a novice broker who couldn't get close to any of those deals, so he found someone who could. He turned to the biggest syndicate producer in the office as a resource for his client.

"I didn't care if I got a commission on the deal," Hank says. "I just needed to get some shares for my client."

Over the next four years, the duo's business exploded, with them providing financial advice on more than $800 million in assets. Over those four years, Hank and his partner built close relationships with about 150 clients who needed—and valued—the full-service financial planning that the team worked to provide.

"To us, it made more sense to be paid based on the client's assets," he says. "I could totally understand why clients would complain when they lost money but were still paying commissions for a trade and that is all they had to show for it."

Hank then started visualizing what types of roles were necessary to provide the many aspects of the wealth management process. Hank sought to bring in-house the knowledgeable professionals and client-service representatives that he felt would offer the type of client experience they are committed to providing.

IT TAKES A TEAM

Hank was pretty lucky from the start. "With assistants like Leah Willingham and Judy Wimpy, you can't help but have a winning team," he says. "They have always made our clients the priority and it shows in the relationships they have built over the years. One of the first questions asked when we moved to Morgan Stanley was, "Are Judy and Leah going with you?"

Hank recalls the potential they exhibited during his early years. "I remember sending Judy to Excel classes because we needed a reporting tool to use for clients. She not only learned spreadsheets, she taught herself how to write programs. Now that is going above and beyond for the interest of the clients."

"The effort that Leah puts in to customer service issues is amazing," Hank says. "You almost have to see it for yourself when she gets on a roll with problem solving for a client."

Service takes you only so far, though. If you aren't making recommendations that ultimately help generate returns, you don't keep those clients for long. But if you can provide the whole package—service and comprehensive wealth management—that is designed to empower your clients in making their investment decisions, you are likely to keep your clients for life, and you are also likely to have a steady stream of referrals from those clients.

"I truly believe that we have to exceed our clients' expectations all the time in order to accomplish our primary focus—showing our clients that they have a personal and trusted financial advisor."

Hank's vision from the beginning was to be able to provide seamless service, anticipating client needs and providing solutions that incorporate all aspects of that client's financial picture. Every client has a financial plan. Every client gets a quarterly performance review. Every client gets regular communications about their asset allocations. Every account is rebalanced every year. Every client gets called on his or her birthday.

Even with this high-end service, it isn't good enough for Hank and team, and they're always seeking to enhance it. For example, Hank is focused even more on customizing each relationship based on the details the client communicates to them; "Instead of listening to client needs and explaining how we can take care of them utilizing our system, we are changing our system based on what the client needs."

"If this were a business of only transactions, we could run it with two assistants. Instead, we have a team of seven people and each individual knows that the clients come first."

The team moved to Morgan Stanley in August 2000. With its broad platform of products and services, Morgan Stanley offered the team the opportunity to take their business to far higher levels.

Hank knew that in the long-term it would be a bonus to both him and the business, but he didn't want to make any quick moves—at least not until he ran into Brian Frank. Having worked with Brian at his previous firm for several years, Hank knew that joining forces with this knowledgeable trust consultant would push both him and his staff to that next level of client service.

When they worked together previously, Hank had seen him in action as a trust consultant and routinely brought him along on client appointments. Hank was constantly impressed with the level of service Brian provided everyone he worked with.

A COMMITMENT TO CARING

That level of caring is something they can't teach you in any training program, which is why he and Hank are such a good fit, Brian says. They share deep, personal priorities and together can bring a combination of services to the table that most financial advisors can't touch.

"Many financial advisors bring in specialists from other areas in the firm to fill in all the other gaps," Brian says. "What we feel like we can bring to the table is the entire process under one comprehensive proposal with us overseeing every piece of the process. We make every effort to ensure that no ball gets dropped, and we'll be there for the duration of the relationship."

That message is delivered from the very first client presentation and is echoed in everything that follows. Together, they go through every investment piece, walking each client through their investment management philosophy and strategies. That portfolio management is then blended with financial planning and estate planning, helping to ensure that each piece of the client's financial picture is working together.

"As we are going down that path together, we are playing the quarterback role," Brian explains, "making sure that clients are also working with their attorneys and their accountants from the get-go."

"We contact our clients proactively to let them know when new issues come up or if there is something we need to be focusing on," Brian says. "That helps us take care of getting their plans in place, certainly, and secondary to that, it also helps to create new opportunities for us from a planning standpoint and new revenue opportunities that help us. But the bottom line is it helps them protect more assets for their estate."

Protecting the estate was a critical issue when Hank and Brian met with a high net worth prospect who had recently been diagnosed with cancer. He had assets scattered across various investment accounts, but the bulk of it was sitting in an individual retirement account. Brian met with him three or four times to discuss the broad issues of estate planning. The prospect also met with an estate attorney he selected to discuss the actions that needed to be considered. The estate attorney started drafting documents, but the prospect just wasn't ready to make any decisions.

Most of the focus through the process was on that IRA. It was important to structure the beneficiary designations so that it was positioned to work with the overall estate plan and help position the rest of his assets in a tax-advantaged manner. Then one night, Brian got a call from the prospect's wife. He was in the hospital and not expected to live much longer. He wanted to meet with Brian and Hank as soon as possible to get everything in place.

"By waiting and not really pushing him or pressuring him on the investment piece, but really doing all the right things first, it led him to this level of trust," Brian says.

Two years later, Brian is still working with the widow to consolidate all his various accounts. She comes by the office every couple of weeks with a stack of financial-related mail that he helps her go through.

"He had stocks with all of the different transfer agents and maybe ten or fifteen brokerage accounts," Brian says. He not only helps the widow sort through all of it, he puts it together in a report that she brings to her accountant.

Along the way, the team also earned the trust of the couple's two children, who have moved their assets to the firm.

That level of trust, though, has to be earned, and sometimes it can take months. The team inherited one client with a $5 million bond portfolio. Having spent most of his career as a bond trader, the client was holding onto a portfolio of long-term bonds that carried a risk of losing ten or twenty percent of their value if interest rates started rising moderately. Hank spent months banging their heads against this client's stubbornness.

"He wouldn't take any recommendation that I made to him," Hank says. "He just assumed that we were trying to make a commission off of him."

About the same time, though, Hank was headed to Mexico for a well-earned vacation the same morning that the client's wife was going into surgery. During a layover in Houston, Hank called the client just to see how the surgery went.

When they got together after Hank's vacation, the client was still trying to figure out why Hank had gone out of his way like that. Finally, he realized there was no hidden motive. Just genuine concern.

"After an hour, he said, 'Just tell me what you think is best.' He trusted me."

BALANCING RISK AND REWARD

That personal attention may be what attracts clients, but no one is going to hang around long if their portfolios aren't keeping pace with their long-term goals. Since most of the team's clients have between $10 million and $100 million in assets, their main concern now is to work with someone they can trust to help them manage those assets to provide a potentially secure future for themselves and their heirs.

"Most of these people have already hit their homeruns," Hank explains. "They don't really care about knocking the lights out. They want to know that the money is going to be there and that it is going to grow at a reasonable rate."

With those goals in mind, Hank and Brian have built a customizable asset allocation model that takes some of the risk out of the market that they have established for each portfolio.

"Our model for investment is a hundred percent simplicity," Hank says. "It encompasses equities, fixed income, alternative investments, and cash. And every one of our clients, for the most part, has a similar model. The differences between one client and another is based on their risk tolerance and their stated goals, so there is more or less equity, fixed income, alternative investments, and so forth."

Hank spends a great deal of time at the beginning getting a true feel for each client's risk tolerance, because what clients think they can handle and how they react to a down market are often very different scenarios. To establish more realistic parameters, they build a model allocation and then back-test it over the past 15 years.

"We will show them exactly how that portfolio would have performed each year for last fifteen years," Hank says. "We'll look at the worst year and ask, 'Is this a situation you could have handled?' "

For example, the portfolio might have dropped six percent in the worst year. Then they show it in dollar terms, illustrating that in one year the client might have lost $600,000 or more, depending on the size of their portfolio. It only takes a few such scenarios to get a real fix on where the allocation should be for each client.

Once the allocation is determined, they start recommending specific investments within each sector. On the equity side, they have put together a model portfolio that tracks the S&P 500. "That's exactly what a client wants," Hanks says.

Even though each client is working off the same equity list, each portfolio is customized. For instance, every recommended trade is analyzed based on its tax ramifications to determine how a transaction will impact that portfolio. If one holding needs to be trimmed to get the portfolio more in line with the allocation model, Hank evaluates the potential capital gains situation. If it is late in the year, he may recommend waiting until January to make the sale to move the tax hit into the next year.

"This gives us flexibility to customize and tailor each portfolio to the needs of the client," Hank says. "As a result, few of our clients have the exact same equity portfolio because of situations like that."

"On the fixed-income side, Hank builds portfolios tailored to the client's individual needs. One of the biggest values we add to a portfolio is the ability to invest the assets in a diverse group of instruments. That diversity can have a dramatic effect on the overall returns. The specialists I have helping me on a daily basis are invaluable. Josh Zucker and Bob Ferrari have been providing me with research and ideas since I moved to this firm. Through them I have added international fixed-income and high-yield and floating-rate notes to provide hedges in different market environments."

Again, though, the real art is in how Hank is able to customize each portfolio within the broader asset allocation parameters that each client follows.

"I am not buying ten million dollars' worth of one bond and allocating it to a hundred people," Hank explains. "I am buying it specially for each account, which means you have to do a ticket for each transaction. There are probably more efficient ways to do this, but I can't customize each portfolio without doing it this way; it's worth the extra work."

"And that is what we do," Hank adds. "We customize."

Once the client makes his or her investment decisions, the allocations are religiously tracked and every client account gets rebalanced once a year.

"I think that is one of the most important things we do for people," he says. "We would not allow an equity portfolio to overrun the bond portfolio. Why would you go through that exercise of determining risk tolerance and building a customized portfolio and then completely ignore it and allow the asset classes to run on their own?"

BEYOND INVESTMENTS

That attention to detail is reflected in the broad range of services Hank and Brian bring to the table. The ultimate goal is to work with every aspect of a client's personal and business finances.

"What's unique about our team is that we have the ability to help facilitate every aspect of a client's financial plan, providing kind of a Ritz-Carlton-like treatment for our clients," Brian says. "Of course, helping clients manage investments is the core of what we do, but we also are able to help clients coordinate the estate planning with the financial planning, and we have the ability and the desire to help clients with the debt side of their balance sheet too."

With all of those capabilities in-house, Hank can oversee the entire plan, hoping to make every piece work in harmony with the client's long-term goals. That holistic focus on each client's total financial picture helped the team land a $60 million account.

The client had been recently widowed and was working with a team of estate planning attorneys that Brian has known for years. On the strength of that past relationship, Brian and Hank were invited to make a presentation to the widow and her team of legal and tax advisors. It was an incredibly complicated scenario, because the estate had been divided into several trusts, but the investments within those trusts needed to be part of one comprehensive financial plan. Their investment savvy combined with their skills in trust services sealed the deal.

"The key was our ability to understand the different trusts that were already created and the different investment allocations that each trust really needed in order to benefit as much as possible from their tax structures," Brian explains.

For example, one of the trusts was a credit shelter trust, which will be protected from taxes until it goes into the next generation. Because of its special tax status, that trust should be funded with growth-oriented assets instead of fixed-income investments. The charitable remainder trust should follow a different investment strategy.

"Without question, I think we earned the confidence of the attorneys and the accountants we work with because they realize that we can speak their language," Brian says. "That adds credibility to both the professional relationships we have and to the client relationships."

SYNCHRONICITY

While the team's mission is to exceed client expectations, Hank's mission is to create a work environment in which that happens naturally. Their top priority is ensuring that everyone understands their role within the team, and, more importantly, making sure that team members understand and respect each other's roles.

Hank wears two hats. His primary function, of course, is to bring in new clients and maintain key client relationships. The less tangible part of the job is his relationship with the firm. Morgan Stanley is one of the largest financial services firms. Hank sees it as his job to maintain relationships with different departments, so that if a client or a team member needs a little extra help or service from another department, they know whom to call for a quick response. "There are tremendous resources available throughout the firm, but if you don't network correctly within the firm, it may be more difficult to take full advantage of them," Hank says.

"My talent is networking within the firm and spending time with clients and prospects," Hank says. "Every minute that I am not doing that is an ineffective use of my time."

That is why it is so critical that the rest of the team works together efficiently, all focused on a common goal and recognizing that the team is much more important than the individual. To make sure that happens, Hank has instituted what he calls a "time block" system, which gives every assistant a two- to three-hour block of uninterrupted time to work on a specific project.

"You can't get anything done when the phones are ringing off the hook and you constantly have to stop what you are doing to take down an order to track down a statement," Hank says.

Instead, every morning the team sits down to go over the priorities for the day. If someone is on deadline with a project, that is their opportunity to say they need a time block that day. When that time comes, everyone pitches in to cover that person, knowing the next day they may need their own time block.

Constantly raising the level of teamwork is especially important when working through an emergency. Hank saw the effectiveness of that team dynamic firsthand one afternoon, while he was sitting on a tarmac in Melbourne, Florida. He was in route to a critical meeting in Palm Beach when his plane was grounded by thunderstorms.

"I am in a panic because I don't want to miss the meeting," Hank remembers.

While passengers were allowed to make calls, his cell phone had no reception, but he could access email through his personal digital assistant.

"Everyone knew how important this meeting was, so they all made two or three calls more than they needed to just to make sure everything got settled," Hank says. "I was overwhelmed, but the bottom line is, when it's time for us to pull together as a team either to take care of a client or take care of a team member, everyone pulls together."

GOING THE EXTRA MILE

It took all of Hank's resources—and ingenuity—to help create, and then keep, one of the team's largest accounts. Several years ago, when the high-tech and telecommunications industries were both booming, Hank got a referral for a businessman who was at the cutting edge of these converging technologies.

Their technology is pretty standard stuff today, but in the mid-1990s, it was revolutionary, and this tiny Midwest company was about to be launched into the international arena with this prospect holding 50 percent ownership in the entire operation.

The IPO was now set to go when a multinational corporation came forward with a deal that was too good to pass up—a combination of cash and stock totaling nearly $200 million, plus paying off that loan. After the acquisition, the stock each owner got in the deal nearly quadrupled. When the dust settled, the prospect was holding nearly $50 million in a single stock, with another $100-plus million in cash and other holdings that needed to be invested.

Through all of this, Hank was acting as the primary facilitator, bringing his financial advice to the table, but the client was still floating on his own with no financial plan, no formal financial advisor relationship, nothing at all to help him figure out what to do with all of this money that he suddenly acquired.

Instead, he had piecemeal relationships with accountants and attorneys but no overarching structure to help the client manage the process. Hank rolled up his sleeves and went to work, analyzing everything the prospect had in place and putting together a detailed financial plan.

Eventually, Hank had earned the client's trust and business. Then the market threw another monkey wrench into the works. The restricted stock the client had acquired in the deal had tripled, but the telecommunications sector was starting to show chinks in its armor. The client was still holding $50 million in stock with six months to go before he could start selling it. Hank knew he had to find a way to unwind that holding, and decided to move it into an investment.

It was a great plan, except the investment had a cap on the amount of that particular sector it would allow in because the investment needed to keep the overall portfolio balanced. Hank, with the strength of the firm behind him, began a full-court press to get the managers to raise that cap.

At the same time, there were problems on the other end. The company had inserted some fine print in the acquisition agreement that blocked the holders of the restricted shares from using them in any hedging strategy. Hank, along with his legal department, worked with a corporate attorney to get the piece of the agreement rewritten.

When the managers finally relented and raised the cap by $50 million, Hank had cleared the corporate hurdle, but still had other things to think about. The extra allocation for the investment was going to be offered on a first-come, first-served basis, so Hank needed to make sure his client was the first in line. He got his client's paperwork in two weeks early.

"I flew out to Lake Powell to get the documents signed because I knew how critically important this was in the long-term to him and his family to get this done," Hank says.

Three years later, the value of the individual shares dropped to around $20 million, but his client's holdings in the investment appreciated to $52 million—in spite of the three-year bear market.

Today, Hank and his team help the client manage every piece of his financial plan, including the trusts in his estate plan.

MAKING WISHES COME TRUE

Given the exhaustive amount of work and effort that Hank and his team bring to every client relationship, it's almost inconceivable that there is time or energy left over for community involvement. But, for Hank, giving back is one of the most important things he does.

He is on the board of the Make a Wish Foundation, on the development committee of his children's school, and president of its booster club. In his spare time, Hank also manages to coach every team his children play on and fills in as voluntary strength coach for the local high school's football team.

"I think most people, when they get out of school and start making enough money to cover the bills and still have a dollar or two left over want to start giving a little back," Hank explains. "I've always felt the desire to do that, but I didn't know enough about charitable giving at first to find something that I was devoted to."

He found it in the Make a Wish Foundation, which grants wishes for children with life-threatening illnesses. A friend of his was on the board and asked him to sit on the finance committee.

"When I started learning about these kids and understanding that these last wishes were sometimes the only happiness that the family had known for the past two or three years, it was easy for me to get involved and to go back to my office and encourage my clients and others to give money to charitable foundations of their choice."

He even got his mother involved. As a high school teacher, she started having students bring quarters to school to build a chain. Eventually, that chain of quarters went all the way around the school.

It may be a given for Hank and Brian, but it certainly is not a given for most financial advisors. That amount of dynamic energy creates almost unlimited opportunity for both the team and its clients.

"I don't think we have any concept of what we are capable of," Hank says. "I think our future is still evolving and growing, so I'm not going to limit us by trying to set up goals. I just know we are all going to show up every day and work our tails off and give every client everything we have."

For Hank, the only goal that matters is having enough time to enjoy his work, his clients, his community, his family, and himself while still being able to provide a level of service that stands head and shoulders above anything else his clients can find anywhere else.

"I want to be able to look back at my career and know that we made a difference in our clients' lives and that I did not forget all the good fortune I have experienced to get where I am."

Chapter 5: Patricia A. Bell

The Right Plan

Merrill Lynch & Co., Inc.
Short Hills, New Jersey

IT TAKES MANY ADVISORS DECADES TO BE SUCCESSFUL IN THE FINANCIAL services industry. Over time—in some cases decades—many realize that the real path to success is to focus on the "right" clients to provide the highest possible levels of service and advice. Pat Bell used her instincts and psychology background to focus on the right clients from her very beginning. Specifically, she was able to attain a high level of success in an extraordinarily short amount of time because of one great idea. Key to Pat's success was defining exactly which market she wanted to target, and for which clients she could provide the greatest amount of value. After that, it was pure determination, hard work, and looking after the best interests of her clients.

PAT'S BEGINNING

Her interest in becoming a financial advisor developed while she was earning her bachelor's degree from University of Colorado in Boulder, with a year at University of Lancaster, near London. Always interested in becoming a psychiatrist, Pat originally planned to major in psychology. With a great interest in an economics class she took, she decided to a dual major in economics. Little did she know how well that background was going to serve her in the future.

While deciding between psychology and a career in the business world, Pat accepted an internship with the National Science Foundation, where she worked side by side with several Nobel Prize recipients. While there, a friend told Pat about her exciting career as a financial advisor and that, with Pat's strong interpersonal skills, she would be a natural at meeting people and building a clientele. Pat thought of it in different terms: "That's when I realized that a career in psychology and a career as a financial advisor are really very similar. As a financial advisor, you are building relationships with people, taking care of their financial needs; it's almost a requirement to understand their psychological makeup." Through a family friend, Pat interviewed with Merrill Lynch and, by October of 1980, began her career as a financial advisor.

Like most successful entrepreneurs, when Pat started in the business, she knew precisely which market she would target and developed an effective marketing plan. Cold calling was not part of this plan, nor did she ever sit around waiting for something to be given to her. Pat had something that few others had: one great idea that would put her in front of hundreds of individuals that fit her target market. Yet while her idea required only a few hours, Pat's greatest strength is that she has always been a people person, and over the years has cemented relationships and confidence by building trust, finding the right solutions for clients, and always keeping the client's best interests in mind.

AN EVENT THAT LAUNCHED A CAREER

Her idea was deceptively simple: She would host a single event. The event would need to attract her target market: women whose families were in the high net worth category, whether they built their wealth themselves or it was part of their family. The result was a decade's worth of leads, hundreds of millions of dollars in assets, and relationships with clients that would last a lifetime.

She teamed up with the local sales rep from a high-end department store and combined a fashion show with a financial seminar. Not just any fashion show, though. Her target market was surrounding affluent communities, such as Short Hills, New Jersey; so, instead of using professional models, Pat went to every women's organization in the area and recruited two members from each to walk the runways.

"It was more common sense than anything. I figured by inviting one or two women from each of these organizations, they would get not only other women in their groups, but their friends to come to the seminar," she says. "If your friend is going to be modeling in a fashion show, you want to go support them."

Because Pat wasn't licensed yet, she arranged for one of Merrill Lynch's cash management account (CMA) specialists to give a brief discussion on money market funds, which at the time were yielding in the mid-teens. It was also a product everyone needs, but, most of all, it's simple and thus understandable to most people. "Of the breadth of products Merrill offers, I wanted to introduce the one product that is right for everybody—money market," Pat says. "I didn't know any of the women, so I didn't want to expose them to anything that might not interest them or not be right for them. Besides, Merrill money market funds are a very nonthreatening product that competes very well against banks."

Pat let the department store, which hosted the event at its location, handle the venue; she handled the refreshments. She knew her target market, so she lined up a top-notch caterer and hand-selected the wine list. She worked with the women's groups to send out the invitations, sending them out herself and making all the follow-up phone calls, thereby collecting the home addresses and phone numbers of each member and introducing herself. When guests arrived, Pat worked the front door alone, passing out the programs and directing the audience to the food and beverages—ensuring that she would at least meet every woman in person who came into the room.

Even with all that preparation, she wasn't prepared for the resounding success of the event. Pat was expecting a few hundred individuals, and so she was delighted when 650 people showed up, crowding the aisles and the back of the room. Even the local newspaper covered the show.

"It was standing room only, and a very festive event," Pat remembers. "We ran out of food. We ran out of wine. The room wasn't big enough to hold all the people. It was hilarious." After the fun ended, Pat was left with a roster of prospects that would take her three years to cultivate. Pat got down to business right away. Shortly after the event, Pat got her securities licenses and began working the list from the fashion show. She called the women at home using the sky-high interest rates on CMA accounts as an attention getter.

"I would simply call them up and say, 'Look, if you have a hundred thousand in your checking account and it's not earning interest, that is seventeen thousand that you are leaving on the table every single year. I don't think that's smart,'" Pat would say.

Neither did her prospects, but invariably the women Pat called ended up explaining that their husbands made all the financial decisions. With the rapport that Pat had already begun building with these women, though, they would usually encourage her to call their husbands directly. They would even give Pat their husband's direct line at the office, advising her to call before 7:00 a.m., before the secretary got in. They would make sure that their husbands took her call. The men took special interest in their wife's new friend, with many sending Pat their cash balances, which they had at their banks.

"I literally would get checks for four hundred thousand dollars or more in the mail, so I opened up all these money-market accounts," Pat says.

The checks may have been coming from the husbands, but it was the relationships that she began developing with the wives that really launched her career and set the tone for the way she would continue building her business over the next two decades. "In those days, these were not joint financial decisions being made, so the wives really appreciated even being asked for their opinion," she says. "And the fact that I had the wife's blessing really helped. My biggest client today tells the story about his wife telling him that she had just met the 'nicest girl.' "

Her success at opening these accounts caught her office manager's attention, and it wasn't long before he was directing new CMA business her way as prospects called the office. In her first year, she was a star rookie, showing great promise. Within a couple of years Pat was the leading financial advisor in her office. By that time, though, interest rates were dropping, making the cash accounts much less attractive. Pat viewed dropping interest rates as an opportunity to begin deepening her relationships with those clients by bringing in new investment ideas.

A HOLISTIC APPROACH

The first thing that jumped up on the radar screen was municipal bonds. While interest rates on money market accounts were sinking, rates on municipal bonds were starting to look good, hovering around the low teens. Add in their tax advantages, and Pat figured these bonds were the perfect vehicle for the very high net worth clients who had $300,000 or $400,000 sitting in their CMA accounts. Again, she started with the wives. One woman would stop by her office pretty regularly just to chat and to drop off checks for $10,000, $15,000, sometimes $50,000 to deposit in the CMA account, so Pat started talking to her about bonds and interest rates.

"Finally, she said to me, 'Let's call my husband.' I called him at his office and showed him some bonds, but he said he had just bought five hundred thousand dollars of them from a competitor," Pat says. That got the conversation going, though. Pat knew this was a product that the client was interested in, and the client knew Pat. The foundation she had built with the CMAs and the close relationship she was building with his wife built a bridge to the husband, who tended to make the final decisions.

"Slowly but surely, I got all the money from the competitor. Then I received all the money from two other competitors the client had relationships with just by servicing the account and anticipating their financial needs," she says. Pat manages more than $120 million for that client today.

Within a few years, Pat had earned the business of around ten percent of the 650 women that showed up that night. By 1985, helping her clients here and there with little boosts in their income accounts simply wasn't enough anymore. Pat was forging strong relationships with both the wives and the husbands, and learned a great deal about their needs, goals, and dreams. In short, she knew so much about them that she felt obligated to do more for them. Pat wanted to be a problem solver, not a product person, so she began offering free portfolio assessments for her top clients—long before the advent of computers and software that could do it for her. Her models were simple but effective, bringing together all of their assets—real-estate holdings, cash, fixed income, and equities—no matter where they were held.

Writing things out on a yellow legal pad, she would show clients exactly how their assets were distributed and whether their current allocation matched their investment goals. More often than not, they didn't. A conservative investor might suddenly see that he had 80 percent of his assets in equities and need more fixed income to balance that out.

With everything laid out in black and white, clients could see their financial disconnects just as clearly as she did. From that point, making changes to the portfolio was not a question, it was an answer.

"It was a done deal that we are going to fix this," she says. "It seemed like a really easy way to then get people to do what I felt was the right action for them to take."

In hindsight, these financial foundations she was building seem obvious, but this was more than a decade before the rest of the industry caught up with her process. For Pat, though, it didn't feel like innovation, it was simply the next step in providing the best service she possibly could for her clients.

"It was really remarkable because now you had a record," she says. "Before that, everything was just in my head. I had a great memory, so I could remember almost anything. But now, I didn't need to; I had all their finances right there in a book."

That gave both Pat and her clients a game plan to work from, and every six months or so she would set up a meeting so they could sit down and review every play. They could see what had been accomplished up to that point and what their next step was.

"The whole idea of planning was the most important evolution in my business," she says of her decision in 1984. "It is one thing to raise the money. It's another thing to do the right thing with it."

A STRATEGIC PLAN

It was the right approach, but it created more work than Pat could handle by herself. She needed someone who could not only take over the administrative chores, but also be her backup with portfolio reviews and client accounts. She had two criteria when looking for her first team member: someone fresh out of college so that she could train them in her way of doing business, and someone committed to staying in the business long term.

Adrienne DiGiorgio had just graduated from college with a degree in economics and was looking for a position in the financial industry. When Pat met her, there was an immediate connection.

"We both just genuinely like people," Pat says. "We are both basically goodnatured, and we are both very open, so it's easy for us to get to know people."

Together, they built a financial planning system basically from scratch, with Adrienne handling the portfolio reviews and research, and Pat working with the clients. They have since hired two additional team members, Kathryn Puorro in 1992 and Cindy Morgan in 1997, and together they provide personal, specialized services to all their clients.

Once the planning started, though, the new challenge was how to invest those assets. Just picking mutual funds or individual stocks without criteria or asset allocation assessment wasn't an option. That's when they tapped into the Merrill's Consults program, finding the right managed money advisor to handle the day-to-day investment decisions based on Pat and Adrienne's portfolio analysis and each client's financial goals.

"We continue to work on that today, and we still continue to work on planning," Pat says. "Believe me, for a lot of people, you can do a plan for them, but it doesn't mean necessarily that they are going to do it right away. Sometimes you have to go over it with them over and over again, until they finally get their act in gear."

Done right, planning is a lifetime process, and Pat's driving goal is to be the one guiding that process. That means staying ahead of the program and trying to anticipate each client's need.

"We solve problems for them that they don't even know they have," she says.

For instance, a few years ago during a conversation with a good friend and a client, Pat learned that the client's grandfather had just died. The grandmother was in her nineties and, as the surviving spouse, would have inherited the entire estate. Pat suggested that the grandmother consider disclaiming her spousal exclusion so that some of that estate could pass tax-free to the daughter and her husband. She did, and two years later, when the grandmother passed, Pat's client ended up saving about $300,000 in estate taxes

"It was just an off-the-cuff conversation that we happened to have because he happened to mention that they were down at the funeral," she says. "I am not a lawyer, but I know a lot about GRAT trusts and by-pass trusts, and private foundations and charitable remainder trusts."

That knowledge and guidance is what has bound her clients to her over the years. And while most advisors reserve that level of advice and service for only the ultrahigh net worth client, Pat doesn't make that distinction. Clients get the same level of commitment whether they have $120 million or $500,000 invested with her. Through the deep relationships she has developed with her clients, she knows them on a very personal level. She knows their families, and she knows their financial situations.

SOLUTIONS-ORIENTED

"We have always been giving private wealth advice to all of our clients," she says. Even if the problem that needs to be solved requires going outside Merrill Lynch for the solution.

Early in Pat's career, she developed a relationship with a local accountant. One day he called her to say that he wanted to introduce her to a nice, elderly couple who needed direction with their investments and a one-on-one relationship. Pat met with them at 8:00 on a Saturday morning. They mentioned that they owned shares in a transportation company, which paid them a "little" dividend every six months. That "little" dividend was over $187,000; so Pat made a point to visit with them every six months, and they would invest the funds into MITs.

Over the years they became friends, and once Pat realized the magnitude of their estate, she suggested that they begin annual gifting to their children and grandchildren. They were reluctant to do so until Pat explained the potential estate tax liabilities. Over time, they also gifted their unified credit. The benefactors, their two sons, were pleased with the advice and the results that Pat had with their parents, and transferred their accounts to Pat as well.

Pat now maintains a multigenerational relationship with the family. Some family members are now deceased, but the relationship has continued to flourish over the years. Pat is close friends with the family, and advises them on all of their financial matters. She works very closely with the accountants and attorneys to maintain a cohesive understanding of all moving parts, including GRAT trusts, GST Trusts, a charitable foundation, mortgages, and more.

Another of her largest clients—a local real estate developer—was approached by one of his leading banks with an offer he didn't want to refuse. Even though he was current on all his loans, they wanted the loans off their books and offered to sell them back to him for roughly 55 cents on the dollar. The only catch was that he had to come up with cash.

Pat offered him a couple of solutions. He could either set himself up as a real estate investment trust (REIT), selling shares to raise the money, or he could use personal assets as capital to finance another loan. He liked the REIT idea; Pat put him in touch with some top REIT specialists so that the client would fully understand the process and meet some of the major players in the industry—and he could seek the most competitive proposition.

Turns out she was right on both counts, and her client appreciated both the information and the effort.

"I knew there was a little bit of a risk that a competitor might try to take him as a client," she says. "But I wanted him to know that Merrill wasn't the only place that I was looking around when I was thinking about solving his problem."

The client ultimately decided not to pursue a REIT with the competing firm, instead asking Pat to take the alternative route that she had proposed: a new LIBOR-based collateralized lending program that Merrill Lynch had recently established. She set up a meeting with the head of Merrill's international bank and structured a deal through which the client could use his securities to pay off the loans and take advantage of the deep discount he was being offered. It didn't hurt that, as a result of the loan package with Merrill, he also ended up consolidating more of his assets with Pat.

Within a year, the client moved $50 million to Pat simply because she was looking after his best interests and solved his problem. "To this day, we still have nearly eight million dollars that we are borrowing under two percent. It's unbelievable."

Still, she didn't push to move all his assets over to her. This was in the heyday of the new issue market, and the client was interested in the hot IPOs. Pat encouraged her client to maintain his relationship with the competition to be eligible for new issue allotments.

"When the new issue market dried up and the guy that he dealt with at the competing bank disappeared, I got the rest of that money, too," she says.

EXPANDING THE BUSINESS

"We try to keep on top of all of our clients' financial dealings," Pat says. Since her early days, Pat's practice has expanded from servicing high net worth families to include ultrahigh net worth clients, with her team serving as an outsourced family office. "We have built a team that is capable of providing high levels of advice and service to both these markets," Pat says firmly. "We are always committed to building on our knowledge and skill set to handle our clients' ever-changing and complex financial needs."

Sometimes, though, it's not just financial issues that are blocking a client's path to success. Often personal hurdles need to be cleared. That's where Pat's background in psychology kicks in. One of her best clients, a well-known corporate executive, had gone through ten financial advisors before meeting Pat. He set the tone in their first meeting by telling her that he had never had a successful relationship with an advisor. However, he also gave her an important tool to work with when he mentioned that he wanted his wife, 15 years his junior, to be more involved in the process.

"I said great, but I prefer that she just come in by herself first," Pat says. "He was very taken aback, but he agreed."

At that first meeting, Pat and the client's wife talked about everything—families, working at Merrill—everything but money, that is. After spending time alone with the client's wife, Pat had a better understanding of the dynamics between the couple when they came in to meet with her together for the first time.

"He was much more outspoken than she was, and she didn't feel like she knew very much," Pat says. "She was clearly uncomfortable because of the situation."

After that first encounter, Pat has always made it a point to try to not have them in at the same time. Ten years later, they are still clients, and Pat has helped them work through every major financial decision, even helping get their children involved. She connected them to an estate attorney to set up a private foundation and a charitable remainder trust, and advised him to gift money directly to his children rather than setting it up in a trust for them.

For another client, Pat was able to provide security in a time of crisis. The client had just lost her husband, and had been referred to Pat to help her put her finances in order and manage her estate. With $700,000 in assets, $500,000 in insurance, and a daughter still in school, Pat's first piece of advice was for her to pay off the mortgage.

"I know a lot of advisors would recommend keeping that money liquid to invest it, but I knew she just wanted security," Pat says. "I thought it would be a nice thing for her to know that she didn't have that payment every month."

The rest she put into a very conservative bond portfolio with just a bit of equity on the side. After that, she set up quarterly reviews with the client. Three years later, the woman is working again, putting money into a retirement account and paying for her daughter's college education.

"But to this day, what she remembers about coming in for that first meeting is my telling her that everything is going to be okay," Pat says. "And it is okay. Her house is completely paid off. She can work for another five or ten years, and she's going to be just fine. To me, that's the most rewarding part of the job, when you empower someone to be able to take care of her family, especially after a catastrophe."

LEARNING FROM MISTAKES

Of course, not every relationship goes that smoothly. Sometimes it's just too easy to put some accounts on autopilot and let things slip through the cracks. That happened with an account that Pat and Adrienne inherited from an advisor who left the business. It consisted of a business retirement account, a personal account, and two smaller personal retirement accounts for both the husband and wife. All totaled, the accounts added up to about $1.5 million.

Adrienne established a relationship with the husband, but it was more transactional than planning. He liked municipal bonds, so she would help him choose those, and occasionally he liked to pick a stock.

"I was just a facilitator for what it was that he wanted to do," she says.

Adrienne barely had any contact at all with his wife—until the day she called to close her account. She had a relationship with another brokerage firm and was consolidating her assets.

"It had nothing to do with the fact that it was a small account; I felt like I had failed because I didn't pay any attention to this person," Adrienne says. "You learn lessons from these things."

Thankfully, it was a mistake that Adrienne was able to correct a few years later. When her client became too ill to continue working in the family business, Adrienne helped the son sort through the documentation needed to take over as president of the company. And when the client eventually ended up in an assisted living facility, his wife sought out Adrienne's help in making sense of some of the legal issues she was suddenly faced with. An attorney that the wife didn't trust had drawn up all the husband's estate papers, and she was planning a month-long trip overseas.

"She was deathly afraid that this attorney was going to somehow take her husband's assets and transfer them to an off-shore account," Adrienne says. "She called me up to see whether or not she could live off of her own assets."

They didn't do a formal financial plan, but Adrienne went over all her assets, both inside and outside Merrill Lynch. They looked at the timing of those assets, the insurance she had, the Social Security she had coming in, the income that she would continue receiving from the business.

"I put her mind at ease, letting her know that what she had and the way things were structured, she was going to be fine," Adrienne says. "She wound up transferring the larger of her accounts in the outside institution here with me, and I am in the process of working on gathering the other assets. I was able to turn it around simply by listening and being available, addressing her concerns, finding out what solutions could be for her, and just helping her understand that someone couldn't come and take the assets. The person at the other institution was not able to do that."

"I have learned from Pat over the years that the biggest thing that you can do is listen to people and address their concerns immediately. That speaks volumes. People are more interested in that and problem solving than they are in just about anything else."

For Pat and Adrienne, that means the personal relationship always comes first. From that core, the rest develops. In fact, it was through a personal relationship with one long-term client that Pat was able to catch a potentially expensive mistake that his lawyer had made. When the client's wife passed away, he was left holding nearly $2 million in his personal account. He needed the income those assets were generating, but, because she had spent years going with him to the track to watch his horses race, Pat knew that the last thing we wanted to do was leave a dime to the IRS.

"I told him that really the only thing he could do estate planning-wise was to set up a family limited partnership and gift away interest to himself," Pat says. "Well, he didn't even know what I was talking about. And when he went to go talk to his lawyer, his lawyer told him it was too complicated."

But Pat knew the client, so she wasn't going to give up on this one. Eventually, the lawyer outsourced the work and the client got the limited partnership. The client lived another 12 years, and when he died the assets transferred smoothly to his son and his daughter—without having to pay a dime of estate taxes.

"They are both very good clients now," she says. "I just tell that story because I think listening to someone and really hearing what they have to say is a little bit of a gift."

GIVING BACK

Hearing what people have to say is a gift that Pat has in abundance, and one that she shares freely with her clients, her colleagues, and her community. For ten years she served on the board of the Inwood House, a home for pregnant teenage girls on New York's upper east-side. Through her guidance, she helped the organization grow from a small institution completely dependent on city financing to a far-reaching inner city resource with a young fathers program, a teen choice program, and a program that brings information on birth control to inner city schools. Today, the organization has stabilized its funding with a broad array of financial support coming from foundations, grants, and public contributions.

Since moving to South Orange three years ago, Pat has been easing out of the Inwood House so that she can become more involved in local organizations, including the Women's Fund of New Jersey (a federation of women's organizations), the Montclair Art Museum, and the Aljira Contemporary Art Center in Newark, New Jersey.

Through all her personal and professional dealings, Pat keeps the focus on just one thing—the relationship. When you get that right, everything else falls into place.

While a one-day event was the foundation of her career, key to Pat's success was her ability to determine the right type of client for her business, predominantly high net worth families. Her ability to ascertain this market was the result of planning that began back in her college days.

The event was highly targeted to the precise market Pat was interested in pursuing; this was part of Pat's strategy the day she entered the business.

More impressive than that early success, though, is the fact that, more than 20 years later, Pat still counts many of those first clients as friends. "We're not in the business of managing assets," Pat says. "We're in the business of relationships."

CHAPTER 6: MEG GREEN

Making a Difference

Meg Green & Assoc. (Royal Alliance)
North Miami Beach, Florida

MEG GREEN WOULD NEVER DESCRIBE HERSELF AS A RISK TAKER, BUT she freely admits to being an overachiever who simply refuses to quit at anything.

When her first husband's company went bankrupt, the former fifth grade teacher got her real estate license and went to work to *help* support the family. After she gave up that career to follow him to a new city and a fresh start, they divorced, leaving her with two small children and barely enough alimony to cover the bills. Her first shot at starting her own business as a financial advisor was nearly crushed under the weight of the collapsing limited partnership business in 1984. Determined, she not only turned it around but became one of the best known advisors in the country, with her own television show and a well-established private practice.

"I don't think there are any of us that are in this business that haven't had things happen to them," she says. "Not by design, necessarily, but, to wit, consider all the money that has been lost in the early 2000s. If you don't learn your lessons from the negatives, then you are not going to be around for the all the positives."

Even today, looking around at all the adversity she has faced down in her life, all Meg can see are the positives.

MEG'S BEGINNING

Born in 1943 in South Orange, New Jersey, Meg grew up in the world of country clubs and cotillions. Even when her father passed away when she was 13, her mother continued to provide her with a sense of security that left her confident that she could do anything.

"My mother was and is fabulous," Meg says. "I was always the most beautiful, the smartest, the best. When you get your parents telling you that, you are going to begin to believe that you are okay."

Along with that sense of self-worth came a very strong sense of values that have guided Meg personally and professionally.

"I grew up in a very affluent neighborhood," she remembers. "All the girls were wearing cashmere sweaters in every color, and they were all wearing Papagallo shoes. You had to have them in every color—the green, the brown, the tan, the black, the navy, the beige, the white."

Meg was allowed to buy only two pairs.

"Not because we couldn't afford it," she says. "But because it was stupid to buy more. I learned that it's not about what shoes you are wearing, it's about how you conduct yourself."

That sense of self-worth and those values built an iron backbone that would eventually support her when life kept trying to knock her down. She got the initial punch during her first marriage. While she had been raised with a strong sense of self, she was also raised with a strong sense of her social standing. She was encouraged to go to college, but not someplace where she would have to work hard—just someplace where she could meet a "nice boy," get married, and have children.

"That was my job—truly," Meg says, laughing at herself.

That severely limited her academic choices. "I could become a schoolteacher, so that if my husband ever leaves me, I can have a job where I can be home with the kids in the afternoon."

That's what she became, living at home and teaching fifth grade until a year after graduation, when she married a boy from her country club and settled into her new career as a homemaker.

"I chose the safe route. I got married, had my Plaza wedding, and then had my boy and my girl," she says. "How smart am I?"

She followed the plan that had been laid out for her, until she found out that life wasn't playing by the same rules. After her son was born, her husband bought a business in Florida without telling her and moved the family south. The business was bankrupt within a year, and Meg's second child was on her way.

"I didn't even have money for baby announcements," Meg says. "We were bust."

CREATING OPPORTUNITIES

She went to work in a retail store owned by some friends of hers. She made enough to cover the $40 birth announcements, but there wasn't much money in selling stuffed animals, so she decided to get her real estate license.

"I was living in Miami Beach and saw that everyone moving in was young, but all the real estate agents were old," she says. "I thought I could sell houses to my friends."

There was just one hitch in her plan. Her friends weren't doctors yet. They were still residents and nowhere near ready to buy real estate where she was selling it. Still, she didn't quit. She juggled work and an infant at home, trying to get listings and spending her weekends sitting at other agents' open houses while her husband stayed at home with the kids. After a year and a half without a single sale, she finally had one that was ready to close. One of her friends had a contract on a house, and she was ecstatic.

That is, until her friend walked into the office a few days before the closing. The friend's husband had found out that someone had died of cancer in the house, and he wanted no part of it. They were backing out of the deal.

"I just looked up and said, 'Okay, I get the message here,'" Meg says. "After she left, I turned to the office at large and said, 'Ladies and gentlemen. It's really obvious that this is not the career for me. It's been nice. Thank you very much. And I'm going home.'"

She sat back down and started cleaning out her desk when an older, retired gentlemen who often hung around the office to pass time came over and sat down at her desk. Reaching into his wallet, he pulled out a worn, torn piece of paper, and on it was a poem entitled "If." "It essentially said, 'If you think you can, you will. If you think you can't, you won't,'" Meg says, summarizing Rudyard Kipling's ballad written in 1895.

"He told me, 'Don't quit. You can't quit,'" she remembers. "'Go out there and say, ''I'm going to do it.'''"

Which is exactly what she did. In the next six weeks, Meg sold six houses, and from there her business skyrocketed. Meg likes to give luck and timing some credit, but it was hard work and creative thinking that generated those sales. And along the way, she learned the single most important lesson in business: You create your own luck.

That's exactly what she did when she was presented with one of the biggest opportunities of her career. She had gone to work with one of the top real estate agents in Miami—"a real barracuda," Meg laughs. The deal was that Meg could take any business that came in while the agent was on vacation. One day a local promoter called: The Bee Gees were in town to cut an album and needed a house to rent.

Meg didn't have any rentals. She told him she'd get back to him that afternoon. She knew that they would be working at Criteria Recording Studios, and she just happened to know the president of the company.

"I called him and said, 'Have I got a deal for you,'" she says. "There's this fabulous house that just fell out of escrow. It has eight bedrooms on the water with a huge guesthouse. You buy the house, and I'll have it rented for you from this company that's renting for the Bee Gees."

She made the sale, got the rental contract, and eventually became the real estate agent for all the Gibb brothers, helping them each buy houses in Miami. Years later, the owner of the record company sold the house and made "a fortune."

Meg became one of the top real estate agents in Miami Beach, but she was still a dutiful wife and mother. So, when her husband was offered a big promotion in exchange for moving to Orlando, she left her career to follow him.

Although his job did work out, their marriage didn't, and one-and-a-half years later they split. Meg found herself with just enough money to buy a $64,000 townhouse in North Miami Beach and alimony of $1,000 a month for a year to get back on her feet—along with a modicum of child support. Going back to south Florida was in the cards, but her old real estate career was out of the question.

"You can't sell real estate in Miami Beach when you are living in North Miami, and I couldn't possibly afford to move back to Miami Beach," she says.

GETTING HER BEARINGS, SETTING HER COURSE

She started her next job search with a list of criteria: She had to have flexible hours because she had two small kids and no one to watch them. It had to be legitimate and upstanding work because that's who she is. And it had to pay a ton of money, because after sitting at the divorce table with her husband and his lawyers and walking away with little, she was never going to put herself or her children in that sort of powerless situation again.

She asked friends for financial advice, but they were of little help. One told her to find another husband; someone else tried to sell her disability insurance, even though she didn't even have job.

A friend of a friend directed her toward her true interest: financial services. He lived in Atlanta and was selling tax shelters. His region covered the entire Southeast, and he was looking for someone who could handle Florida for him. Meg didn't even know what a tax shelter was, but she agreed to go to a training session and find out what it was all about.

"I had my thousand dollars a month for a year, so I figured this would be my learning experience," she says.

Along the way she learned a few lessons that weren't in the prospectus. He came to Miami, taught her about tax shelter products, and told her to prospect accountants and lawyers. She set up an office in her townhouse and pulled out the phonebooks for Dade and Broward counties, calling every tax lawyer and CPA listed. By December, the tax shelter season was closing fast, and she hadn't had one sale. On December 26, he called her from Atlanta and told her there was a hot prospect who wanted to meet with her immediately.

That day she sold a large tax shelter. In January she went to a national tax shelter conference, and that's where her true education in the business began.

"There were three women and ninety-seven men," Meg remembers.

Meg's real luck, though, was that her roommate wasn't part of the tax shelter crowd. She was a certified financial planner from California, and Meg kept her up all night by peppering her with questions.

"I had never heard of certified financial planners," she says. "I said, 'Tell me what you do, and how you do it.' It was just what I needed. I needed someone to tell me what to do—what to do with my IRA, whether I needed a will or not. I never knew this type of planning existed; I didn't even know what questions to ask."

By the end of the conference, she also had the answer for what she wanted to do with her life. With her commission from the tax shelter, Meg financed her start as a financial planner. She called around, found a local financial planner and asked him for a job. He didn't have any openings, but he invited Meg to come to his office and be a fly on the wall while he taught her the business. Going to night school, Meg earned her CFP®, passed her Series 7 and insurance license, and earned her principal's license. She was off and running, and started building a client base.

Suddenly, she came to a screeching halt. On Friday the 13th and a week before her daughter's bat mitzvah, the financial planner she had worked with told her he was out of business, and the office would be closed in two weeks.

Meg initially interviewed with all the major securities firms. Then she decided to follow her instincts, and her second husband Richard's advice, to remain independent. He was a real estate broker, and he had just opened an office on Biscayne Boulevard that had an empty office with a private entrance. For Mother's Day, he offered her the space and some secretarial backup until she could get on her feet, and put up a wall to give her a substantial space. "That was a great gift," she says with a laugh.

By May she was up and running as an independent office, clearing through Integrated Resources, which is now a part of Royal Alliance. She had her own shingle and her own office, but this was the spring of 1984, and the oil and real estate markets were melting down around her.

"This was a very dark period of my life," she remembers. But, again, Meg Green simply wouldn't quit. She slugged it out, helping her clients in any way possible and scrambling just to keep her own footing.

It was a tough fight, but Meg had been through enough to know that the only one she wanted to have to depend on for her professional success was herself. One year into the business, another shoe looked like it was about to drop. Integrated Resources was floundering, and one day three men walked into her office with an offer they told her she couldn't refuse. With Integrated on its last leg, they were going to take over Florida, and they would "let" her keep working for them.

"I told them that if they were going to take over Florida, then I would take one-third of the state, but that I wasn't going to work for them," Meg remembers. "They told me they could really help my business because they knew the ropes. I told them, 'I'm sure you do, but I'm going to be swinging on my own.' "

And swing she did. Right over the fences. Within just a few years after Royal Alliance picked up the pieces from Integrated Resources, Meg was their top advisor five years in a row, and she hasn't let up the pace since.

FIFTEEN YEARS OF FAME

Once again though, Meg found her greatest success by creating her own luck. In 1985, over a year after setting up her own shop on Biscayne Boulevard, she was still trying to find her rhythm and not having much success. She decided to try seminars, and hooked up with a wholesaler to put on a dog-and-pony show for her clients and prospects. When she was stuffing the invitation envelopes one afternoon, a salesman walked into her office—"a very nice, tired looking gentleman," Meg says.

"His shoes were a little scruffy and there was a little shine on his suit, but he was really trying," she remembers. "He was selling hundred dollar memberships to the Chamber of Commerce, and I thought if anyone needed to make a hundred dollar sale, it was him."

While Meg was writing out a check, he was checking on the invitations sitting on her desk and asked if he could come. She said, "sure," and he came—along with three other prospects. The seminar wasn't exactly a resounding success, but a couple of years later the phone rang. It was the guy from the U.S. Chamber of Commerce. He had moved on, and was now the business manager for a local radio station, and they were looking for someone to do a money show on Saturday mornings.

Since Meg's husband Richard was in real estate, he was envisioning a husband and wife show on money. Richard wasn't interested, but Meg certainly was. She was becoming increasingly frustrated with how little the public understood about finances and investing, and she was tired of seeing people getting ripped off.

"I already had in the back of my mind that someday I wanted to be able to teach the public about money," she says. She thought maybe she could pursue some media opportunities after her daughter graduated from high school, but this was an opportunity that she couldn't pass up.

She has never done radio before, but figured she had nothing to lose because they surely weren't going to hire her anyway. So she went to the meeting with the program director and laid it on the line.

"I said, 'Look, first of all, if you want to do a stock and bond show, like, ''should I sell my Exxon,'' I'm not interested. But if you'll let me bring out all the underbelly of money, all the mistakes that people make, then I would be interested in your job,' " she says.

They not only wanted that type of show, they wanted Meg enough to pay her $75 a week to do it. Granted, $75 wasn't exactly big money, not even back then. But this was at a time and in a medium in which most advisors were paying the stations to put them on the air.

Meg grabbed at it, and quickly learned once again how naïve she was when it came to business.

"I was there because I was getting the opportunity to teach the public about money and getting paid for it," she laughs. "It never occurred to me that this was marketing for my business."

It didn't take her long to figure it out, though. Preparing for her first show, Meg was so convinced that no one would call that she called her entire network of friends and family and made them promise to listen and call in with questions. She needn't have worried. The phone lines lit up the minute she went on the air, and when a new program manager took over the station six months later, he boosted the show to four hours.

"He's a client today, of course," she laughs. "They all are. You can run, but you can't hide."

The biggest surprise for Meg, though, wasn't that the phone lines were lighting up at the station; it was that her phone at the office was suddenly ringing off the hook. She never gave her business name or number out over the air.

"I always felt that would be a tacky thing to do," she says. "Especially since I was getting paid to do a show that was strictly educational."

They found her anyway. Within six months she was getting many new clients a week from her radio show, and that didn't count the number of people who called but she turned away. Clearly, the radio show had tapped into a deep public need for information and clear, honest advice, and, after two years of local coverage, her program manager told her she should go national. He could connect her to his contacts with American Radio Networks, which could broadcast the show on subscribing stations coast to coast.

Within a few weeks, Meg went national. The network set up a dedicated phone line and microphone system in her new offices.

"It was hysterical," she says. "My husband and my children were my program directors. I would sit there in front of the microphone with my headphones on, and one of them would field the incoming calls and write, 'George from Medford, Oregon' on a yellow pad. If they could have seen us."

From the outside looking in, the setup may have looked like amateur hour, but the program was nothing but first-class. Between the national and the local shows, she was good enough to get the attention of the local public television station.

"The general manager called me up and said, 'I've never seen what you look like, can you convert to television?' " she says. "I told him I didn't think I would scare anyone off the box, but that I had never done television."

Of course, lack of experience had never stopped her before, and this time was no different. Sight unseen, he offered her a one-hour live show every week, replayed twice through the week, and he was willing to give her total control. She could be the director and the on-air talent, and he would provide the cameramen and the engineers. The only hitch was that she had to come up with a not-for-profit sponsor.

It meant a lot of work, and another very steep learning curve, but Meg was up for the challenge. She decided that this would be a very low-risk way to learn the ropes in television, so she signed up the College for Financial Planning as her not-for-profit sponsor and was on the air.

It didn't take long for her to figure out that television was a long way from radio. Her first day on the air she ran out of material 20 minutes into the one-hour show, and not one person had called in. Her husband was watching, though, and he put in an emergency call to her mother. She lived in a different county and didn't get the show, but he gave her the number to call, and Meg's mother became her first caller.

"I did that for six months, but that's where I learned television," she says. "I would watch myself afterward and think, 'Oh my gosh, what am I doing? You have to learn interview skills. You have to learn where to look. You have to learn what to do with your hands, but I had a chance to watch myself for six months with practically nobody else watching.' "

To further boost her presence, in the early 1990s Meg took a gamble by creating *Meg Green's Financial Workout*, a video distributed in retail stores that helps individuals build a financial plan. While she invested nine months in the project and earned only enough royalties to cover her expenses, the media exposure was incalculable.

The video, along with her personality and financial know-how, and her huge media presence during Hurricane Andrew earned the attention of the local NBC affiliate. The station tapped her to come over to the big time.

"By then I was ready for NBC," she says. And national television was ready for her. Meg spent 13 years on television, building a local and national following—and wearing herself out in the process. Because of her video and all her shows, she made all the talk show rounds, logging in appearances on Joan Rivers, Sally Jesse Rafael, and even Oprah. She was even offered her own high-paying show on CNBC, which she declined for fear of spending too much time away from her family and practice.

"Television keeps you out there," she says. "Everyone sees you, so they all think they know you. They follow you up the escalator asking you if they should sell their Magellan."

"My media career was awesome for a long, long time," she adds.

She was on air every Saturday morning locally and making guest appearances on many national shows, but the glamour had long since worn off. She and her husband found an ocean-front dream home on the tip of the Baja peninsula and she decided it was more fun to be there than on-air on Saturday mornings. After 13 years broadcasting on weekends, Meg has given up her show, but still answers financial questions in *The Miami Herald*'s Sunday business section.

LEVERAGE YOURSELF

Thankfully, Meg learned early in her career that she couldn't be in two places at one time. While she was out educating the public and bringing in the business, someone else had to be at the office, answering the phones and servicing the clients. When she was first starting out, she shared a secretary with Richard, but one of her early mentors quickly convinced her that was not enough.

"He told you that you can't grow until you leverage yourself," she says. "He told me that I had to hire an assistant, not just a secretary but an assistant who could really leverage my time."

She said she couldn't afford it, but he convinced her that she couldn't afford not to.

"So I choked up and hired someone, and, lo and behold, if I was in a meeting, she'd be answering calls," she says. "Suddenly, I was leveraged."

But hiring people is not the same as building a team, and, over the next few years, Meg had a revolving door on her office.

"I didn't realize how much people needed to be managed," she says. "I would hire people, but for one reason or another they just didn't work out."

Meg admits that one of the big reasons they didn't work out was that she just wasn't very good at managing people. It was another long, steep growth curve she had to face, but thankfully she didn't have to face it alone. In 1998, she hired Diane Plucienkowski, CFP®, and it was a perfect fit.

"Managing people is one of her missions in life, and boy is she good at it," Meg says. She also helped Meg realize that one of the greatest strengths a leader can show is in understanding where their weaknesses are and bringing in the right people to shore them up.

"I think those of us who succeed in one way are probably lacking in a lot of other ways," she says. "The way to really succeed is to recognize your strengths, recognize your weaknesses, and then get somebody strong to cover those weaknesses."

Diane understands people, and she understands the systems that need to be in place to get—and keep—an operation moving smoothly. Meg gives her most of the credit for closing the revolving door and for building a cohesive team to help manage the nearly 500 families that have become clients over the years.

Diane is an important cog in the Meg Green & Associates' wheel, as president of the financial planning services division and manager of the human resources end of the business. The third leg of the stool is Todd Battaglia, MBA, who joined the team in 1999 and is now a partner and president, heading up the investment management division. The three of them manage a staff of seven other professionals, working together to service all the needs of their clients.

Together, they provide a unified front for the rest of the team, setting the standards for client service and setting an example of how the team can and should work together. Central to both of those is always placing the client first. Everything that goes on in the office, from how jobs are organized to how people are paid, reflects that commitment to client service.

First, Meg makes sure that her people are taken care of. Salaries are very competitive, and she pays everyone's health care, including disability. What sets her office apart, though, is how people earn bonuses. Everyone draws from two bonus pools. The first one is based on assets under management—not on commissions generated.

"I don't want anybody ever making decisions based on money," she says. "I think that's where people make their biggest mistakes."

Meg's role is the rainmaker. The rest of the team's job is to keep the clients happy once she brings them in the door. That means that the clients stay and the assets grow. When that happens, everyone gets a bonus—the same bonus.

"I don't care what your job is," Meg insists. "I don't care if you are a secretary without a license, or a trader or a financial planner, every job is important, and everyone gets the same bonus."

The second bonus is what Meg calls the "incentive bonus." Anyone in the office can earn an extra $2,000 a year just for thinking outside the box, and it can be applied to any sort of creative thinking, as long as the team member is going that extra mile and making a difference for the client or their coworkers.

There are four categories for the "incentive-bonus," but probably the most important one is being supportive of peers.

"If you come in late everyday or snip at everybody in the office, you are not being supportive," Meg explains. "You will get your salary and you will get your team bonus, but you will not get the 'incentive-bonus.' Of course, if that happens too much, you probably won't have a job, either."

Meg tries to keep bureaucracy and meetings to a minimum, but every Monday morning starts with a staff meeting to go over "La List," which includes anything and everything that people are working on. That way everyone is always up to speed on what is going on with clients or prospects and is available to field a call or fill in wherever necessary. The team also goes over the entire calendar for the week, so everyone knows who is coming in, what they are coming in for, who is meeting with them and what background information they need going into the meeting.

"Everyone needs to be aware of everything, because we're a team," she says. "It's not very fancy, but it's my management style. What you see is what you get."

The biggest challenge is making sure that everyone is satisfied in his job and growing both personally and professionally. Meg not only encourages her employees to move up the ladder, she pays them for it, covering tuition costs and giving them the time they need to complete certification courses.

"I am more of a mentor than a boss because I don't quite know how to do the boss thing," Meg confesses. "I haven't figured that out yet."

She must be getting something right as her door stopped revolving years ago. Most of her team has been with her for several years now, and the additional hires are filling new positions created by growth, not replacing employees who didn't work out.

More impressive than her staff retention, though, is her client retention. Meg has maintained one of the highest retention rates in the industry. She can name the few clients who have moved on over the years, tell you why they left, and in many cases tell you how they came back.

A TEAM EFFORT

Meg's name is on the door, but the minute a client walks through it, they know they are working with a well-honed team of professionals.

"Everyone who is a client of this office knows that they are a client of the team. There is no, 'I work with Todd' or 'I work with Meg,' " she says. "We don't have any of that stuff."

Everyone has his or her job to do, and everyone pitches in according to the job that needs to be done. If a client needs to know what the minimum required distribution is or needs their charitable remainder trust recalculated, Kevin McGann handles it. If a client's CPA needs to know a cost basis on something that was sold, they talk to Mallory Mangrum. Tere DaSilva books all the appointments.

They even share the birthday calls. Every morning the client calendar is pulled up and a memo is sent around the office alerting all to any birthdays. Team members take turns making the calls.

"I don't feel compelled to make all the calls," Meg says. "Someone will say, 'Oh, I'll call her,' and you'll hear someone else saying, 'Tell her I said hi.' It's really nice."

The final, but most important member of the team is the computer system. Richard set it up for her when he found out that she had stopped taking on new clients because she couldn't handle the work. He found a computer expert and together they designed a customized system that is scalable enough to grow as fast as she can grow the business, and flexible enough to handle any and every client, product, or service.

"When I am talking to a client, I can look at my screen and know everything I need to know," she says. She can see how his fixed income portfolio is allocated, where it is performing, and where it might need a little tweaking. And if he wants to know where it is today compared to three months ago, all Meg has to do is plug in the date he wants. It also keeps track of every conversation anyone in the office ever had with the client.

The system even breaks the client book down by activity and assets under management, with each client assigned a different color so each team member can immediately identify the type of client on the phone, even if they don't recognize the name. Pink is for the top 150 clients, and black is for the bottom tier.

"I can go into the computer and find out every single trade that was made and which account it was made in," she says. "There is nothing that I can't tell you about this client or this portfolio."

That level of information and client contact is invaluable, and you never know when you are going to need it. Recently a long-term client passed away suddenly. When his son called Meg, though, she had everything right there, including the name and number of the client's CPA and attorney. She had instant access to IRA accounts, his beneficiary statements, how it was to be divided, and a detailed record of every required minimum distribution the client had received.

"It's just awesome," Meg says. "When his son came in this morning, we had everything ready for him that he needed to sign, we knew everything we needed to do and where we all needed to go from there."

This instant access to comprehensive client information is also mission-critical to another one of Meg's client service directives. No voicemail. Ever. No one even has a voice mailbox. Every client calling in talks to a live person, and anyone who answers the phone can get the client the information they need.

"If I call somebody's office, I want to talk to a live person and I want to get served immediately," she says. "We like to spoil our clients."

CLIENTS COME FIRST, LAST, AND ALWAYS

Internally, the team works as a cohesive unit. Externally, clients get seamless support and customized service. Clients can choose how much or how little advice and planning they want, and they get to choose how they pay for it, on either a fee-based system, a commission, or a combination of the two.

The difference in the customized service Meg and her team deliver is clear from the first time a prospect walks into the office. First, there is not one piece of financial planning software anywhere in the building. Obviously, there are programs out there designed to make financial planning faster, easier, and cheaper, but that's not why Meg's clients come to her.

"Everyone is different; so everyone's plan has to be different," Meg says. "We have guidelines, but it is all handwritten, and it is all about that particular client."

And because each client is different, Meg insists that financial planning is much more an art than a science.

"I think one of my talents, if you will, is that I can figure out what somebody needs to know, and then give them that information in a way that they need to hear it," she says.

It is a skill few advisors have mastered, but one all should develop. For Meg, it consistently sets her apart from the competition, especially when competing head to head for big accounts. Recently she was asked to be one of three presenters for a group of doctors interested in buying annuities.

"I knew that if you sat down in front of a bunch of doctors and started talking to them about basis points that you were going to lose them," she explains. "So I talked to them about their security. Don't give them something they don't want. Find out what it is they want, and then provide the solution. That's what we do."

To do that, Meg listens carefully to both what the clients tell her and what they *don't* tell her. They may tell her they are conservative, but then want a financial plan that is going to return 12 percent or more. She will watch the interactions between a husband and wife, and, if the wife starts fading into the background, she'll pull her out and look for her feedback as well. She also watches body language so that she can gauge when someone is getting nervous or confused.

"Understanding people and their needs is the most important element of financial planning," she says. "Because when you can do that, you are hitting the bull's-eye every time."

You are also getting the type of personal knowledge about each client that you need to make sure you are always doing the right thing based on their personal situation. For example, the state of Florida has a quirk in the laws governing ownership and title of assets. Assets titled as "tenants by the entirety" instead of the more common "joint tenants with right of survivorship" offer much greater protection from lawsuits.

One of her clients is very active in the community and sits on several boards, including the board of a local bank. The bank got sued, the board got sued, and he got sued. Meg knew the law and knew him, so all his assets were titled properly so that the client was protected from the suits.

"It was just because we are always thinking about the right way to do things," Meg says.

And you never know when each client is going to need that attention to detail, so you can never afford to let anything slip through the cracks. A few years ago the daughter of one of Meg's clients was going through a particularly nasty divorce. Unfortunately, the son-in-law was running the family business and was in line to inherit it if something happened to the mother. The client called Meg in a panic, desperate to get her son-in-law off the legal documents and out of the business; Meg found an attorney and scheduled to meet with the two of them the following week.

That wasn't good enough. In Meg's mind, this needed to be handled immediately. Within Meg's network of professionals, she arranged to have a simple will created, outlining her wishes; two people in the office witnessed their signatures. That weekend, the woman was killed in a car accident. They found the will in her purse, and it held up in court.

"I knew what needed to be done to keep her protected until Tuesday," Meg says. "And we are always going to do what needs to be done to protect people."

Granted, these are tough conversations to have with clients. No one wants to focus on the worst-case scenario, so that's why Meg always gets all the negatives out on the table and dealt with very early in every client relationship. She makes sure all of those contingencies are confronted and handled with before they start talking about investing.

"It doesn't matter what your portfolio looks like if you have a serious illness and don't have long-term care insurance," she says. "Most financial advisors look at the money but don't see the person attached to that money. I think the whole difference here is that we believe that, if you take care of the person, the money comes along with it."

WOMEN OF TOMORROW

Meg can talk for hours about the business she has built and the clients she has helped over her two decades in the industry, but what really gets her emotional is when she starts talking about a regional group she helped start when she was at the local NBC station called "Women of Tomorrow."

She and a network of professional women go to the local high schools and provide one-on-one mentoring for young women at risk. They talk to them about staying in school, not getting pregnant, developing a career. They use their own experiences as examples for these young women, and then provide scholarships for the girls who stay in the program and go on to college. She still tears up when she remembers one of the first scholarship award lunches she attended.

"Most of these girls don't invite their parents or grandparents, but I was sitting at a table with an older woman and her granddaughter, who had cerebral palsy. She was very disabled but a very bright young woman, and we were giving her a scholarship and a computer," Meg says. "The grandmother told me that this was the first child in her family to go to college, and that she was a throwaway child. She said, 'My son and my daughter-in-law didn't want her, so I said I'd take her. Now look at her, getting a scholarship and going to college.' "

After the girls finish college and start their own careers, they often come back and become mentors themselves.

"It's really, really special," Meg says.

She also finds time to volunteer with several other local charities, including The Wellness Community, an educational and support center for people with cancer, and she was recently voted onto the board of the new Aventura Hospital and Medical Center.

When work and community service become too much, she and Richard disappear to their second home in Los Cabos, Mexico, where they can relax and spend time together. Still, she never lets herself get too far removed from the office. Richard has set up a home office down there, complete with a DSL internet line and a phone line with a 305 area code so she's always just a local call away from her clients.

Watching her flow seamlessly through work, family, and community involvement, Meg almost makes it look easy. It's not, but her philosophy is deceptively simple.

"Do well for others and you'll be rewarded in the long run," she says. "And always follow your heart."

CHAPTER 7: DAVID NOVELLI

A Virtual Family Office

Smith Barney
Houston, Texas

DAVID NOVELLI BUILT A HIGHLY SPECIALIZED TEAM THAT CATERS TO *helping clients achieve their goals and fulfill dreams.*

For David, perfecting a client's plan can take time. For one client, David and his team spent three years getting the right structures and investments in place.

The client had sold his interest in a family-owned business, netting about $30 million, which he had invested in bonds along with some tech stocks that had climbed through the roof during the late 1990s. David and his team worked with him to set up a family foundation and funded it with those highly appreciated stocks. When the market was soaring in early 2000, David and his team convinced him to diversify those shares inside the foundation, where that appreciation could be shielded from capital gains taxes. He got out before the market downturn, protecting both portfolio and his family's future. The client, who could have sustained substantial losses, is forever grateful for David's advice.

Now they are working with him to build an estate plan that can shield the rest of his assets from taxes, while providing for his family and his philanthropic objectives.

David credits his team for this and many other positive client experiences. David says, "The work of all the people on our team provide this client—and every other client—a positive experience and credibility to the advice we provide. Our client experience is clearly the work of a team of highly qualified professionals who work together for one common goal: to provide exceptional advice and service to every single client."

FAMILY AFFAIRS

Central to each of these client relationships is a comprehensive family wealth management plan designed to address both the financial and personal priorities of the entire family, not just the primary investor. So the first step in that relationship is to spend the one-on-one time it requires to truly understand the entire family. That means bringing everyone to the table and finding out what is important to each family member.

"Our first introductory meeting usually includes a quick summary of our strengths and capabilities," David says. "Then we complete an exhaustive inventory of the client's financial circumstances. We want to understand the client's income statement and balance sheet. We're looking for a great deal of granularity with respect to their assets and liabilities. We want to understand how they are structured, where they are invested, what type of successes they've had with those investments in the past, and what types of failures he or she has had. And then we want to get a really keen sense of what their priorities are. What do they want to accomplish?"

"People usually have a great deal of personal meaning attached to their wealth. For some, it's an opportunity to be philanthropic and give back to their community. For others, it's the opportunity to enjoy the fruits of their labor with family and friends. Some see wealth merely as a means to ensure the future prosperity of their children and grandchildren."

"We want to understand what this affluence, what this wealth, what this success means to our clients," David says. "Then we want to understand very clearly what their priorities are; from this we're able to construct an all-encompassing task list to meet those objectives."

That task list lays out all the strategies available to best meet that client's goals. If the client is focused on philanthropy, for example, the task list will focus on creating vehicles such as a family foundation or establishing an endowment strategy.

"We deal with structural issues," David says. "Are assets for this client better held in a 529 plan for college planning, or should they be in a trust or custodial account?"

David's team analyzes every option and then screens potential solutions against each client's immediate needs, long-term goals, tax liabilities, and the assets available. Are the assets tied to a single concentrated stock position? If so, how should that position be unwound? Is the client interested in philanthropy? What is the best tax structure for charitable giving? Should they use debt to finance some of their strategies?

"We want to make sure we evaluate all these options so that we recommend the appropriate solutions," David says. "The devil is in the details. Which strategy, ranging from a family foundation, a charitable gift fund, a charitable remainder trust, a charitable lead annuity trust is the best strategy for this family in this circumstance to accomplish the goal that was defined in their priorities?"

Only after these decisions are made do they begin the more traditional discussion about asset management, because often the client needs to understand the context for making what can be difficult financial decisions.

FINDING THE RIGHT SOLUTIONS

One of David's clients is a senior executive with a large publicly held company who has most of his assets tied up in a concentrated stock position. The client has watched his net worth shrink from $100 million to less than $50 million because of pressure on that company stock, but he is still reluctant to let go of it because of his long-term optimism for the company.

"This is commonly a very difficult thing for officers of companies who have created substantial wealth through their investment of that single company's stock," David says. "We've been working on helping the client get to the point where he can rationalize his decision about diversification."

They are helping the client make important decisions by keeping him focused on the three primary goals he laid out during their first meetings: to ensure a comfortable retirement, to provide for their daughter's financial security, and to diversify that single stock position.

David's partner, Diane Gonzales shares, "The first step was to suggest the client sell ten million dollars worth of stock and invest the proceeds in municipal bonds. We showed the family that the bond portfolio would generate a minimum income of three hundred and fifty thousand dollars, which they had determined they needed to maintain a comfortable lifestyle."

The second step was to run Monte Carlo-style simulations on what a broadly diversified $10 million equity portfolio would look like in conjunction with the bond portfolio. He then compared this against what they could expect from their single stock position. By focusing on the client's stated objective of receiving an 8 percent annualized return, David and his team showed the probability of meeting those objectives while lowering the overall volatility of the portfolio.

"We are helping the client better understand both the cost and the opportunity of maintaining a concentrated stock position because volatility has both a positive and a negative impact on long-term performance," David's partner Jeff Kirkham explains. "Sometimes clients are unwilling to sell because they believe in an upside potential of their stock. But they often fail to understand that there is also a downside potential of the stock. We are just trying to quantify for the client the probability of both the upside and the downside and compare that to the same for a diversified portfolio."

Another client is a retired software executive who is living off the cash flow from a substantial municipal bond portfolio. The rest of his assets are growing in a diversified equity portfolio that is overweighted in a concentrated position in his former employer's stock. He has been holding onto the stock in the hopes that the company could be bought out, but that optimism has blinded him to the very real downside risk of the stock, which is trading around $15 a share. The team developed similar probability studies and illustrated to the client the risk of holding the concentrated position.

This is where the strengths of working with Smith Barney and Citigroup become evident. David is tapping into Citi's vast corporate resources to build a customized protective hedge on that concentrated stock position. Using a variable prepaid forward, the client can participate in the stock's appreciation up to $20 a share, while locking in any downside risk at the then current price of $15.

"That gives him some upside potential along with some liquidity to take advantage of current market opportunities," David says.

Working through these complicated scenarios takes time, patience, and the entire team working toward the same mission of helping each client achieve his or her personal goals.

"What we are trying to deliver is a group of honest, highly competent people who are fun and enjoyable to work with and who are reliable, dependable, and capable," David says. "In that process, we can ensure that our clients, who have very high expectations because of their own level of success, are making steady progress toward their financial and life priorities."

DAVID FINDS HIS CALLING

Looking back over his academic career, David Novelli describes himself as a "late bloomer." He had spent his high school years living in the long shadows of his older siblings, one of whom set several Texas State and collegiate records in distance running, graduated magna cum laude from Rice University, and was a Rhodes scholar nominee.

"People kept telling me I should be more like him," David says. "But I wasn't really focused on achieving great things."

In many ways he still isn't, at least not for himself. Instead, David focuses on achieving great things for his clients. Any personal success he has achieved for himself has always come as a result of helping his clients and teammates meet their own personal goals. That was the cornerstone of his business plan when he became a financial advisor in 1992, and it is what consistently sets him apart from the competition.

David and his partners, Diane Gonzales and Jeff Kirkham, have designed an entire team around servicing the complicated and demanding issues facing affluent families. Building what David describes as a "virtual family office" made up of a CPA, two CFP®s, and a recently minted MBA, the three have recreated the same type of professional financial services offerings to which most of their clients are accustomed. David explains: "Our clients are senior executives running large public companies, and they are accustomed to having financial teams supporting their most important professional decisions," David says. "We function as the financial team supporting their most important family financial decisions."

The level of expertise they have developed in-house allows the team to provide much more comprehensive financial modeling and support than simply investment management. They manage their clients' liabilities as well as their assets, providing advice with respect to wealth transfer planning, philanthropy, and even their family dynamics.

"It's about the people, not about the performance," David emphasizes. "We have to be focused on our clients' concerns and problems and then build our practice around the clients' needs and expectations."

COMING FULL CIRCLE

That client focus has helped David build one of the industry's most impressive financial advisory practices in the country, but it's a far cry from what he thought he would end up doing. By the time he graduated from Strake Jesuit College Prep in Houston, David's primary objective was just to get out from under his own family dynamic. He headed to the University of Texas because that's where most of his friends were going and where he wouldn't be in the shadow of his older siblings.

At college, "there was a point of maturing where I realized that if I was going to succeed, it was going to be up to me," he says. "I think I shared the same characteristics that my siblings had. We are all pretty driven people, but I just hadn't discovered that about myself yet."

The point of that discovery came in his first accounting class. At the time, David was majoring in electrical engineering, but he was more engaged in friends than his studies. Accounting struck a chord.

"It was the first time I began to achieve at the University of Texas," he says. "It was like a light went off, and I had a real connection to what I wanted to do. They say that accounting is the language of business, and the whole idea resonated with me."

By his senior year, he had raised his grade point average from C's to nearly all A's, and had passed the CPA exam before he even graduated. That academic success pushed him to the front of the line when he started interviewing for jobs, and he left college with offers from each of the what was then the Big Six accounting firms.

He accepted a position in New York with one of the these firms and ended up in the financial services center, a relatively new offshoot to the firm's traditional accounting business that was focused on Wall Street. After a few years a friend of his at a securities firm started a full-court press to recruit him onto the firm's trading desk. The job was as a sales coordinator, working as a liaison between the financial advisor and the traders on the taxable fixed-income desk to handle custom orders from wealthy individual and institutional clients.

To David's dismay, just as family dynamics pulled David out of Houston, it was family that brought him home. Six months into the new job, his father was diagnosed with cancer and died just a few months later.

"It was heartbreaking for everyone in the family," David remembers. His siblings had scattered around the globe, leaving David's mother home alone to cope with her loss. Within a year, he knew he had to go back home, so he started calling his firm's branch managers in the Houston area, asking if they had a job for someone with his skills.

FINDING HIS NICHE

He had never really seen himself as a financial advisor, but the only job he could find at the time was as an assistant to two of the firm's top producers making a nominal salary plus a portion of the revenue that he generated.

But he wasn't coming for the money, rather for his family, so he made it work until the two partners jumped ship and moved to a competitor. They offered David a 50 percent hike in pay join them. "I'm not that smart, but at least I could do *that* math!" David recalls.

"A few years later, I was planning to propose to my wife, but I knew I couldn't support her and raise a family on that modest compensation," he says. "I went to the partners and asked them how I could transcend to a more significant role within the team."

They struggled for a solution. The partners were unwilling to share their business, no matter how hard he worked for them, so again

David relearned the lesson he was taught in college—that his future was up to him. Even though he doubted his abilities, David decided to take a chance as a financial advisor, sketching out a business plan on a legal pad one long Saturday afternoon at his fiancée's apartment.

"I realized that there were two things that needed to happen in order for me to be successful," he says. "First, I would have to talk to people whom I would most likely have something in common with and, second, I would have to have some mechanism through which to generate business."

As a CPA, he figured that his accounting background gave him an in with the local CPAs who were likely to be involved with the executives of publicly traded companies. His strategy was to go after the administration and execution services for their employee stock options.

"I reviewed my plan with the branch manager," David remembers. "He said, 'It'll never work. I'll give you six months. Good luck.' "

That was all he needed.

"I was convinced that if I could sit down with chief financial officers and other people in treasury departments, then I could get an opportunity to help executives exercise stock options," he says. "This would put me in situations where money would be in motion. I was looking for a significant catalyst, such as a liquidity event with the options, restricted or founder's stock that would generate an opportunity for me to offer financial planning and other services."

That's not exactly a fast-track strategy for success as it's a long, arduous process of relationship building. Nevertheless, David knew that over time it would be the best way to capitalize on his accounting background and truly add value to client relationships. It was also one of the few areas in financial services in which he truly had an edge over his competition.

"I would not have said at the time that this was cutting-edge or anything like that," he says of his early days in the business in 1992. "It was just what was most apparent to a guy who had come from a public accounting background and was working in a brokerage office."

He pulled together his initial prospect list by culling the Rule 144 filings of all the publicly held companies in the Houston area, and looking for the ones who offered option plans that would meet his demographics: executive option plans that had few disbursements. Then he would track those companies' stock prices.

"There is a correlation between the strike price of the option, the amount that's 'in the money' and the rising price of a company's stock," he explains.

The flex point in that correlation is where significant amounts of money start to move, so that is where he positioned himself. He was at the right place at the right time when two local technology companies were just beginning to make their moves, and they became two of his first corporate clients for execution services. That put him in front of the senior executives he ultimately wanted to do business with. Even today, David gives more credit to his timing than to his own innovative thinking.

"It worked for a lot of reasons that are not necessarily about me," he says. "It worked because people were beginning to emphasize stock option plans. It worked because they are complicated transactions to complete and because at the time there were no vendors in that business providing good service."

It also worked because when he got the go-ahead to exercise options for senior executives, he would ask for the opportunity to come in and sit down with their families to discuss their goals and objectives. Through that entrée, David brought his unique accounting perspective and began the broad discussion of financial planning, rather than just investment options.

"We talked about exercising these options not in the context of how to invest this money, but mostly in how they could structure their resources to accomplish what they had identified as their personal and financial priorities. We were really driving to use my unique background to establish a prudent and responsible monetization strategy to accomplish these goals," David says.

He got their attention because it was a conversation that many executives had been too preoccupied to focus on. He earned their business by following up those initial meetings with a detailed report that restated their priorities, and he presented a strategic and comprehensive plan for achieving those priorities.

He knew he was going in the right direction, and within a few months the business started taking off, despite his branch manager's dire warnings. Working through referrals, he managed to earn one of the technology company's business from a major Wall Street firm within two years of that first transaction.

DEFINING THE PRIORITIES

The big turning point didn't come until 1994, when he was vacationing with his brother's family at their lake house. Over the course of the weekend, David's brother invited the people next door over for dinner. As luck would have it, the neighbor was a cofounder of what is today one of the largest computer makers in the country, but at the time it was just a small company generating about $80 million in revenue.

Still, David kept in touch, and nine months later, when the company was readying a secondary offering, the prospective client contacted him about making a presentation. The company and its executives already had relationships with other advisors and, of course, their underwriter, but he wanted to give David a chance to make a pitch for some of the business. The individual was offering 10 million shares at $30 each—$300 million total.

David was given 30 minutes to make his presentation, so he headed off to two meetings in different parts of the country with a more senior and experienced specialist in tow.

"I was still finding my way, and was doing a good job, but I basically told him that I would lead the presentation," David says. "He was surprised by my taking charge, but I was really clear on what I wanted to say in those thirty minutes."

He wanted to cover three points. First, he wanted to make it clear that he wasn't there to sell anything. His job was to provide asset allocation advice based not on what has happened in the past within certain asset classes, but with an eye toward what might be happening in the future, based on each client's personal goals.

"I told him, 'What we want to do with our asset allocation effort is to help you avoid a tragedy,' " he told him. " 'We want to give you a chance to get off the freeway before a crash happens.' " Then David outlined the in-depth research he conducts on all the investment managers he recommends who would invest the proceeds.

"I call it the four "Ps," We believe that, if we know the people, their philosophy, and their process, then we have a better sense of the contributing factors that can help determine their future performance," he explains.

Finally, he told them that, as the new guy coming onto a team of existing advisory relationships, he would be responsible for finding solutions that would complement their existing managers, not duplicate their efforts. David got the mandate and the relationship grew to over $100 million.

"It was probably that event that gave me the confidence to know that from a competitive perspective I was no longer an inexperienced guy trying to build my business, but a guy who was capable of addressing even the most complicated and sophisticated situations," David says.

TEAMING UP

His strategy not only got the attention of clients and prospects, it also started getting the attention of some of his colleagues. Though they didn't necessarily understand what he was doing, they could not deny what he was accomplishing. Another advisor in his office, Pat Condon, proved successful at earning the personal business of several local corporate executives, but stock option execution administration was outside his area of expertise. Pat recognized they shared the same values and passion for their work and approached David about joining strengths and becoming partners.

Early on they started digging into a small niche within stock option administration. They also focused on directed share plans, through which employees are able to buy shares in a company during its initial public offering

"Pat and I became quite proficient at the rules and regulations associated with these types of transactions," David says.

More importantly, these transactions brought David and Pat into the planning process long before any offering was launched. This meant they were working closely with the founders and executives of these soon to be public companies before their IPOs launched them onto their competitors' radar.

The strategy also positioned the pair to take advantage of some unique opportunities that were starting to develop in the financial services industry. Around the mid 1990s, their firm initiated an acquisition that David and Pat felt was detrimental to the service they were providing their clients. They started shopping around for the firm that they felt was best positioned to offer their clients the best experience.

Smith Barney was an exceptional fit. The firm was formulating its own business plan to build a corporate client group. They joined the firm in January 1995.

"Smith Barney's extraordinary platform enabled us to compete effectively and offer the hands-down best service for company founders and senior executives for large corporations who are dealing with complicated financial issues," David says. Issues that David and Pat were already on top of: diversification, asset management, regulatory, and legal issues surrounding options programs, family wealth, and multigenerational wealth transfers.

As their success in this burgeoning area grew, so did their team. "One of the things that I learned from my two first bosses is that teams are not only about leveraging your own effort," he says.

"They are really more about developing talented people to be successful and independent within the team. It's critical for a team leader to say, 'I am going to help you be successful whether you continue to work for me or not. And while you are working for me, this will be your responsibility, this will be your compensation or your share of revenue in our team environment.' "

Using that formula, the team has grown impressively within the Smith Barney system. Pat and David are the leaders, taking on the responsibility of maintaining their relationships with key corporate clients and working with the senior executives of those corporations. Backing them up are seven financial consultants who provide reinvestment services to client employees exercising stock options.

As the business has grown, David and Pat have remained partners, but each has taken on a specific piece of the work, building their own divisions within the practice. While still responsible for managing significant stock plan clients, David heads up a private wealth management team, and supporting him are two of his own partners. Diane Gonzales handles private wealth management service, while Jeff Kirkham focuses on new business development. They have a dedicated staff that supports their efforts

"I am working with the most affluent individuals and families within these corporate clients," David explains. "We are also establishing relationships with affluent and super affluent families that are not affiliated with our corporate clients."

David meets with a lot of prospective clients, some of whom are not in a position to make a change. Regardless, the team makes the time to share their philosophy and approach. David sums it up this way, "I tell prospective clients, 'There may not be a catalyst now, but like most people, you will likely encounter an issue or an obstacle, whether asset or liability based in the future. When you do, let us know. We're pretty good at coming up with solutions and I'm confident we'll be able to help you.' "

ALWAYS GIVING

Giving has been a mantra of David's since he entered the business—whether it's giving to Smith Barney—in terms of ideas, mentoring other financial advisors, providing clients high levels of advice and service—or to his community. He and his wife Amy are active in a number of charities and nonprofit organizations. Besides being on the board of trustees at his children's school and his high school,

David is an elder in their church. As a family, they sponsor a child in an inner-city Houston school

"We are always looking for ways to give back," David says. "We believe that, of everyone who has been given much, much will be demanded. We want our family's life experience to be a manifestation of this philosophy."

CHAPTER 8: LOUIS CHIAVACCI

Exceptional Value

Merrill Lynch & Co., Inc.
Coral Gables, Florida

HOW'S THIS FOR ADDING VALUE? LOUIS CHIAVACCI AND TEAM provide a comprehensive financial plan that an outside consultant would charge $25,000 to $100,000 for ultrahigh net worth individuals *before* they become clients. Or how about his value-based investment strategy that left clients virtually unscathed through the down market . . . or his high level of service, which clients have claimed doesn't exist anywhere else?

Adding value and building trust are the cornerstones of Louis's business, which consists of 45 clients with an average net worth of $65 million. He and his team currently manage $1.2 billion in assets.

Trust, incidentally, is the main reason Louis became interested in the securities industry.

In high school, Louis was determined to enter the U.S. Naval Academy. He had the grades, but was required to undergo a series of interviews. One interviewer in particular intrigued him, a retired Naval Commander and Blue and Gold officer named John Jackson who was a financial advisor with Merrill Lynch. Louis was admitted to the academy and remained close to John, who encouraged Louis to start investing in the markets. Louis became fascinated with the markets and in particular with John: "John's clients absolutely loved him," Louis says, clearly still in awe of his mentor. "When he decided to retire, his clients wouldn't let him. He had the one hundred percent trust of his clients, the foundation of any great client-advisor relationship. Out of pure dedication to his clients he stayed in the business another ten years to serve his family of clients."

During two years at the academy Louis developed habits that would last a lifetime. "I learned the meaning of hard work and discipline," he says "I never worked so hard in my life." These habits would later play a crucial rule during the development of his business and maintaining disciplines in his investment approaches.

Louis transferred to Indiana University, where he first earned his bachelor's degree, then an MBA in 1986. His first job was as a sales associate in training at a Wall Street private banking firm. After 11 months he was relocated to a regional office in Miami. The bank's process demanded that he open one new account every six weeks; clients had to invest a minimum of $5 million.

As a rookie out of business school, building a high net worth book of clients was challenging. Louis knew he needed to work smart and fast as he had to meet quickly approaching goals. He figured that networking was out of the question for him, as he had little to offer CPAs and attorneys in return for their referrals. The discipline he learned at the academy served him well when cold calling, working from 7 o'clock in the morning until 8 o'clock at night. "It was painful making those calls and sending out extra letters," he says. "It's always easy to avoid doing something that's uncomfortable, such as receiving rejection. I always had the mindset that there was only upside." Louis saw many others fail because they couldn't take the rejection. "I learned quickly that if you're calling on the right types of people—those for which you can best offer your services—and you're always polite and professional with people, no matter how many times they hang up, you can always call back and they may be willing to listen to you."

Louis focused his calls on two segments: corporate executives and bank owners, whose companies were being taken over during the consolidation in the banking industry in the late 1980s. This market seemed right for Louis, who sought sophisticated investors who would understand the value of the investing discipline he was developing.

When calling prospects, Louis' priorities were to build a rapport, gain an understanding of their needs, and then try to land a meeting. "It was a challenge trying to create compelling reasons for high net worth clients to spend their scarce resource, time, to talk to me over the phone or meet in person," Louis says. "I constantly sought ideas that they would find interesting so I could land a meeting." One of his first prospects was the chairman of a large public company. "I was always the first one to fax him significant news articles or research about his company. He knew that most articles were going to be published, but he liked to see them right away." After Louis sent the article, he would follow up with a phone call, always prepared to discuss the news. "I was constantly getting in front of prospects with something they'd be interested in, and I would never waste their time." Once on the phone, he would learn as much as possible about them so he could add more value to future conversations and to better offer them solutions. "I always wanted to have substantial dialogue with the prospects; you can't rely on pleasantries, because they are short-term, and the chances of winning business are diminished because you can't waste a prospect's time." Louis persevered in finding a reason to follow up with another phone call or to arrange a meeting.

Over time, Louis developed a pipeline of high net worth prospects and opened a dozen accounts over two years. From the beginning, Louis focused on being a portfolio manager for his clients, primarily with a value-based approach. "When I walked into a prospect's office I wanted him or her to know that I was more knowledgeable than any of my competitors," he explains. "At the age of twenty-four I couldn't rely on playing golf with a guy who just sold his company for a hundred million dollars. Instead, I would show him ideas and talk to him about strategies he wasn't hearing elsewhere."

Once Louis built the foundation of a clientele, he shifted from prospecting almost 100 percent of the time to a balance of prospecting, managing the assets, and client service. "At this point you must appropriately allocate and budget your time and work efficiently." Louis says. "The most efficient way to accomplish this is through implementing some degree of standardization across your client base, so you don't have disparate portfolios or different types of clients that require varying types of specialized needs. In regards to the portfolios, I always tried to use my best ideas across every portfolio with varying allocations. I focused on developing my own value-based investing approach; it was a niche I was comfortable with and it helped me to position myself as a specialist."

Louis continues to discuss the right types of clients: "One of the biggest mistakes rookies in this business make is they will take any type of client. On one hand they need the business in order to generate revenue so they can survive; on the other hand, if they're not equipped to handle the business then they're going to lose it anyway. If a rookie focuses on one or two types of clients, they can build a niche with real specialized services and build a scalable business."

As Louis spent more time managing portfolios and serving clients and less time prospecting, he felt the need to pursue smarter prospecting methods, primarily through referrals. Louis explains: "Business begets new business. Once I introduce an idea to one client, it's not unusual for him or her to say, 'I have a friend that may be interested in this' or 'I have a relative that would like to learn about this.' These referrals are typically similar to the clients, such as being ultrahigh net worth or a high-level executive, and they tend to have similar needs."

For example, in the early 1990s a client in Tampa, Florida referred a friend who was a New Zealand resident and became a client. One day Louis presented a private equity deal to the new client. The client immediately suggested that Louis show it to several of his friends, while he was in the country. Two of the friends became clients.

"A real key element in being successful in this business is knowing what your circle of competency is, and staying in that circle. For example, we don't try to manage 401k plans or executive compensation plans. We know what our specialty is and we try to do it exceedingly well. If a prospect asks for these services, we refer them to someone that we feel is highly qualified to serve their needs. For our ultrahigh net worth clientele, we'll move beyond our circle of competency only to accommodate someone's needs, such as when a client is looking for a new mortgage or wants to finance a large purchase, such as a plane. We believe in specialization, working with clients who share our investing philosophies."

Those whose portfolios he managed were well rewarded. His team's "core" portfolio—primarily large-cap U.S. companies—returned 24.41 percent per year from inception in 1994 through 2002, versus 13.30 percent per year for his benchmark, the S&P 500 index.

Louis manages the portfolios and investment strategy with partner Mike Nies, a CFA® (Chartered Financial Analyst) and CIMA® (Certified Investment Management Analyst), who joined the team in 1999. Mike is the former CFO of a private company; he is a graduate of the U.S. Naval Academy and attended BUD/SEAL training before serving as a Navy Pilot throughout the United States and abroad, including combat air operations over Bosnia Herzegovina. Ken Chan, formerly involved in portfolio management and research at a major bank trust company, performs stock market analyses.

"Our team generates investment ideas through a variety of methods, including the screening of financial databases, industry resources, independent research and ideas from Merrill," Louis explains. "If a security appears attractive, the next step is detailed quantitative and qualitative research." The quantitative approach leverages Merrill's powerful research. For new ideas, the universe begins with the S&P 500, keeping the top 200 as dictated by Merrill's recommendations. Out of those, the 75 companies with the highest ROE are kept.

Stocks considered typically meet the following characteristics: companies that are industry leaders in product development, market share, or pricing power, with international growth opportunities. Fundamentally, the company's balance sheet must contain low debt relative to enterprise value and free cash flow, with free cash flows and intelligent management of excess cash; revenue and earnings growth must be sustainable and consistent. "We invest in companies that we believe trade at a substantial discount to what we consider to be their true business value," Louis explains. "We are patient investors, not market timers. We believe that over time the price of a stock will rise to reflect the value of the underlying company. Most purchases are viewed as if we were buying a piece of a business, not just a stock certificate." Management must be shareholder-friendly with a high level of ownership, and shares must be highly liquid. When customized for each client, tax implications are measured, along with consideration for other equity holdings.

"The value philosophy rests on the principle that the market is not always priced efficiently," Mike says. "Value investing is predicated on the ability to find undervalued securities. We view growth and value as two sides of the same coin. In this context, value investing is simply buying growth at a discount. Paying a reasonable price, with a sufficient margin of safety, in an enterprise that can grow is essential to long-term investing."

The sell discipline is equally as rigorous. The team monitors for diminished fundamentals, in extended valuations, negative changes in business outlook, or failure to execute the business plan. As a position increases, the holding may be gradually sold to reduce overconcentration, or reduced in order to pursue additional opportunities. Also, selling may occur to realize tax advantages.

"Our sell discipline is consistent and well defined," Louis says. "Because we buy companies that trade at a discount to intrinsic value, we are much more likely to average down when a stock price declines than to sell. We will, however, sell a stock when the underlying business fundamentals change for the worse, or if the stock price appreciates to our 'intrinsic value' price target."

While this conservative approach has proven outstanding returns, Louis admits he'd rather underperform the market than take more risk with his investors' money. "We know we will underperform the broader market indices from time to time," he acknowledges. "Since the best way to create wealth is by compounding your investment returns year after year, we measure our success by our ability to create an environment in which compounding will flourish. This means trying to deliver consistently positive returns over a prolonged period of time. It also means avoiding 'The Big Loss,' which is the mortal enemy of compounding and may take years to overcome. Our bias toward value investing was really the premise on which the team was built," Louis says.

Mike adds: "We don't judge success on a short-term, quarter-to-quarter basis. Warren Buffet has said that 'compounding is the eighth wonder of the world.' Our investment philosophy aims to minimize factors which prevent the power of compounding from working to the fullest extent possible."

Like Buffet, Louis and team stick to their value-based disciplines. As the bubble was inflating in 1998, with the S&P returning 28.34 percent, the core portfolio trailed by over thirteen percentage points; in 1999 the core portfolio returned 22.22 percent, in line with the index. "I was taught to buy low and sell high," Louis says with a chuckle, then points to reports on the table that prove his unwavering faithfulness to his value-based strategy. "At times, we may have felt a bit foolish—oftentimes wondering if we were missing something—for not jumping on the bandwagon, but we stuck to our principles and everything we've learned over the years. We understand our circle of competence, and not straying is an important part of being successful. Our clients are sophisticated individuals and rely on our honest advice and thorough understanding of the markets; one way we earn their trust is by being consistent and sticking to our discipline." Louis' clients stood by his side during the down markets.

All but one, that is. And from this client, Louis will forever blame himself for not trying harder. In 1998 Louis earned a referral who sold his engineering-parts manufacturing business in the 1980s for over $100 million. After the first meeting, the prospect asked Louis to model a $5 million portfolio. Based on the prospect's objectives, the team put together a plan that included an allocation of 26 percent to high-quality, short-term municipal bonds, 10 percent to high-yield corporate bonds, 34 percent to domestic equities, and 10 percent to international equities. Ten percent was appropriated to real estate and 10 percent with futures managers. Louis singled out a dozen portfolio managers, each with long-term performance records that would be used for each investment, plus their performances versus benchmarks and correlation analyses among the managers and asset classes. Also included in the analyses were complete risk measures, risk-return and market-line analyses, proposed portfolio versus the single components, historical best and worst performances of portfolio, and more. This plethora of data was then inserted into analyses that used Monte Carlo simulations to provide a range of expected returns over varying timelines.

The team also provided intensive historical relative-value analyses and economic scenarios for each asset class that justified asset allocations. All in all, the analyses showed that the portfolio would provide far less risk than an all-equity portfolio.

Impressed with this work, in early 1998 the family engaged the team with an initial investment of $35 million. The assets were allocated according to the proposed plan. With almost no exposure to technology stocks, in 1998 and 1999 the diversified portfolio performed according to plan, but behind the technology-laden Nasdaq and S&P 500 indices. In December of 1999, only weeks prior to the peak of the tech bubble, the client fired Louis, citing underperformance and an allocation in REITs. "Although we realized we were missing a major move in the market, and even lost a client because of it, we stuck to our principles," Louis says. "To us, it's more important not to lose money than it is to make money." In early 2000, the client found an advisor who would invest most the portfolio in high-growth stocks, only to see a substantial portion of his net worth vanish in the ensuing months.

"Losing him was one of the biggest mistakes we made in the business," Louis says. "But losing that client made us a better team. We realized we lost the client not just because of underperformance, but also because of how we communicated performance with him. We should have done a better job educating the client. And I shouldn't have let him jump in the market with or with out me." At the time of Louis' recommendations, REITs were yielding almost 10 percent and trading at almost a 30 percent discount to net asset value. "We perform extensive relative-value analyses for our clients to determine which sectors are expensive and those that are inexpensive," Louis explains. "Thankfully we have built tremendous confidence and trust among our clients; otherwise they may have thought we were crazy at the time."

This proprietary relative-value analysis incorporates Merrill's quantitative research, which enables the team to rebalance portfolios at opportune times. Louis describes the asset class orientation: "Simply put, is growth expensive relative to value?" In 2002 the team determined that the high-yield bond sector represented compelling value as compared to investment-grade bonds. "We incorporated this value-based discipline into each clients' overall investment strategy, with the exception of those clients for which we felt these bonds were not suitable." Louis continues to discuss the importance of his asset class strategies: "Asset allocation is by far the greatest contributor to a portfolio's total return. This is one of the drivers of the investment strategy that we produce." In the REIT example, the late 1990s was a time when investors were chasing high-growth stocks, not old-economy stodgy REITs. In Louis' mind, that was the best time to enter that market. "Historically, REITs have traded in a range of sixty-eight percent of net asset value, or NAV, at its trough to a peak of one hundred and thirty percent. The mean is one hundred and two percent. In 1999 we were buying the REITs at approximately seventy percent of NAV." Louis compares the spreads, or price differences, between the different sectors, adds economic variables, and determines where value exists. Over the next few years, REITs became one of the best performing asset classes. In retrospect, investing in REITs instead of technology stocks in 1999 and 2000 was a product of our capital allocation process. "This disciplined approach helps to preserve our clients' wealth."

During the course of frequent communications with clients, "We have very frank discussions with clients about how painful it is to lose money," Louis explains. "Of course by the time the late 1990s arrived, investors seemed to forget the meaning of losses." During the discussions, Louis builds models to show clients the impact of losses on their portfolios. Additionally, the team's detailed quarterly reports act as a reminder of the disciplined approach, need to rebalance, and the importance of sticking to the long-term game plan.

As the bubble continued to inflate in the late 1990s, Louis' relative valuations were off the charts, pointing to severe overvaluations in several sectors of the equities markets. Even though clients' portfolios were balanced according to Louis' models, he became further convinced of an impending down market. "I was concerned that a major market downturn would adversely affect the securities industry," Louis reflects. "We believed that if we offered superior value for our clients, including comprehensive service and advice, we would be well positioned to capture market share in the event of a downturn."

Although Louis' proven portfolio management skills remain consistent from his early days, the late 1990s brought one transformation to his service offerings: "The biggest difference in my business is my team of specialists, versus the beginning when I only had a team of two—my assistant and me." In 1998 Louis moved his business to Merrill Lynch, primarily for the firm's deep resources for HNW (high net worth) individuals and the support they provide teams. "Merrill supported my decision to build a team of specialists," Louis says. "After interviewing many firms, I chose Merrill because I knew my clients would be best served there."

Under the new structure, Louis classified his investors into two groups: customers and clients. "Our customers, typically a family office, buy products like hedging instruments or loans," Louis explains. "The relationship tends to be institutional in nature; they seek particular and sophisticated solutions." For customers, the decision-making process is made collectively, as a consensus, with the family office, accountants, etc. Louis makes it clear to all involved that when several voices contribute to the decision, it is indeed a joint decision that doesn't rest on him. Conversely, when he and team are the sole decision makers, he takes full accountability. "When we structure a *client's* portfolio, on the other hand, first we form an opinion, then offer the client a financial plan and asset allocation strategies. We offer a menu of products, from REITs and managed futures to private equity and distressed debt. We make judgments, among which choices are most attractive and what's suitable for the family's needs." Louis and the team make 95 percent of the decisions for clients.

When Louis arrived at Merrill, he was surprised by the firm's determination to offer financial planning to all the firm's investors. "This was the first time I really got a close look at comprehensive financial planning," Louis remarks. Somewhat skeptical, he tried Merrill's HNW financial plan for a client. He took a comprehensive view of the client's entire financial situation and provided the information to Merrill's financial planners. Several weeks later he reviewed the plan, and presented it to the client. The client had never before seen such detailed planning for his unique situation. The client was hooked and so was Louis.

"I felt like I was looking into the future," Louis recalls. "When I left that meeting, I was determined to incorporate a high-level, senior financial planning professional on our team to deliver very personal value-added financial advice on areas ranging from estate planning and wealth transfer to portfolio management and private banking. I would create a team of specialists that would focus on HNW individuals, a one-stop shop for all their financial needs. Our HNW clients value their time, I was determined to make their lives easier."

Louis immediately set out to find a top-notch professional with extensive comprehensive financial planning experience. After several months, Louis and Mike found the perfect match in Michael Beckerman, who spent almost ten years at a Big-Four accounting firm as a senior investment advisor and senior consultant for the firm's individual clients. He also managed wealthy families, HNW individuals, and corporate executives, offering estate and retirement planning as well as insurance, stock option, and income tax planning. With a master's degree in taxation, and professional designations ranging from CPA, CFP® (certified financial planner), PFS (personal financial specialist), and CIMA® (Certified Investment Management Analyst), few were better qualified for the position. The team also hired Belkys Pereda to provide further depth to the group's financial planning by providing investment research and analytical support. Belkys has an MBA and CFP® designation on the way, and she previously held these responsibilities with a major corporation.

To provide exceptional service, Louis and partners Mike Nies and Michael Beckerman hired operations specialist Kim Lemmon, who entered the business in the early 1980s. Another key hire was Sana Fuerth, who has 15 years' experience in operations and client service.

With the team in place, most clients received a high-end comprehensive financial plan. Clients were pleased with the level of detail and ultimately felt more comfortable with their financial situation, strategy, and plans for the future. Some ultrahigh net worth clients were surprised to learn that there was no additional charge for the plans, considering they had paid thousands of dollars for the same type of planning in the past.

When the bubble started to deflate, though Louis tried to prepare his clients well, he was still surprised. "I didn't expect the bubble to continue for as long as it did," he says, "nor did I expect the ensuing bear market to be as severe as it actually was. Our disciplines kept our clients' portfolios intact because of our value bias, disciplined asset allocations and relative-value approaches. Additionally, our financial planning model and the newer wealth management approach (estate planning, wealth transfer issues, income and capital gains issues) combined to offer a very high-end service for our clients." With this value proposition, clients showed their appreciation with phone calls, letters, and referrals.

In 2002 Louis received one such valuable referral. The individual had fired his existing advisor for lack of competence, and was interviewing at least five potential replacements. The prospect had sold his company for stock which subsequently appreciated five-fold to over $220 million. His number one objective was to reduce his risk and diversify. The prospect gave each prospective financial advisor the information necessary to construct a strategy.

To start, Louis' team analyzed the family's balance sheet. His cash position was $15 million, with concentrated stock of $172 million and collared stock of $9 million. Other investments included $3.2 million in large-cap stocks, $3 million in private equity, and $20 million in real estate. They estimated his one-year after-tax total return to be 9.3 percent, or $20.6 million.

Based on this information, the team analyzed three situations: Scenario A was a base case, consisting of selling the concentrated stock in the open market for $181.7 million, based on an average share price of $44 for the shares not collared and $32.7 for the collared shares, pay the capital gains, then diversify. Louis describes the advantages: "It is very simple, it would more than meet his investment needs and the new portfolio would consist of dramatically lower risk. The growth from the portfolio and the excess cash could be used to reinvest and ultimately pay an even higher cash flow. The disadvantage is a large initial tax bill, and no benefit from any further price appreciation in the concentrated stock because it would be sold in its entirety."

Instead of selling the stock, Scenario B entailed contributing $50 million of the concentrated stock to an exchange fund and entering into a prepaid forward contract to protect the stock's downside. This allowed the stock to retain some upside potential and generate cash flow that would diversify the holdings. Then $35 million of the proceeds would be used for a tax-harvesting indexation strategy, offsetting gains with losses to deliver a higher after-tax return. The remaining $72 million of restricted stock would be sold to pay taxes of $14.5 million. The exchange fund and prepaid forward transactions would be utilized as components of the new diversified portfolio. "In Scenario B there are substantial tax savings, far lower—but still modest—risk, and substantial upside potential in the company stock due to the prepaid forward transaction. The disadvantages include a big tax bill, although $20 million smaller than in Scenario A, and upside for the company stock is capped."

Scenario C utilizes four techniques to help the investor diversify his concentrated position: $35 million into a tax harvesting indexation strategy using the S&P 500, a prepaid forward contract on $50 million of the concentrated stock, $50 million into an exchange fund, and the remaining $72.6 million of stock into a CRUT (charitable remainder unitrust) with an annual 7 percent payout. Louis points out that, while Scenario A begins with a starting value of $180 million because of the tax hit, Scenario C theoretically starts at $225 million, not $222 million, because the net present value is added due to the tax benefit of the CRUT. "This scenario provides a high degree of diversification, participation in the upside of the company stock, far less downside than the initial portfolio, and pays no capital gains taxes to achieve diversification. Furthermore," Louis adds, "he would not utilize any aggressive tax strategies since these are all IRS code-driven." The plan includes disadvantages of annual trust filings, a large irrevocable transaction, and the loss of CRUT assets in the event of premature death, but could be offset by purchasing life insurance in an irrevocable trust.

The client told Louis that he, his lawyers, and accountants had never seen such detailed and thorough modeling and appreciated their consultative approach. The client said: "I have never seen anything like this." The client chose Louis and his team over the competing advisors.

In a similar situation, Louis was competing for the business of Tim Gannon, founder of Outback Steakhouse, after his company went public. Tim praises Louis: "When we took the company public back in 1991 every firm on the street came in to pitch the founding partners for our personal investment business. Louis was in that group and is the only advisor of the bunch that we are still working with. He is the last one standing."

"We tend to win the business because of our intense preparation and our approach—we're not selling, we take a consultative approach toward modeling the choices the prospect or client faces," Louis explains. "We always clearly articulate the disadvantages, and lay out all options in straightforward terms for each strategy. And above all else, Michael Beckerman's depth of knowledge and awareness of the nuances clearly differentiate us from others."

Once he has a client, Louis maintains ongoing communications over the telephone and in person, whether the client is on the other side of town or the other side of the world in New Zealand. Additionally, the team prepares quarterly reports that clearly state the clients' objectives and current assumptions, such as economic forecasts and opinions on the direction of interest rates and currencies. The report details the holdings, broken down by sectors and asset classes, as well as recommended allocations. The performance numbers are listed, as well as the client's starting point, or initial deposit, subsequent deposits, and how the portfolio is performing against appropriate benchmark indices. Louis showed me an actual quarterly report, covering the client's identity: "We were down 5.74 percent in 2002 versus the S&P 500's loss of 22.03 percent," Louis says. "Of course we never like to lose money, but the client was very pleased." Louis turns several pages to show evaluations for each of the client's portfolio managers, comparing their risk-adjusted performance versus their respective benchmark indices. Toward the end of the report is a page recommending next steps for each client, such as recommendations to rebalance the portfolio or strategies to accomplish a client's objective, such as buying an airplane or yacht. "This ongoing communication is vital. We refuse to lose a client due to a lack of communication," he demands, referring to his previous mistake of not better educating a client.

To provide the highest value proposition possible, it's understandable Louis would offer his clients a comprehensive plan, which is valued between $25 thousand and $100 thousand at a consulting firm. But why offer it to prospects? "Our prospects are mainly referrals," Louis begins. "Oftentimes it's a sister, son, friend, or colleague.

Because these are relationships of our clients, we feel compelled to offer them one hundred and ten percent of our services, as if they were already clients. There's no greater pat on the back from a client than receiving a referral, who has given us a glowing recommendation. We take this business very personally."

"From another business perspective, we often receive referrals from prospects," he says, describing quality referrals as the best way to grow the right kind of business. "Also, offering them a free experience of our comprehensive services enables them to better determine if we are right for them, and we can determine if they are right for us."

"The more value we offer our clients and prospects, the better we seem to become," Louis says proudly. "Whether it's our comprehensive plans, our investing and asset allocation strategies, or our friendship, we all benefit as a result of the relationship."

In addition to sharing knowledge with his clients, he dedicates much of his free time to the industry and his community. He frequently lectures financial advisors about best practices and how to service high net worth clients, and he serves on the board of the University of Miami Center for Ethics & Public Service, and as an adjunct professor, teaching an investing course to attorneys seeking their master's degree in taxation.

CHAPTER 9: REBECCA ROTHSTEIN

A Preeminent Platform

Smith Barney
Los Angeles, California

THE REBECCA ROTHSTEIN STORY IS A TRUE AMERICAN SUCCESS STORY. As one of Wall Street's most successful women, her story confirms that determination, integrity, doing what's best for the client, and good old-fashioned hard work can be a potent recipe for success.

"Considering where I came from, I still can't believe this is me," Rebecca says. "I keep thinking somebody's going to knock on my door and say, 'This is not your life—we're just kidding.' It's incredible to imagine that I am able to help so many individuals as a career."

Rebecca carries a small slip of paper wherever she goes. She's had the words memorized for years, but there's something about holding it and reading its message that gives it its greatest impact. It's a simple but profound message she read from the book *The Four Agreements: A Practical Guide to Personal Freedom* (Amber-Allen Publishing, 1997).

> Don't take anything personally.
> Be impeccable with your word.
> Don't make assumptions.
> Always do your best.

From early in her career, Rebecca has approached her business and her clients from a solutions-oriented perspective, more interested in helping clients achieve their goals, objectives, and dreams rather than generating sales. The book gave clarity and voice to the natural instincts she was already following and helped her focus her own energies on the issues that matter most: her family, her clients, her firm, and her team.

REBECCA'S BEGINNING

Born in Winnipeg, Manitoba, Rebecca was a high-school dropout, unsure of what she wanted to do with her life. She worked odd jobs in the retail industry and moved to Los Angeles, where she worked for two department stores. She married Ronald, whom she still describes as her "true love," when she was just 20. Soon after marriage, they had three children (and now has four), she was traveling constantly and still managed to earn her high-school equivalent GED and attend a trade school for design and merchandising. But the choice to work was out of necessity as her husband was still establishing himself in the entertainment industry. Rebecca describes those days as "challenging, yet motivating and fun."

One night, Rebecca and Ronald were tossing around ways that she could earn money without having to do so much traveling. Because she had an interest in helping others achieve financial success, he suggested that she consider becoming a stockbroker. "I said to him, 'Who would want to hire me as a stockbroker?' "

Within a span of a few months, "I convinced my mother to pay for my Series 7 class. I passed the test, received my license, and started at a small retail brokerage firm in August 1987."

Based in Los Angeles, Rebecca is now a financial advisor with Smith Barney. Hundreds of millions of dollars were entrusted to Rebecca when the market bubble burst in the early 2000s from both new clients and existing clients that were empowering her as their primary financial advisor. Not bad considering it was the most challenging bear market in nearly three decades and thousands of advisors were leaving the business. While Rebecca makes her success look simple, her fortitude and strong positive state of mind helped her to overcome virtually all the struggles that normally plague rookies.

REBECCA'S START IN THE BUSINESS

Starting her career at a small firm, Rebecca had no formal training, no mentor, and nobody to show her the ropes. "I had to figure out the whole business myself," she says with a laugh. "Because I had no training, I was very careful never to answer a question unless I knew the correct answer; if I didn't know the answer, I would be up front with the individual, and tell them that I would call them back with the right answers. Over time, she took every opportunity to further her knowledge by reading everything she could get her hands on relating to investments. She also found the right professionals from which she could access information and developed a network of people that would support her. "I once called a trader and said, 'Could you please teach me everything you know about California municipal bonds.' The trader took the time to teach me, then I called the client and spoke with credibility and conviction." Slowly but surely, Rebecca developed enough knowledge to build a basic business consisting of stocks, bonds, options, and to lesser degrees annuities and lending. "Because individuals always have a wide array of financial needs, there's always business to be done," she says. "You just have to figure out what to do."

Rebecca had a daily goal of setting up five appointments, either by telephone or in person. While most in the business—or any business, for that matter—consider cold calling tedious and degrading, Rebecca loved it, calling it exhilarating and dynamic, and never feeling a sense of rejection. She explains: "It was just me, a desk, a phone and a stack of leads, and I kept telling myself. 'I'm going to get there.' "

When making a call, she quickly learned to break the ice immediately and developed a cold calling strategy that proved effective. "The approach was designed to overcome the resistance that many investment professionals face when canvassing for new accounts," she says.

Though she did not realize it at the time, Rebecca was already following the first agreement, don't take anything personally. She remembers well an angry response she got from one cold call when the prospect admonished her to never call him again. Rebecca calmed him with steady reassurance instead of a brash sales pitch. "During the call, I would say, 'I can't imagine how many cold calls you've had and how many people have tried to get you to do business with them. All that I ask is to please not hang up on me. If I can convince you in the next two or three minutes that I am a worthwhile person to speak with, then we will continue to talk. If I don't, then please feel free to hang up.' " Rebecca found that, while seemingly simple, being up front and open with prospects and clients is an essential part of developing trust. Moreover, she was speaking from the heart: "It wasn't a manipulative tool to get business. Instinctively it felt like the right thing to say. After all, people feel bad when others hang up on them. This is always how I communicate with people."

During these calls, Rebecca would refrain from asking for an order. "That's the biggest mistake that people make when speaking to someone for the first time," she offers. "How can you earn trust when you're only looking to make a sale?" Rebecca simply wanted to introduce herself and make people feel comfortable and give them confidence in her abilities. More times than not, prospects would appreciate her sincerity and give her the opportunity to continue speaking. "I know that I am technically a salesperson but I consider myself an advisor. I am very sincere in what I speak about, and I'm very interested in knowing who you are, what you do, and what I can do for you. I try to be frank and honest all the time, and I'm never pushy." It's clear that when Rebecca finds the right solutions for prospects or clients, her enthusiasm and conviction are evident in her presentation.

Rebecca learned what clients want from their advisors, particularly high net worth clients: someone who is willing to take the extra step to understand exactly what they need. That philosophy is central to the second agreement: Be impeccable with your word. For Rebecca, that means always keeping the focus on the client—listening intently and speaking the truth with integrity.

After the initial call, Rebecca offered to send prospects information at no cost or obligation and extended an invitation to meet with them personally if they felt she could help. This sincere and subtle approach paid off. Her success rate was an astounding 5 percent, bringing in one new account for every 20 prospects she spoke to.

Her first year in the business, she surpassed her own best year's earnings as a buyer in a department store. Adding to her pressure was her determination to maintain and build deep relationships with her clients. To accomplish this, she hired her first assistant, Catherine Buckingham, in 1991. Out of Rebecca's pocket, she paid Catherine a salary of $20,000 a year. "I told her at the time, 'Hopefully, it will get better.'" Catherine agreed and has been with Rebecca ever since. Catherine and Rebecca are years-long friends; in fact Catherine is godmother to Rebecca's four sons. "Catherine knew me when I was studying for my Series 7 examination," Rebecca says fondly. "I've earned the trust of my clients, and I trust Catherine unequivocally."

As her formula for establishing trust and initial rapport began to kick in, as well as the added service provided by Catherine, so did Rebecca's number of new accounts. By year two, she was on the fast track, but faced one challenge: She lacked a plan. She was opening accounts for anyone who was willing to invest with her, but had no real idea of how to build a business. "Although I was doing pretty well," she remembers, "I didn't have a vision for the type of practice I wanted to build. I didn't have anybody to help me. I had no mentor. I had nobody to take me under his arm and say, 'Here, let me show you how to build the right kind of business.' And so I just hunted and pecked as best I could."

Rebecca leveraged her newly formed relationships by asking clients for referrals to their CPAs, attorneys, and other professionals, including their business managers and agents. When she called these professionals, she would introduce herself, explain her mission, and request a meeting to describe her firm's capabilities. "Everybody appreciates this approach," she suggests. Over time, Rebecca became a key referral source for these professionals. For many, she is now their largest source of referrals.

The referrals she received had a wide range of needs, some of which she could not answer. But Rebecca didn't try to create the impression that she was an expert in every area. Instead, she found people who could answer the questions. In doing so, she not only built credibility but a network of sources that could provide her with expert guidance in a variety of areas. "Within a couple of years, I was able to gain a good understanding of the major topics of our business. And as my business grew, I became even more knowledgeable by the very nature of hands-on experience, so I didn't need to say, 'Hold on, I'll find out.' I already knew the answer." One of Rebecca's remarkable traits is her dedication to building knowledge and skills to provide the best possible service for her clients.

One of her sources included the research department within her firm. With a specialty in all areas of technology, health care, biotechnology, and regional banking, she was able to position herself as a credible source of information in these sectors. "I used this as a springboard to get in front of new people and say, 'We just initiated coverage of XYZ. May I send you the report?' I became knowledgeable in these areas, and I had contacts within the research and investment banking areas to further help my clients."

Rebecca made it a priority always to follow up with clients and prospects on a personal finance issue or after she sent a prospect a research report. "Too many people just don't follow up," she says. "They forget to say 'Did you find that report interesting?' or 'You once mentioned an interest in this company; we just released a research report that may interest you.'" Rebecca says follow-through is a crucial part of the relationship-building process.

While Rebecca's business was growing dramatically at this time, service quickly became her biggest challenge. In fact, Rebecca's business was growing so rapidly that she could not service all her clients' financial needs. Consequently, she was losing opportunities to grow and expand her practice. While her employer's entrepreneurial culture was appealing, she was convinced that having a broader platform would provide her more traction: "My clients only had some of their money with me because of the firm's limitations; in order to take my business to higher levels and provide the best possible platform for my clients, I would have to provide them a full suite of products and services."

This dedication to her clients spurred her to make the next critically important decision of her professional life: to leave for a larger firm with a broader and deeper range of products and services. Additionally, because her business had grown remarkably, she now sought additional forms of support that would help her take her business to far higher levels.

UPGRADING TO SMITH BARNEY

In 1999, Rebecca made a list of about 15 firms that she thought she might want to join. Rebecca was most interested in finding a company that could help mold her business into one that would provide her clients with the highest possible levels of advice and service. Citigroup became an obvious choice.

In addition to Citigroup's vast resources Rebecca received a call from a Smith Barney manager who simply said: "I'd like you to speak with Bob Perry, our branch manager in downtown L.A. If he can't convince you in five minutes that we are the best place to be, then I promise I will never call you again."

Rebecca's straightforwardness and easygoing sense of humor prompted her to laugh and say, "I'll meet with you just so you never call me again." The next morning at 5 a.m. in downtown L.A., Rebecca met with Bob, "who would eventually become one of the most influential people in my professional life." She took the job, which included new office space that was customized for her and her team's needs. This was just her first experience with Bob and an indication of the impact that he would have on Rebecca's business in the coming years.

When Rebecca joined Smith Barney in 1999 and became aware of what she calls "the great panacea of products" that the firm offers, from alternative investments and hedging products to managed futures and consumer lending, she knew her business could continue to grow. "It's just amazing what you can do at a firm like this," she says. "There's no reason for a client to go anywhere else." Still, the growth that she would experience even surprised her.

A TEAM THAT WINS FOR CLIENTS

Bob spent a great deal of time with Rebecca, detailing her business and writing her business plan. "We started by closing the door and sketching out plans on a whiteboard. He said to me, 'Let's talk about each of your team members. Tell me the areas in which they really excel and what jobs you feel they should be responsible for.' Then I brought each individual in the room and asked them to describe where they feel they excel and where their interests lie within the business.

"While I've always known that I can read clients very well, I realized my observations about my team weren't parallel with their observations. There were a series of concentric circles among their skills and responsibilities. I had failed to do a good enough job in developing them into their own areas of expertise."

Bob's first piece of advice was to streamline Rebecca's team by creating distinct job descriptions, with each becoming a specialist in his area. "After a series of meetings and conversations with each team member, we clearly defined the responsibilities in which they excelled and wanted to own. Until that point, the business was growing so rapidly it was more of a catch as catch can," Rebecca says. "For example, before we made any changes, whoever answered the phone was the one that opened up the account, initiated the transfer, got the client information, followed it up, and so on. There was almost no organization."

"Over time, as our business continued to grow, they were earning more responsibility, and feeling a true sense of ownership and pride." Rebecca's next step was to assign backup responsibilities so that they would always be covered if one or more people were out of the office or unknown events required additional assistance in a particular area.

Today, Rebecca's team consists of five assistants, three of whom have been with her since the early 1990s. Catherine remains Rebecca's customer service representative. "When I am on the other line and I know I need to talk to that person, I can say to Catherine, chat with this person for a minute, I will be right there. She's very southern, very polite—really sweet and warm. Catherine also handles all of the administrative responsibilities associated with estate trust lending. In addition, she conducts my scheduling and travel planning."

Rebecca hired Herman Quispe out of UCLA when he was working as a teller at a bank. "As head of operations, he is a pivotal member of my team," according to Rebecca. "He handles the flow of work that goes through the team and oversees all of the assistants." Herman controls trading activities, manages all the information about news and how it affects the client base. "He works very, very diligently to expand his knowledge and to make sure that the business is running smoothly at all times," she explains.

John Vukson is Rebecca's analyst. He conducts all the research on money managers and alternative investments in addition to all of the reporting. "We have five different reports for clients that go from the basic to the most sophisticated," Rebecca explains. "I tell

Catherine which report I will need for what client. Catherine tells John. He generates the report. I review it, edit it, and bring it to John, who takes my corrections and comments into consideration and generates a final report."

Tim Leonard monitors all the performance of the alternative investments and oversees the accuracy of the client profiles. "I am a stickler on making sure that client profiles are accurate at all times," Rebecca explains. "For example, I want to know ahead of time that a client is turning seventy and a half and has to make an IRA distribution. Tim handles this responsibility for me."

Finally, there is Sherry Strand, whom Rebecca calls "the queen of getting us through the day with optimal efficiency." She adds, "We have an enormous amount of money movement that occurs. She opens accounts. She does all the transfers. She makes sure that all the appropriate paperwork is on file for every account, and she has excellent customer service skills."

Rebecca describes the team's culture: "We're on a mission for every single client. At the end of the day, we know that we're on top of our clients' financial needs. To accomplish this, we focus on teamwork, close communications with each other, and we enthusiastically support one another. We focus on what's best for the client, the firm, and our team." Herman adds, "If there is ever a problem, there is never fingerpointing; we're solely focused on solutions."

Critical to her ability to service these clients is the team Rebecca has built around her. Everyone has a clear job description and understands how he or she each fits into the overall management of the office, but they also understand that their disparate jobs all revolve around the single mission of servicing the client. It goes without saying they are all committed to following the fourth agreement: Always do your best.

A TIGHT SHIP

With the team in place and processes established for advice and service, The Rothstein Team now runs like a well-oiled machine. Interestingly, her so-called "sweet spot" for a typical client relates more to how they fit into the Rothstein network than the size of their account or their financial goals. Rebecca describes her clients as "a broad clientele of families that are fun to work with. I'm in this business because I love it," she says. "So I'll only do business with people that I enjoy and can add to my network." Her "fun" clients tend to be "very interesting, very intelligent, and well connected."

Professionally, they tend to be corporate executives, entrepreneurs, and individuals in the entertainment industry. It's important that I appreciate doing business with them, and that they appreciate the service, advice, and relationship I can offer them on a personal level in order to provide them the best possible service. Within this network it's important that we can share ideas and inspire each other both in personal and professional ways. This is the basis of the partnership we form with each client."

"I am very good at positioning myself as a quarterback," Rebecca continues. "I am not an expert on charitable lead trusts or charitable remainder trusts. I am not an expert on dynasty trusts or which states are taxing distributions from 529 plans. I am, however, an expert on understanding what the client wants and putting a person in front of them that is an expert in those areas.

"When you try to be all things to everybody, you dilute yourself. But if you position yourself as a person who is a quarterback, or relationship manager, you gain credibility. You know that you've put people that are experts in those areas in front of your clients." Accordingly, Rebecca is sure to learn as much as possible about each client and prospect in order to fully service his or her financial needs. "This begins with every single prospect or client meeting," she says.

"Before we even set up a meeting, I discuss a tentative agenda with the client or prospect to ensure that I'll be addressing his or her objectives and expectations. I'll tell a prospect or client: 'Let's set up this meeting so that we meet your expectations.' Too many times financial advisors will meet with prospects or clients and discuss a particular subject, when the individual was expecting to discuss other items." An agenda is forwarded to the client to edit or for approval. If changes are made, they are incorporated into the agenda, then sent again to the client or prospect for approval. Once approved, Rebecca will outline what she plans to present and discuss, and give a copy to John, who develops the presentation. Rebecca prepares for each presentation by studying the data and reviewing the agenda the night before. "This is how we develop a presentation that is completely tailored for each individual."

Once Rebecca finalizes an agenda, she then establishes which firm experts she wants to have at the meeting. "This substantiates our depth of expertise when we meet with the prospect or client. After we've shown our expertise, then we position our team of five and explain each member's function, as well as the client's interactions with each."

Rebecca also stresses the importance of impressions, whether first or last. "When meeting with a prospect, offer a firm handshake, and look the person straight in the eye. Whether for a client or a prospect, dress appropriately for the meeting and always look professional.

"The advisors I compete with tend to go for the kill," Rebecca says. "I don't feel the need to win the first time I walk in the door. I assess the situation and take my time. I have never asked for the order at the first meeting. I want to understand the areas in which they're experiencing deficiencies or concerns about achieving their goals—directly from both the husband and the wife. I give their input a lot of thought and prepare a plan that I believe is the absolute best solution for their needs."

A few years ago she was referred to an entrepreneur who had recently taken his company public, netting him $250 million and the attention of half a dozen major securities firms and banks that wanted to land that account.

Each advisor had the same data from which to prepare a plan, but, while the competition rushed to show off their wealth management software, throwing together financial plans in that first meeting, Rebecca stuck to what she does best, getting to know the individuals and assessing their needs. She also listened to the client's wife.

She earned the business before she even presented a plan because she followed the third agreement: Don't make assumptions. The other advisors assumed that they knew what the client needed, and they assumed that the wife had little or no input in the decision. Later, the couple told Rebecca that listening to the wife helped put her over the top. Her competitors completely ignored the spouse, leaving her feeling "utterly disrespected."

"While each presentation is customized to each prospect's or client's needs, the only common thread in my presentation is the Smith Barney and Citigroup story," she explains. "I am very proud to describe the breadth and depth of the firm and its incredible platform." This is crucial to Rebecca's business because, no matter the market environment, she is delivering solutions that range from stocks and bonds, to lending and alternative investments, to insurance and annuity products.

Consequently, she is able to handle all areas of her clients' financial needs, from traditional investments and estate planning to alternative investments and consumer lending, her clients enjoy a one-stop financial offering and remain well diversified (for example, at the time of writing, 15 percent of her business is lending-related and 15 percent is in alternative investments). Meanwhile, Rebecca benefits from a satisfied client base and revenue that is diversified across numerous products and services. And because her clients know she offers a one-stop financial offering, she has positioned herself as the first person her clients call for any kind of financial need. Keeping an eye on all assets is also important to her: "You have to know where they are, what your clients own, what their investment criteria is, what their goals are," she says. "The best way to help clients is to know how everything fits together."

The team also tracks all financial data relating to their clients, from reports they run every day that show the performance of each client's alternative investments to news stories on all securities in which clients hold positions. "If there is news about those investments, we look at the information and decide whether to contact the clients to discuss these details with them," Rebecca says. "I have a stack on my desk, everything that happened in my client's portfolio in the prior day. For example, when a company reports earnings, I call clients when the news is released and let them know whether the company met, fell short, or beat their earnings expectations. If there is other information on these stocks, such as splits, dividends, restructures, etc., we make a determination on whether to call clients regarding these details. I'll call a client on the phone that has ten thousand shares of Cisco and say, 'Just wanted to let you know that Cisco is reporting on Wednesday and we are expecting them to report XYZ. I'll keep you posted on it.' Then I'll circle back to them after the report has been released and give them the news and my analysis. We're always on top of their finances so they can have peace of mind."

THE PRIMARY ADVISOR

Rebecca believes that it's essential to be a client's primary financial advisor. "To truly offer superior service, it's important to be the first person that a client calls for any piece of financial services business that they do. To be successful, you must be the first line of defense." Rebecca also maintains that you must know the client's exact situation, including where all the assets are and how they relate to the client's overall picture. "You have to know what the client owns, where the assets are, what their investment criteria is, what their investment goals are and really keep a very close eye in order to protect their interests."

Rebecca adds that advisors should not attempt to make a sale every time they are in contact with their client. "Don't convey a message that you're out to make money," she emphasizes. "Instead, the message should be along the lines of, 'Tell me what's new in your life.' I like to prove to them that I'm doing everything I can to bring them closer to their goals. In other words, I treat them the way I would want to be treated."

As relationship manager, Rebecca is confident of the support Smith Barney offers: "I have absolutely got the support of everybody in the firm. Everybody. No matter who you are in this firm, you have that kind of support—that's the kind of firm this is. This is an entrepreneurial firm filled with smart people. Sandy [Weill] sets the tone for this firm; he is one of the greatest entrepreneurs ever, and doesn't want anybody at this firm not treated well. As a result, it permeates every little nook and cranny of Smith Barney that this is a place where we are all here to help each other."

Rebecca discusses the nature of her client relationships: "When managing someone's money, it's crucial to form a partnership, a shared commitment to ensure success. This includes a commitment to do the best possible job for them, and for the client to be open with their needs, expectations, and developments in their lives that may affect our planning. Rebecca takes pride in reviewing and updating clients' goals and objectives on a regular basis. "It's a very important aspect of my full-service offering; to find answers—even if the client doesn't know the questions, I will pull it out of them, then form a vision of what they want. Then my job is to execute the strategies that will bring them closer to their financial goals.

Rebecca continues: "An advisor's job is to align his or her interests with their client's interests. It's very important. People who are new in the business are so anxious to make money, so many of them will put themselves first. You have to align your interests with your client's interests. And once you've done that you take the conflict out of the relationship. In the old days, when I first entered the business, the inherent flaw was that every time you executed a transaction for a client, you got paid. So you were given an incentive to trade by getting paid. Once you align your client's interests with your interests, the relationships will foster and both the client and the advisor will do well."

"Aligning interests is best done by creating a fee-based arrangement," says Rebecca. "Of course, it doesn't make sense for every account. When a client prefers a transactional relationship, I make it very clear to the client: 'I will always act in your best interests. But understand that under this relationship, I will earn a commission regardless of whether or not you make money.' I believe that always being direct in a client relationship is always the best choice. Always."

"This is just common courtesy," Rebecca underscores. "Treat people the way you want to be treated. Don't tell people you want to make money for them. Ask them how they are doing, what's going on with their lives. Get to know them personally because when you do, you get to know their needs, and the better you know their needs, the better you can do your job."

IDEAS FOR ENDURING SUCCESS

Rebecca boils down her success: "I am amazed that so many advisors aren't focusing on the service aspect of our business," she says. "This is the easy secret to my success. We're not reinventing the wheel, and we're not restructuring the way the financial markets work. This is just a service business. I am successful because I help my clients achieve their financial goals, and the best way to accomplish that is to cull from my clients what their real plan is, what their real hopes are, what their plans for the future are; this includes establishing relationships with the children and other relatives of her clients. I build deep relationships in order to discover what their true needs are. Then we execute a plan."

"In most cases I actually help them congeal that point of view. And then we go about the business of setting up, initiating, reviewing that plan so that they have what they need. I never lose sight of the fact that it's not my money; it's their money. And I never lose sight of the fact that the responsibility I have is planning for their retirement, their futures, their children. Because of that responsibility we constantly obtain updates about their situations, review risk assessment, spend time going over where we are in the plan, what their careers and income look like. As a result of this constant contact and great service, my turnover in my client base is negligible and referrals are high."

Of course, this extraordinary service doesn't happen without teamwork and hard work, "which is the core of my success," she says. She still shows up at the office at the crack of dawn every business day and doesn't leave until she has made at least 100 phone calls, and to this day she still makes that same number of calls, though it's now weighted more toward clients.

Rebecca places great importance on having a high energy level and maintaining the right attitude. She says she wakes up every day with the goal of "doing the best job that I can. That doesn't mean I am looking to overachieve every day," she says. "I just seek to do the best job. That's all I can realistically expect from myself."

And if you make a mistake, "Be easy on yourself," she says. "For example, when the uncertainty surrounding the 2000 presidential election carried over into the following day, I should have contracted my clients' equity holding until the issue resolved itself. But I didn't until May or June of the next year. It was the biggest mistake I ever made. The way I rationalize it is that a lot of people did the same thing."

More advice on the mental side: "Keep your ego in check. When you're successful, it's easy to think, 'Look at how good I am.' But you always have to remember that you are no better than anybody else. You just happen to make a little bit more money. I never forget where I came from."

Then she turns to her first rule: Don't take things personally. "There was a time when I would agonize over what I did to make a client leave me. I came to realize that it's not personal. Sometimes people meet other people that have a better fit for them. Sometimes they get married and their wife's brother is a financial advisor. Sometimes, as was the case during the market downturn that dragged on through 2003, investors may think if they move someplace else their situation will improve. When you are an overachiever, it's really hard to accept this. But try to do your best to acknowledge it."

Rebecca believes these four agreements are the driving force behind her ascent in business, and in life. "Every second of every day I just try to do my very best, whether it's for my clients, my firm, my family or myself," she says. "And if there's ever a day where I don't feel like I'm giving my all, I just pull out this little piece of paper."

HARD WORK

Rebecca's hard work is also shown in her high level of persistence, especially if it means doing the right thing for a client or prospect. For example, in 1998 Rebecca began calling a high net worth client hoping she would get the opportunity to manage a greater portion of his portfolio, valued in the tens of millions of dollars. At the time, she managed about 5 percent of his assets. She called him for about a year, establishing a good rapport. "He would laugh because I tried so hard," she recalls.

One day, the client agreed to meet with her and shared information about an account that he had at another firm. The client was upset because he said his accountant told him that he had lost $5 million in equity positions in 1998, a time in which stock prices couldn't move high enough. The prospect showed Rebecca the statement, and she noticed that he was short a number of large-cap tech stocks.

"I looked at him and said, 'Do you realize that you have unlimited risk in this portfolio?' I said my words loudly and slowly so they would resonate with him. He said he didn't understand. I asked him, 'Do you know what it means to sell short?' And he said he really didn't. 'Please explain it to me.' So I did.

"He was a busy man who had made a vast amount of wealth very quickly in life, so he had entrusted many decisions regarding his finances to other people. When I took the time to explain things to him, he said, 'How long would it take to transfer my money to you?' I told him one day. He said, 'Please do it.' I had the account the next day."

Over the next year, Rebecca not only helped the investor restructure his portfolio, she periodically showed him how much money he would have lost if he had kept his portfolio intact at the other firm. "The losses," she recalls, "would have exceeded $10 million within a year, and he would have been forced to close positions to meet margin requirements."

Rebecca is a big believer in providing services that don't immediately result in production but have tremendous value in building good will. And quite often she will invest an inordinate amount of time to make this point with her clients and to set a good example for her team. "I recall a situation in which a client needed to obtain certain documents to close on a mortgage but was having no luck," recalls Herman. "It was the eleventh hour. I was calling everyone to try to get the information. The realtor was doing the same. Rebecca got involved and started calling everyone she knew. She was finally able to contact the senior vice president of the institution that was lending the money and got him to fund the loan."

It wasn't the first time Rebecca had pulled off a minor miracle. Another time, an ultrahigh net worth client asked Rebecca to issue a credit card for each of his employees. "This is an example of Citigroup's ability to get things done. We were able to mobilize various departments within Citigroup to get this done," she says. Within 48 hours, all necessary documentation and credit limits were in order and the cards were mailed overnight to the client. The next morning, Rebecca received a call from the appreciative client, who had just received the cards: "This is why I do business with you."

UP BUSINESS IN DOWN MARKETS

During the market bubble in the 1990s, Rebecca remained determined to keep her clients focused on their goals and objectives via disciplined investment strategies and asset allocations. Her clients, while somewhat envious of eye-popping technology returns, were confident in Rebecca's wealth-management and wealth-building strategies. During this timeframe, her network continued to bring in new business.

From January 1999 to December 2001, her business literally doubled, then continued to grow through 2003. Some of this success was the result of clients' wealth preserved from much of the market downturn, resulting in earning a greater portion of her clients' assets and an abundance of referrals. However, Rebecca cites two other rationales. First and foremost, she credits her team: "During this period, all of my assistants made a significant contribution to the growth of the practice," she says. "Additionally, Bob Perry taught me how to organize my business, how to create and build a book, how to leverage a franchise, and how to maximize the potential of assistants and give them the incentive to help grow the business."

Part of this advice included tapping into Smith Barney's, and its parent Citigroup's, vast resources. She attained this goal by diversifying her practice away from traditional business. Approximately 40a percent of her practice is fee-based equity business, and about 30 percent is nonfee-based equity and fixed-income business. Alternative investments and lending comprise the other 30 percent of her business.

She also broadened her client base. Although a significant portion of her business comes from professionals in the entertainment industry, such as writers, directors, producers, and performers, she serves the needs of many different types of investors, from working class individuals to chief executive officers with multimillion accounts.

LOOKING AHEAD

Rebecca is thankful for her lot in life: a successful marriage, healthy and happy children, and a booming business. Today, she gives herself plenty of personal time to do things she loves: spending time with family, cooking, baking, running, reading, biking, and sailing when she visits her second home in Malibu. She says it gives her life the balance that she needs to be a healthy person, a good mother, and the best advisor she can be.

But Rebecca has no plans to slow down anytime soon. She says she would like to expand her business to include more private and investment banking as Citigroup has provided Smith Barney with an excellent lending platform. "Even though interest rates have risen from their lows, we're still in an environment where interest rates are so low that one of the best tools that you have in your tool chest is lending," she offers.

She also has an interest in getting involved in politics and may even run for public office, probably at the state level, sometime in the future. For some time, she has been involved in charitable work, something that she plans to do more of in the years ahead.

No one doubts that Rebecca Rothstein will be successful in her new endeavors. She certainly feels the same way. "One of the most beautiful feelings in life is to know that you can accomplish anything, even when the odds are seemingly not in your favor," she says.

What Rebecca Rothstein has accomplished is testament to the fact that boundaries are nothing more than limits human beings place on themselves.

CHAPTER 10: WANDA AUSTIN

Up Close and Personal

Legg Mason Wood Walker Inc.
Newport News, Virginia

If one thread runs through the life and career of Wanda Austin, it's family. As a girl, she helped to raise two younger siblings while her mother worked three jobs. As an advisor, she's built an energetic and close-knit team that's become a model for the profession. As for her clients, Wanda treats them as no less than kin.

And that's not the only constant for this tell-it-like-it-is financial pro. She's a big thinker for whom details matter. She sets the highest of standards, above all for herself. She's dogged when it comes to success. And Wanda is no wallflower when it comes to asking: Where's all your money?

There is nothing arm's length about Wanda, who has an almost larger than life quality that defines her every endeavor. Just consider her team, which has been dubbed, quite accurately, "The Wanda."

It's not unusual for Wanda to open a client meeting saying, "I want to know everything about you. Be prepared to talk. And to tell me about your life and your family and what you are trying to accomplish." And talk, they do. As Wanda puts it, "People call me and ask, 'Can I buy a couch?' "

It's relationship building practiced at the highest level, probably the driving force behind this former receptionist's remarkable success. But the real story starts with a little girl in Portsmouth. Virginia helped raise her two siblings, starting when she was just a third grader herself. "Even at eight, I was thirty-five," Wanda says about her early years.

It was not a picture-perfect childhood: Her father abandoned the family when Wanda was little. Her mother, one of 16 children, worked six days a week to keep the family afloat. "As a result of that, I had to pitch in for the family to survive. We struggled," says Wanda. "It's not something you would want to happen, but it did so you come out fighting."

Wanda credits her childhood and the lessons learned with the success she enjoys today. But even now, deep into a rewarding career, she takes nothing for granted.

"First of all, I like being successful," she says. "And so I have to have ways in which I can track and measure my successes. At the end of the day, I have to be able to say, 'Okay, I've put in a ten- or twelve-hour day and either I've seen this many clients and uncovered this amount of assets or solved this many problems.' I've got to know that at the end of the day I was successful. I want to be able to say that I put in a good day's work. I've done what I set out to accomplish," she adds. "I also believe if you do it and do it the right way, then you will be successful."

BUILDING A CAREER

Wanda was working long hours as an assistant marketing director at a Virginia mall in the late 1970s when she decided it was more important to be home with her young daughter, Christina. Even then she was a self-described workaholic and she ended her stint as a stay-at-home mom a couple of months later to take a job as a receptionist for Wheat First Securities. It would prove to be a life-changing event.

"I decided this is really neat. This is exciting. This is something different," Wanda says about those first few months on the job. "I really have a way with numbers. I love people. I like solutions." Wheat First recognized Wanda's potential and had her registered as an operations manager where in the early 1980s, she traveled from branch to branch, helping streamline procedures. Along the way, she began assisting advisors with clients.

Then the by now single mother concluded: "I need to do this on my own."

In 1987, seven years after she was hired as a receptionist, Wanda Austin was one of 11 rookies (the only woman) in Wheat First's training program. All but three of them washed out. "I'm very appreciative to Bill Butler, the newly hired Branch Manager in the Newport News office for his support and encouragement. He was repetitive and consistent with words of encouragement. Bill felt very strongly that there was a place in the industry for women as Financial Advisors. And continuously encouraged me with these words: 'Wanda, you can do it.' "

Like most rookies at the time, Wanda built her business through systematic cold calling. In her case, she was pitching municipal bonds—a reflection, she says, of her own fiscally conservative nature. "I was like a machine. One day, I made twelve hundred dials," she recalls. "It was really important to me. Having observed many new rookies in our branch as well as others, it became evident to me that activity was the early sign of success or failure. In order to build a successful business, you have to have clients to advise. It's a matter of numbers and I was determined to be successful." Wanda still has a trophy her fellow rookies gave her after that twelve-hundred-dial day, "Dialing for Dollars" as we referred to it. Inscribed on the memento: "I beat the guys."

Wanda has also used community contacts to introduce herself to prospects, including the Junior League of Hampton Roads, Kiwanis Club, Food Bank, Salvation Army, Habitat for Humanity, and the Girl Scouts. She held seminars, networked, and gave talks. "It was about getting out there. Exposure. I have a lot of clients that are still clients because of that," she says. "Anybody that would listen to me, I would talk to them about their futures and goals. All I had to do is get in the door. I think people realized that I really do like them and I really do want to be a part of the solution. As a result of that, if I can get in front of someone ... they became clients. Because I do enjoy it ... people sense it and get excited. At the time, it was a matter of gathering assets. Now, it's about being part of the family and accomplishing their goals."

Wanda's personal and professional worlds converged in 1988 when she married John E. Decher, III who was a seasoned financial advisor. By then, Wanda was beginning to focus on financial planning, and with Decher's expertise in research, analysis, and portfolio management, the two seemed readymade business partners. They made it formal in 1992, when they began converting their business to a fee-based practice. Along the way Wanda hired several support staff. Among them were her longtime registered associate and retirement specialist, Janet Medina; Kathy Jones, the Registered Marketing Associate; and the team's Operation Manager and Associate Portfolio Manager and her daughter, Christina Austin. They all have earned various licenses, a result of a continuing education emphasis that Wanda holds almost sacred. Be, do, have! Determine what it is that you want to be. Then do what it takes to have what you want.

"I really encourage them to continue to get educated. Because that's where my education comes from," notes Wanda, who is a huge proponent of industry educational programs. "I got so involved in my business that I decided to pursue it from within the industry with all types of courses relating to financial planning and wealth management. You can't have enough knowledge. I feel like my time was better spent on an educational opportunity relating to the investment business. From that standpoint, you cannot afford not to expand your knowledge of products, changes in laws, tax and planning strategies and, demographics. Our business is forever changing and creating new opportunities. That's part of the excitement and the challenge."

AN EARLY MOVE TOWARD COMPREHENSIVE FINANCIAL PLANNING

From the outset of her career, Wanda gravitated toward comprehensive financial planning. "I like this," she says. "I like sitting down. I like you telling me about your family. I like finding a solution." Each initial client interview begins with a customized profile with Wanda asking questions, taking notes and collecting financial statements. Afterward, Christina crunches the numbers in a financial planning program that spits out essentials on estate taxes, asset allocation, investments, and retirement plans. Wanda will typically make follow-up phone calls prior to a second appointment when the information is reviewed and a game plan designed. Meanwhile Janet follows the trail carefully during the first year—even teaching clients how to interpret their statements.

"Once we get to that point where we are getting down to investments, people will say to me, 'How am I going to pay for this?' And I will say, first of all, let's figure out what we are going to do and then I'll tell you how you are going to pay and what's in your best interests," says Wanda, whose practice is roughly 40 percent fee-based. "And then we go through a checklist."

It is an exercise that helps demystify the planning process.

Afterward, Wanda will tell clients to expect a call from Janet. "When you get your statement, Janet will give you a call and she'll walk you through it. It may take two or three of those statements for you to feel comfortable with it. And by the time you come in for your next quarterly review with me, you still may have questions," notes Wanda about her everything-on-the-table presentation. "So people pretty much know what to expect from us. And they expect me to ask: 'Where is all your money?' They come out of the process knowing that I might have been joking about it but they expect that type of a question from me."

HIGH TOUCH

The thorough, high-touch approach doesn't stop after the initial contact is sealed—far from it. The team's top 50 clients are contacted on a monthly basis. Then there are the birthday cards, Christmas cards, and the quarterly reviews, which give Wanda additional opportunities to dig deep with clients.

Her directness plays well with her southern accent and charm. With her pleasant and engaging smile, she continues: "I'm saying, now, okay, what haven't you told me? What have you got stashed away? And they'll say: Oh well, I've got this stock over here. And why don't I have it?" The response from a client is always a chuckle. "'Why are you keeping your money there when I can do all of these things for you? We help you pay your bills. We help plan for long-term care, education planning, retirement planning—all this other sort of stuff. In order for me to do a good job, I need to see it all.' Well, once I see it, we consistently ask for it, and eventually we get it all. I'm patient!"

MANAGING PORTFOLIOS

On occasion, Decher, an advisor since 1969 and a highly regarded money manager, is brought in to consult when appointments are focused solely on a client's stock portfolio. In fact, Wanda credits Decher with shielding their clients from the worst of the three-year market downturn in the early 2000s. "Our clients came out of this really well. They didn't see huge losses. And that really came from Decher's experience. Where I am a total optimist, he is more of a pessimist," says Wanda. "So when things started to turn, he's very quick to recognize the fact that things aren't working out. As a result of that, we pulled money on the sidelines." Christina, among with her many other duties, assists Decher with the managed portfolio.

To watch "The Wanda" work is to watch a pretty seamless operation. In fact, the teamwork is so smooth that all five members are often mistaken for family. But its success hasn't come without trial and error. Efforts to bring on a junior advisor have failed—something Wanda hopes to get right one day. "I'd like to bring on a partner so I can spend even more time with clients and prospective clients at their kitchen tables. That's the only way in which I really can leverage my time," she says.

Meanwhile, Wanda's team continues to be a model of success.

A TEAM MODEL

In fact, after joining Legg Mason in 1998, the firm dispatched a team-building group to Virginia to study "The Austin/Decher Group" and give it pointers on how to improve. After observing for three or four days, Wanda notes, "Basically they said, 'We should be using your group as a model throughout the firm.' "

What does Wanda attribute her team's success to?

"Years of making mistakes," she says. "I have learned that every team member has strengths and weaknesses and his or her own area of expertise. What seems to work best for us is when we are able to match our strengths with our tasks and expand on those skills. Rather than try to change the person to conform to the job ... I try to allow the person to create the job (or value) for the team. This has worked for us. At the end of the day, each team member feels that they have used their strengths, whether it is putting out fires, organizing a project, or crunching numbers, for the good of the team. It took years to figure that out. And that's why we have a difficult time bringing in a new person. The last was a gentleman that had been in the business for about three years—and he stayed with us for eight months. It just threw the whole thing off. I said, 'This is not working.' I cut my mistakes. That's also happens to be our philosophy when investing in stocks. You let your winners run and you cut your losers. You pick the weeds and water the flowers. Well, when I make a mistake, as hard as it is, I cut my losses. And if you ask any of these ladies, they think we are the best in the industry. We are very tight and genuinely like each other. There are other teams where nobody gets along. You can feel it and your clients can feel and I don't want to work that way."

The remarkable teamwork of the operation allows Wanda to work at what she enjoys most: the client interface. She calls it "Wanda's road tour." It's not unusual, for instance, for a meeting to take place at a client's home. "I really enjoy just sitting down at the kitchen table. It gives me a real feel for their family. You can get a better sense of what they are telling you and what their risk tolerance is, and their lifestyle. I like to get out and just see people. I would hate to be in the business if it was only about investments and not the solutions."

Clearly, for Wanda, it's not just about investments. She has taken clients' pets to the vet for them. She's called on clients in nursing homes. Recently, she flew to the other side of the country to help a client's widow settle his estate.

"Our clients find it a pleasure to work with us. At the end of any quarterly review, I will say: 'Is there anything that we can do for you that we haven't been doing?' Has there ever been a time when you've called in and not gotten a solution? It's all about solution," says Wanda.

Wanda believes the customized service sets her team apart.

PART OF THE FAMILY

"Everyone says this, and that's why I hate to even use it, but we are part of your family. We do multigenerational planning. I need to know who your children are. I need to know your grandchildren. I need to do those 529 plans. I need to address that long-term care situation because I want to preserve your money and do a good job for you and your family," she says. "We are organized. We are honest. And we are conservative. We listen to what your needs are."

A client once told her she knew more about him than his wife. "I tell people: I want to know your needs, your wants, and your desires. And that's kind of the way we start. And I tell them the more information you can give me, the better job I can do for you. And eventually, I'll know everything. They laugh. I say: 'Eventually, I'll have all your money,'" says Wanda. "And they laugh. And it just happens because I continue to ask the questions."

In one notable instance, Wanda approached one of Decher's long-time clients—a retired CEO with a major national company who had parked a stock account with Decher. "Decher had been doing business with him for years. And I said: Why don't we have all of his money? I know he has more money than this." The next time the client came in, Wanda interrupted the 'man's man–type' meeting. "And I said: 'Where's your money?' And of course, his chest expanded. He says: What do you mean? I said: 'I know you have more money than this. You are a very successful man.'" Wanda then left the room, returning minutes later with a new account form. The client signed the form, transferring a significant sum. "Just like that," says Wanda. "It was just a matter of asking for it. And enjoying it. Then I said to him, 'I know you have more than that.' And I will eventually get it all. Because we do a good job."

GETTING PERSONAL

Wanda won't take a check from a prospect until she's done a complete and thorough client profile. And she requires no minimum although she has divided her book into A, B, and C client tiers.

"And of course we are always trying to uncover more assets from the C's. That's why I think it's really important to profile your clients," she says. "I had a gentleman come in recently who said: 'I want to give you a check and here's what I what I want you to do with it,' and I said: 'Well, before you do that, I have a lot of questions to ask. And if you find I'm too personal, just say so. I want to know: Where are your kids? Your will? I want to know everything about you. I want to know your dog. I want to know anything that you can possibly tell me because'—and I always say this—'the hardest part is not the investment. It's finding your comfort level and finding out your risk tolerance and what you want, what you need and what you expect from me. Because, at the end of the day, I want to feel good about the job I'm doing. Without this information, I can't possibly do a good job for you.'"

In addition to digging deeper into clients' lives and earning assets, Wanda is now building her business on word of mouth from other professionals as well as clients, many of them women. "It's just worked out that way," she says. "Probably some of the greatest referral sources that I have are female physicians, female attorneys, and female CPAs." In fact, it's not uncommon for a prospect to seek out Wanda because she is a woman.

"You do get clients that call in and ask specifically to talk to a female broker. All the things that women do well as far as nurturing relationships are perfect in this industry—even though it hasn't been recognized over the years. I think women have an ability to listen and they have a tendency to want to take care of people. As a result of that, I think we are very detail-oriented," says Wanda, who looks no further than her own mother for a role model. ("If she had had an opportunity for a higher education, she could have done anything," says Wanda about this "very sharp lady." As it is, her mother has been an owner in several businesses: a restaurant, a consignment shop, and a rental business.)

A little note on Wanda's telephone says: "Ask for referrals." The command also shows up on the weekly to-do list she gets from her team and occasionally on the daily email that Christina sends, reminding her: "Here's where we are. Here's where you need to be." Now that the markets have recovered, Wanda has begun to solicit referrals again.

HAND HOLDING

"We really spent most of the last few years protecting our clients and holding hands and maintaining relationships. We really didn't have a whole lot of panic but it wore me out. In the negative market you had to carry me out of here. But it was the right thing to do. You're going to hear from me in the good times but you definitely need me in bad times. I met with clients regularly, many more often than quarterly and told them: 'This is what's going on. I can't tell you how long this is going to last. But here's what we are going to do to protect your assets. Here's how we're going to handle this. This is how we are going to get through the storm.' I'm very proud of this—but it really wore me out," says Wanda. "After we weathered the early 2000s storm, I began asking them: So, do you have anyone else that we can help? And that's happening a lot now." Between protecting clients' downside through the downturn and constant hand-holding, clients have been delighted to provide referrals.

Wanda is driven by the desire to help clients. Her competitive nature pushes her to be the best within her branch, and even at Legg Mason. "We have a business plan," Wanda begins. "We write down our yearly, monthly, and daily goals and commit to meeting or exceeding them. At the end of the day, my day-timer tells the story. I track the number of meetings and people I have spoken to. If I don't have the numbers there, then I know why. I just didn't work hard enough."

DAILY, MONTHLY, AND ANNUAL GOALS

One day, Wanda foresees building a team that might include a CPA and an attorney. "Basically, we're striving to build a money center," she says.

And Wanda likes what she sees when she looks into the future.

"I think the business is changing a bit, which I think is a positive in that you are not just encouraged on the production side of it. It's the building of the assets and the relationships. When I started in the business things were different—you were measured solely by the production, which is a horrible way to do business and a horrible way to build your business. I would say for new financial advisors, it is relationships. It is taking the time, early in your career, to build the foundation for a long-term relationship. And I think it's very important to find a niche you are comfortable with. And teams? I think teams are going to be very important going forward because there is so much product and so many different directions that you can take your business. It's virtually impossible for one person to do it all and do it well."

Wanda considers herself lucky that she has built a practice that is measured not by production but by people—her team and her clients. Her family, as she would call them.

"I'm going to keep doing all the things that I have done in the past that have worked for me. I like relationships so it's all about relationships. It's all about building that trust. It's all about being that hub. Being that center of influence. I don't want [the hub] to be the attorney. I want it to be Wanda. I just want to continue doing what I'm doing—just in bigger form. We are honest. We have fun. And we want our clients to enjoy doing business with us, making money, and building a successful investment plan."

"There are some things we can't do. But the majority of things, if there is a way in which we can do it, we will do it. That's where our business will flourish—because of the relationship. I think it's that simple, really. I truly don't think there's anything complex about it. It's just a matter of where your comfort level is. And what you do well and how hard you are willing to work."

She pauses. "Of course, not everybody can have a Wanda."

CHAPTER 11: RON CARSON

A Passion for Service

Carson Wealth Management Group (Linsco/Private Ledger)
Omaha, Nebraska

PRIOR TO OUR INTERVIEW, RON CARSON TREATED ME TO A TOUR OF *Carson Wealth Management, including introductions to the team and a fascinating account of the "Wall of Thanks." I asked Ron about one letter, which said "... when my husband passed away, I didn't have a clue about what needed to be done with our estate and, I really didn't care ... thanks to you and your team for all your knowledge and for giving me peace of mind." Ron explained the deep relationships the team develops with each client, and how they earn their trust every single day. "This woman's husband has leveraged our team for all aspects of their financial lives," Ron explains. "Once her husband passed away, she really realized how dependent she and her husband have been on our trust. And now she relies on our trust every single day." Remarkably, this was just one of dozens of letters on the wall, with hundreds like them in Ron's files.*

"Our mission statement is to provide peace of mind to your financial security," Ron says. "We'll provide this by offering the highest level of service in both communication and education."

They key word here is "service," and it is the only product Ron sells. Everything else is ancillary to the mission. He has even gone so far as coining his own phrase to describe the level of service that he is committed to providing and the level of service that his clients have come to rely on—seamless proactive service, or SPS®.

It is seamless in that he has developed a finely tuned system that ensures every piece of every client's financial plan is working in harmony toward his or her ultimate financial goal; proactive in that every member of the team is trained in, and compensated for, anticipating client needs rather than reacting to them.

"If you talk to any one of my staff people, they not only know the mission statement, but they can tell you what our values are and things that we want to accomplish," Ron says. "We have our vision, our mission, our commitment to deliver to our clients and so we are all moving in a common direction, together."

That level of commitment, though, is a two-way street. Through the relationships that he has built as a representative of Linsco/Private Ledger and the trust he has developed with his clients over the years, Ron has built more than an advisory practice. He has built a family that sticks together through good times and bad. In the rare occasion that a client actually leaves the fold, they usually come back. That was the case of an older couple who left a few years ago.

The gentleman was in poor health, and they thought it was important to set up a trust as part of their estate plan. At the time, Ron didn't have in-house trust capabilities, so the couple worked with a local bank, eventually transferring over all their assets to the bank. After the husband died two years later, the wife called Ron.

"She asked if there was any way we could handle her accounts again," Ron remembers. "I assured her that we could and she was so relieved. She said, 'You know, from the day we left we knew we had made a mistake. We didn't get nearly the service we had gotten from you. We didn't get phone calls like we used to get. They didn't recognize our anniversary. We really felt like we were a part of a family when we were with you.' "

Her husband couldn't bring himself to ask if they could come back, but after his death she couldn't face her future without Ron's support. This is a scenario that is played out regularly among Ron's clients and his team members, but no matter how many times he hears it, he never takes these deep relationships for granted.

Ron and the team stay in constant contact with each client—either electronically, by telephone calls, in person, or via U.S. mail—an average of 100 times a year. And just to make sure clients are always happy with their experience, Ron routinely sends out questionnaires making sure service is always living up to their expectations.

"One of the questions we ask on our survey is, 'What is unique in your dealings with our firm?' " he says. "Two things always stand out. The most common comment they make is that they feel like they are part of a family, and they all appreciate the level of communication that we have with them."

A FAMILY TRADITION

With hundreds of clients and a team of 11 managing assets that are nearing a billion dollars, committing to and delivering that level of personalized service would feel like a Herculean task for most advisors, but it's all in a day's work for Ron, who learned the art of multitasking from a master: his father. Growing up on a farm, Ron understood early in life that the workday doesn't end at 5 p.m. It's just time to start work on the next project.

"When I say we worked sunup to sundown, seven days a week, we worked sunup to sundown, seven days a week," he says. "My dad couldn't keep a hired man around very long because he didn't believe in breaking for lunch. You brought it with you, and you didn't get off the tractor to eat it. So anything that I was going to do after that was going to pale in comparison."

While in school, Ron didn't get summer breaks. That was time spent in the field. When winter came, they were cutting firewood and selling it. On the side, his father ran close to a dozen small businesses. He made and sold insulation. He was a pilot and ran a small charter service. He had an auction company, and once sent Ron off to Kansas City so that he could cry his own auction.

Eventually, Ron got the entrepreneurial bug and started his own private enterprises. In high school he had his own consignment shop and even ran his own trap line.

"I literally would get up way before school in the morning and go harvest all my pelts," he says. "Today I can't even imagine doing that because I hate killing anything. But in those days, I could make two hundred to four hundred to five hundred dollars a morning, harvesting mink, raccoon, and muskrat out of my traps."

That was big bucks back in the 1970s. Still, it was just a sideline. Ron also ran a small fireworks distributorship through which he imported fireworks and sold them retail. He even hired local kids to go out into the cornfields to pick up the ears that the combine knocked off. He would dry it, bag it, and sell it as popcorn.

"My dad started me on this thing, and then I had this entrepreneurial bent all the way through," he says. But it was his mother who got him interested in the financial markets. She was the one responsible for marketing the family crops, so she started following the futures market, getting up early every day to check the latest grain prices so that she could hedge at least part of the crop against fluctuations in the market.

"She would try to sell half of each crop into the futures market, and became very successful at it," Ron says. Almost too successful.

"That was when my dad had the bright idea that if we were so successful at hedging, maybe we should speculate," Ron says. "So they ended up where they were speculating heavily in the commodities market, and it came very close to breaking my parents. They got in on the wrong side of the market when the Hunts were involved in trying to corner the markets in soybeans and silver."

Ron learned two things from watching his parents through that experience. First, he learned he had a fascination for how the markets worked. More importantly, though, he learned that you had to know what you could afford to lose.

IN THE BEGINNING

Ron moved from popcorn and trap lines into financial services while he was at the University of Nebraska at Lincoln, where he injured his knee and was offered a scholarship to redshirt. Again, he was following his father's lead; among all his other lines of business, his father got his insurance license and started selling universal life policies. He thought insurance might provide a good side income for his son, too, so Ron had his insurance license before he had his high school diploma.

"Here I am, playing football, trying to keep my grades up, and he says that since I'm going to have all this extra time now, I should be making money," Ron laughs. "I literally started this business cold calling on life insurance products out of my dorm room in Lincoln."

"I *hated* it."

It wasn't the cold calling he hated. It was the product he was selling, but he didn't know enough about other financial products at the time to know the difference. He just knew that trying to force something onto someone that they probably didn't need just didn't feel right. Finally, he discovered mutual funds, something that he truly believed could provide a service and fill a need for his clients.

"I started making a lot more money," he says. "After I got my mutual fund license, over the next year and a half I made about ninety thousand dollars, and I thought, 'Man, this is a great business.' "

Diversification into the equities markets was an easy story to tell, but interest rates were still relatively, high—in the 8 percent and 9 percent range. Most of the prospects he was calling on were farmers, who thought they took enough risk every year just putting a crop in the ground. They wanted their hard-earned cash tucked away in a bank account.

"It was like pulling teeth," Ron remembers. "I would see people that had two hundred thousand, three hundred thousand, or four hundred thousand dollars in CDs and in money market accounts. I remember a local savings and loan offered a ten-year CD at over 10 percent. The financial markets were not doing much better than that. Farmers, of all people, they are the quintessential gamblers but still it was a tough sell getting them to convert."

That was when Ron got his first lesson in building trust through education. That was long before mutual fund companies had to report their performance by using net asset value, so when his clients got their statements in the mail, they had no idea what they were reading, much less the value of their holdings.

"It was like the reports were in Greek or Braille or something," Ron says. "I remember sitting down at farmers' kitchen tables, explaining the reports to them and holding their hands and saying, 'No, you really do have this money here, and if you wanted to get out of it today, here's what it would be worth.' "

It was rewarding, but exhausting. At the time, Ron was doing everything himself, running his business out of his car, logging tens of thousands of miles a year crisscrossing the Nebraska prairies, making house calls, and beating the fields for client. He rented out access to an executive suite, where he had a receptionist answer a phone for him and a conference room available in the rare occasion that a client would come to him.

That seat-of-the-pants existence couldn't last very long, though. Ron got a wakeup call when the receptionist at the office suite phoned to tell him that one of his clients was in the lobby and wanted to meet with him. Ron's cover was blown when the client realized that his financial advisor didn't even have his own office.

"This was a guy that I had just sold a three hundred thousand dollar mutual fund, and I guess he started worrying about it, so he wanted to talk to me," Ron says. "This was my biggest ticket to date, and I was terrified."

The receptionist couldn't even put the client on the phone for Ron to explain the situation because it was a busy switchboard. When he finally did meet with the client, Ron explained to him that he was just getting started in the business, but assured him that the money was invested just as the client had wanted. Ron laid out all of the reports on the mutual fund, and the client did some checking around on his own. The client not only stuck with Ron, but he became one of his leading supporters. That client has since passed away, but his wife is still with Ron.

In fact, many of those early clients are still with Ron today, including his first $100,000 client who now has over $1 million invested with him. Spending that time and developing those relationships built a foundation that has carried him through both rough spots in the market and rough patches in his personal life.

MAKE-OR-BREAK TIME

Ron can still remember the exact moment that he hit the wall. In hindsight, he calls that moment his "breakthrough," but at the time it was one of the darkest moments of his life. He was 25 years old, making more money than he had ever dreamed of, but he had set a pace for himself that he simply couldn't maintain. He knew it was bad when even his father told him he was working too hard.

"I got burned out," he says. "I got to where I hated this business. I can still remember the intersection I was sitting at over here on one hundred and eighth and L streets. I had had several appointments stand me up that day, and all I had to look forward to was a ton of paperwork that I had to do. I was making pretty good money, but I was working all the time. And I thought, I am either going to quit this business or I am going to figure out a different way to approach it."

Thankfully, he found a better way, almost by accident. Out of frustration as much as anything else, Ron started flipping through his client list and came across the names of people he genuinely cared about. People that he wanted to talk to.

"I thought, 'I'm just going to touch base with my clients,'" he says. "I called them up just to see what was going on and to ask if there was anything I could do for them."

That was a new sensation for both Ron and his clients.

"In the past, the only time I ever called anybody was when I had something to sell, or when he or she had money that I wanted," he remembers. "There was always something in it for me, because back then that's how this business worked. They were shocked that I didn't have some other agenda."

And Ron was shocked by the warm reception he received, so he started calling all his clients. The feedback was so positive that he started doing other things to make contact with his clients and help define the kind of service that they were looking for. He put together a rudimentary questionnaire, asking about things like the date of each family member's birthday and favorite hobbies.

These first bits of personal information seeded what would become an exhaustive database of personal and financial information. He started calling clients on their birthdays. And when he met with them, he would explain to them not only their finances, but his business model as well.

"I would talk to them about how I get paid," he says. "In those days it was all commission-driven, so I explained to them that I wanted to be in the business of helping them attain their goals, not in the business of constant marketing. The more I explained what I was doing, the more receptive they were in providing the names of other people I should talk to."

The meetings were followed up with letters that would always close with a reminder that Ron would love for them to introduce him to someone that they thought would benefit from working with him.

Soon he was hosting events for his clients and his friends, and that was the beginning of what Ron calls "love affair marketing."

"I have taken that concept into our process today, and we are always trying to take it to the next level," he says. "Like today. I have to catch a plane later, but on the way to the airport I'm going to call some clients who are celebrating their fifteenth anniversary."

The clients will get more than a phone call today. They will also receive a bottle of their favorite wine; Ron just happens to have that piece of personal information in the database. And a couple of other team members who work with the clients will call today too.

"We'll make a big deal out of it," he says. "Almost like it's their birthday. We'll make them feel special and feel like they are a part of this family."

This level of detailed information that Ron accumulates about his clients, along with how he uses his understanding of each client to deepen and enrich his relationships, is what sets Ron apart. Most advisors have a database of personal client information, and everyone sends out birthday cards to their clients. Ron is always challenged to take it to the next step, to make each relationship even more personal.

"Information is like paint," he says. "Anybody can get some, but in this organization we have become information artists."

RELATIONSHIPS FIRST

When he is not meeting with clients, Ron spends his time traveling around the country trying to teach other advisors about his unique brand of relationship marketing. It's more an art than a science, though, so it's not something that is easily taught.

"I tell all of the advisors that I work with that the quality of their advisory practice is in direct proportion to the quality and the depth of the relationship they have with their very best client," he says.

Still, too many advisors want quick fixes and immediate results without putting in the work that is required to build a long-term commitment. Recently on a conference with several advisors, Ron was challenged by one rookie who didn't want to hear about Ron's "passion prospecting" and "love affair marketing" process. He was just looking at the assets Ron has under management, and insisted that his success had to be based on performance. He wanted to hear that secret.

"He said, 'Well, obviously since you have raised all of these assets, you must have a performance advantage,'" Ron laughs. "I said, 'No. I have no performance advantage. No one has a performance advantage. It's all about intimacy.' I told them that they should never try to sell performance, because that's a losing game. As soon as your performance isn't where someone thinks it should be, they are gone."

Nobody knows where the market is going, Ron insists. But you can learn how to manage downside risk so that you can help your clients get where they want to go no matter what happens along the way, making adjustments where necessary.

"My philosophy is simple," Ron says. "Either the world is going to come to an end or it's not. And if it doesn't, people are going to still need to turn on their lights, drive their cars, drink Pepsi, and all that. So the markets might go down, but they are probably not going to go to zero. And if they go to zero, that means the world would have had to come to an end and it's not going to matter. So don't worry about it."

Instead, focus on the things you can control, he advises, such as client communication. Because when the markets turn down, that is when customer service becomes crucial. Ron had one client turn his entire account over to him during the worst stretch of the three-year bear market.

"He told me that when the markets were good, he really didn't care about the service he was getting. He didn't even think about service," Ron says. "When things started going down, though, he never heard from anyone so he never understood what was happening or whether his other advisors had a plan. That's when he realized he needed and wanted service."

Ron credits his SPS approach to client service with the fact that his numbers never fell during the prolonged bear market. Assets under management stayed steady, and since the market began its rebound, he is seeing a surge of new assets coming in.

"I really attribute it to these other services that we provide," he says. "We either provide the services in-house or someone from our team will work with their CPA or their attorney, just so there is a dialogue and so they can see we are being proactive."

BUILDING A TEAM

Just as the level of an advisor's success is directly proportional to the depth of his or her relationships, the depth of those client relationships is directly proportional to the kind of team put into place. Ron realized that early on, and began outlining the ideal organizational chart long before he could even afford to hire people to plug into all of those spaces.

"My ultimate goal was to have my day structured so that I only did the things that I love to do and that I was good at," he says. "That was a pretty small list, so I wanted to hire a staff to do everything else."

In the early days, his name appeared in all the organization boxes. When he finally reached the point where he felt comfortable hiring someone, he sat down with a chart and started prioritizing the skills he wanted to bring in based on his own weaknesses. He checked all the boxes of the tasks that he hated and that he wasn't very good at—which usually ended up being the same thing—and wrote a job description based on filling in those blanks and started searching for a "team leader," even though at first that person would be leading a team of one.

"When I interviewed her I said, 'Here's what you are going to be doing, and here's where I want to go,' " Ron explains. "I told her that I wanted to grow to the point where she would start bringing in people to assist her."

The long-term plan was that as the team grew, he could keep moving some of his boxes down to the team leader, who in turn would move some of her boxes down to the next person in line. That way somebody worth $20 an hour wasn't spending time doing a $5-an-hour job, such as filing. Nearly 22 years later, Ron is still working off that same basic organization chart, continually filling in boxes as growth demands.

"It's a whole process," he says. "You start with the organizational chart, and then bring one person. Your key person. They are the most important person in the foundation because that is the point from which you are going to begin building your team."

His first team leader left after a few years to be a stay-at-home mom, but Michele Schreck has been filling in the boxes for Ron for 11 years, helping him direct the growth of the team toward his ultimate goal.

"I eventually want to get to where the six most important things I've got to get done each day are things I love to do," he says. And he's almost there. "Rarely do I have to put something on my list that I don't like to do."

Having a nice, neat chart in hand, though, is not the same as knowing precisely when and where to start adding people and services. Even when he knew he had to do something when his business hit a plateau, Ron still wasn't sure what the next step should be.

"I knew I really couldn't handle a lot of additional clients, and I got to thinking about what was missing in the services that we were providing," he remembers. "I was constantly frustrated because I would sit down with a client after the fact and realize that they had a bunch of gains somewhere else that I didn't know about and we didn't take the capital losses against it. Or they didn't maximize their 401(k) contribution. Or they didn't do any planning beforehand."

He also knew from talking to his clients that most of them weren't particularly happy with their tax advisors. So he went back to his most trusted resources for guidance: his existing clients. He sent out a survey explaining that he was thinking about adding a tax planning and preparation service. Clients had a choice of three boxes to check: Yes, I would be interested in having you do my taxes and my planning; I am not interested in having you do my taxes, but I would consider it a value-added service; or I am not interested in either.

The top two boxes were checked in more than half of the cards that came back, so he added a tax planning service, and hired Paul Beveridge to head it up. When he started thinking about adding an estate planning specialist, he went back to his clients for guidance. That addition turned out to be an even bigger hit, for both Ron and his clients.

"We were also frustrated because a client would go out, go to an attorney, get all of these trusts set up, get everything done, and they wouldn't tell us about it," he says. "They thought the attorney was going to retitle all their assets and everything, but it inevitably turned out that they would spend all this money on estate planning, but nothing flowed the way they had intended for it to flow."

Ron knows that his practice cannot offer legal advice, so he did the next best thing. He convinced the largest law firm in the city to lease space in his building and staff it with one of their top estate planners. Julie Hoffman, the estate specialist on Ron's team, works closely with the almost in-house legal team to draft the necessary documents and then ensures that estate plans flow smoothly with their overall financial plan. If clients already have an attorney, she works with their counsel to make sure everything works together.

"Julie is the point person who has the responsibility of retitling everything and then writing the memo about how everything is set up and how their estate will flow based on the documents that they have," Ron explains. "And every two years, Julie pulls out and goes through a checklist of questions to update that."

Julie also works closely with Linsco/Private Ledger's private trust company in Chicago, so the firm is now able to provide trust capabilities as well, building additional synergies under the estate planning umbrella. Obviously, there is a charge for these services, but it's just to cover the costs not to make money, Ron says.

"We make our money on the asset management side of the business," he explains. "But I am constantly dripping on my clients to get feedback on these additional services."

Thanks to that constant system of feedback that Ron has built in to the day-to-day operations, the firm has also added an insurance specialist—not because Ron wants to get back into the insurance business, but to make sure clients have all their bases covered in their retirement and estate plans.

CREATING SYNERGIES

With each piece of a client's overall financial plan working in harmony toward a single goal, success becomes self-fulfilling.

"For instance, even if Paul is not doing their taxes, that high net worth person sees Paul connecting all their dots, and they see they are getting a higher level of service than they got before," Ron says. "We are getting the benefit of the intimacy that they feel or the improved relationship because we are doing something for them."

That invariably leads to additional business for the firm—sometimes from sources they never even contemplated. Recently, Ron received a call from a key client—the CEO of a local corporation with a significant 401(k) plan invested with the team. The chief executive was calling to tell Ron that he was transferring $700,000 of his personal account over for Ron to manage because of the extraordinary service he received from Julie.

"He has his personal assets invested with three financial advisors, including us, but he told me that he wanted me to know that we were getting the money because he was so happy with the way she had taken care of some of the details in his estate plan," he says.

During her routine estate plan checkup, Julie discovered that the client's plan had not been funded correctly. More importantly, neither the client nor his business partner had realized that their life insurance policies had lapsed, which meant that the primary piece of their estate plan was not funded at all. They thought everything had been taken care of, but their attorney had died a year ago and several important details had slipped through the cracks. That is, until Julie did her regular account review.

"Everybody thought someone else was keeping an eye on it," Ron says. "As a result of Julie's seamless, proactive service, we not only received an additional $700,000 in assets to manage, but we ended up writing a nice life insurance policy too."

The final key member of the team didn't come on board as a result of a client survey. Ron decided to fill in that box in the organizational chart himself when he sat down to review his personal goals and long-term plans. One of his most important goals was to be able take summers off to spend that time with his kids.

"It's not really off, off," he explains. "I work from home during that time. I get up early to catch up on what's going on in the office, but once they are out of bed, I'm taking them to swim team or playing basketball with them."

He's been able to do that since bringing on Dennis McMillan as a partner.

"He has been in the business longer than I have, and I've known Dennis forever," Ron says. "I brought him in to run things while I'm taking time off. He's a principal in the firm, and he's also listed as comanager of this branch. He has total authority to do anything that I can do, and he can sit down and meet with any of my clients. He's the only one that I really have that much confidence in that he can handle the more complicated issues."

Dennis and Michelle work closely with Ron to keep operations running smoothly, but they have plenty of backup. One individual is dedicated to the team's 401(k) business and several associate wealth advisors handle smaller accounts. Jenna Starmer handles special events, along with managing compliance issues. Rhonda Corliss manages new business issues, and Jamie Johnson is responsible for all updates. Jane Vlcek is director of "first impressions" and Mark Lookabill is responsible for client contact.

"We are very proactive in making calls to our clients," Ron explains. Mark, with assistant Heather Jonas, also handles all the trades.

"I am always branding," Ron explains. "I don't want people to say it's either Ron or nothing, because then I have not institutionalized the relationship. I want this to be like the Lexus experience, and by doing that I've built something that's really worth something because I've proven that I can be away from the business. It still continues to function and grow and make people happy. We are a very systems-driven organization. So, as long as we follow the systems, everything is going to run well."

WINNING MEANS NOT LOSING

Ron is a big believer in systems, and he has a written formula for everything that happens in the office, including wealth management.

"I keep it very simple," he says. "I tell clients that I believe in asset allocation. I don't believe in the use of leverage. I built portfolios based on each client's downside risk, not upside fantasies."

While most advisors talk to their clients about how much money they are going to make for them, Ron goes straight to the hard truth.

"I tell them how much money I can lose for them," he says. "Most people are shocked when I tell them that I guarantee that at some point in the process, they are going to lose money. When they understand that, though, that is when we can start determining how much fluctuation they can stomach."

Since most of his clients have already hit their homeruns, he sees his job as making sure they don't end up losing the game. He does that by illustrating the teeter-totter effect of asset allocation. When one asset class is up, another is usually down. He shows them charts of sample portfolios to explain that a portfolio with 75 percent in stocks and 25 percent in bonds is actually less risky than being 100 percent invested in bonds.

Once the client's goals and risk tolerance have been determined, he matches them with model portfolios that he has developed over the years, running the full spectrum from aggressive growth to conservative income.

"Almost all of the assets we manage reside in two balanced portfolios, growth and income, and growth and income plus," he explains. "I will walk through each of the asset categories we have and discuss whether they should own a mutual fund or individual equities."

Some clients prefer owning more individual stocks, while some are more comfortable with mutual funds, so Ron will construct a portfolio based on those personal preferences. Then he constantly monitors the performance of each portfolio, making adjustments when necessary.

Just as important as knowing what to buy, though, is knowing what and when to sell. To ensure that portfolios are always working at peak performance, he has automated every element of portfolio management, including the development of a propriety software program that tells him when it's time to take some chips off the table and reallocate some of the assets.

"It's an unbelievable program," he says. "It measures more than six hundred different qualitative factors and tells us when to make our moves."

Using the program, Ron got out of Intel when it was in the low-$30s range and moved those dollars into Liz Claiborne, which has been a strong performer. He also credits the program with getting his clients out of Sun Microsystems just before it crumbled and into PriceLine.com in time for that takeoff. It also signaled a sell on Microsoft stock before that fell.

"With all of its recommendations, I've only ended up on the losing side of one trade," Ron says. "It got us into Disney, which is down about one percent."

The program's greatest value is that it instills a very strict sell-side discipline, a quality that many advisors, including Ron, often lack. He points out that people are better at looking for winners than knowing when enough is enough.

But Ron doesn't leave it all to computers. He reviews his holdings list everyday, and screens the list against news headlines. He also measures each stock or mutual fund performance against its benchmark.

"There has to be some human element involved," he says. "I like what Warren Buffet says—'Find a trend and then throw yourself in front of it.' "

So when Ron sees a trend, he's not afraid to be overweighted in certain sectors. For instance, he has been overweighted in energy since 2001, and he started cutting back on his long-term Treasury holdings when interest rates bottomed out in early 2004, moving fixed-income assets into dividend-paying stocks.

TECHNOLOGY: THE SILENT PARTNER

Technology has become such a dynamic presence in Ron's business that he has integrated it into every level of customer service and client interaction. He took a leap forward with new account-aggregating software that allows the client to log into one site and view all of his holdings, no matter where they are held. The program consolidates everything from bank checking accounts to credit card statements to frequent flyer miles.

"They can even set up alerts on the account to remind them of their wife's birthday," he says. "We have an electronic vault that allows us to scan things like their trust documents and powers of attorney, complete with their signatures, so we can forward it anywhere it needs to go. This is what is really going to propel my business into the future."

Ron's team inputs each client's entire financial plan, so that from any computer in the world, the client can go into the program and track each account that is relative to that plan. The software even allows users to flag certain accounts and automatically sends email alerts based on pre-established parameters.

For instance, if a client wants to keep $10,000 in his checking account, a designated person on Ron's team gets an email when the account slips below that level so they can wire money into the account. Similarly, if they don't want an account to get over a certain amount, the team gets a flag to take money out of the account and move it somewhere else.

It has already become a central part of every client account and a PowerPoint presentation when he is meeting with prospects. When he really wants to impress clients with the power of the program, Ron brings them into his "Wall Street Room," a high-tech command post with a 10- by 20-foot drop-down screen and surround sound system.

"I show this service to my high net worth clients, and they tell me that this is exactly what they want," Ron says.

Technology is also what allows the team to manage multiple complex relationships—another rung in the ladder of seamless proactive service. All emails, along with any other outgoing correspondence, are embedded in each client's file. Ron can access the system and see an automatic update of all their assets and see what services they are using—and where they might appreciate some proactive service to fill in a gap in their plan. It shows who last contacted the client, why, and what the results of that contact were.

"I can't even name all the processes that we have been able to automate with this system," Ron says. "I can look at every conversation anybody has ever had with any client and what was discussed. If someone sends us a referral, the system will automatically generate a thank you letter that goes out. If it's their first, second, or third referral, there's a different letter that goes so they are not getting the same stuff."

"By having these systems in place, it has been the equivalent of me having two more people on my staff because it makes everyone that much more efficient. But more importantly, it allows us to make sure nothing falls through the cracks," Ron says.

That is a benefit that clients notice and appreciate. Ron's single largest client, who has about $300 million invested between Ron and two other advisors, recently told Ron that he had just come into another $25 million. This time, though, he wasn't going to divvy up the money. He was giving it all to Ron.

"He said, 'I want you to know that your fee is higher than the other two advisors, but you give me by far the best service. We feel the most comfortable with you and your team and that's why we are giving it to you,'" Ron recounts.

SPS AND LOVE AFFAIR MARKETING

That commitment to service has become a passion for Ron, and one that he has managed to instill in his entire team.

"It was born the day I was ready to quit the business and called that first client for a reason other than business," Ron remembers. "It really wasn't just one thing, though. It was lots of little things that added up."

And he is still adding up those "little things" by constantly encouraging his team to come up with what he calls "random acts of kindness."

"How can we do something totally unexpected for the client?" he asks. And it's not a rhetorical question. He and his team spend a great deal of time and energy discussing this very topic. Part of the team's annual goals—along with a piece of everyone's compensation—is tied to the answers they can come up with.

"We just had our quarterly meeting with the entire team, and one of the questions we always ask is, 'What can we do that is not expensive but will totally wow them?'" Ron explains. "We have to come up with six creative things to do every quarter to stay top-of-mind with our clients."

One way they do that is by communicating with top clients nearly 100 times a year. Fifty-two of those contacts are through the Carson Wealth Report Management reports—weekly updates on clients' finances. Then there are the regular "drippings" with updates and newsletters. And on top of that each client gets called at least once a month. Ron personally handles all the birthday and anniversary calls to his top clients, no matter where he is or what he is doing.

"We even know what type of coffee they like," Ron adds. Recently a client arrived early in the morning—before the cookies, which are a mainstay in the receiving room, arrived. The client joked that he should have arrived a few hours later. In the middle of the meeting, Jane served freshly baked chocolate chip cookies. "You talk about a raving fan," Ron says with delight.

"I don't care if I am in Germany or Australia, I always call my clients," he says. "I never have any downtime."

The real fun—and the real work—goes into dozens of client events he hosts every year—all part of "passion prospecting." By connecting his own passions with those of his clients, Ron can continually develop the personal relationship far beyond the professional one.

"Whether it is bringing in an economist to speak or a wine-tasting event or a football game, we can connect through shared interests, so obviously we get great participation with those events," he explains.

One of the most important things in an affluent person's life is his or her kids and grandchildren, so there is always a heavy focus on finding ways to recognize something that is going on in a child's or grandchild's life.

The one caveat Ron offers concerning this ultrahigh level of service is that it has to be consistent. The worst mistake you can make in client service is to create expectations that you can't maintain. With that in mind, Ron never leaves anything to chance. He and his team are constantly updating their client database. Whenever staffers are on the phone with any client for any reason, they pull up the profile and see if there are any blanks. He is even updating his phone system so that, when a client calls in, the system recognizes the phone number and automatically brings up that screen for whoever takes the call.

Ron ticks off the detailed personal information that he keeps track of. First, there is the obvious—family names, ages, birthdays, anniversaries, etc. But Ron wants to know it all—what kind of car they drive, what kind of wine they prefer, if they prefer to receive flowers or a plant, what newspapers they read, what types of movies they like, and what television shows they watch. Do they play golf or tennis? Do they go to the theater? What accomplishments are they most proud of, and what are their future goals?

"As you can imagine, there is so much that you can do with this kind of information," he says. "And our system will say automatically, 'Okay, this person's birthday is coming up, she is an A-plus client, so the budget is this. She doesn't drink, but she likes baskets of goodies.' "

The system even emails the supplier they use for the baskets, and the vendor emails them back confirming that the basket has been sent.

"It's happened. It goes into the records, and no personal contact even had to take place," Ron says. "All the processes are automated."

Those personal touches, when combined with Ron's professional proficiencies, are a can't-miss combination for clients and prospects. At a recent wine tasting event, a client brought in a friend who loves red wine almost as much as he loves playing golf.

"We hit on all cylinders," Ron says. During the conversation, the prospect said that, although he was pretty happy with how his money was being managed, he had really enjoyed the evening and would like to come in and talk to him.

When he came in, Ron showed him the E-Money demo, and that was all that the client needed to see. He was ready to send his entire $8 million portfolio over immediately, but more importantly than the money, Ron wanted to build a strong foundation for a long-term relationship.

He had the prospect meet with Paul Beveridge to go over past tax returns. He sent over all his trust documents for Julie to review along with Mike Schilken, the attorney Ron works with. Mike put together a detailed analysis showing how the estate would flow under the current structure. Jocelyn Schreiner evaluated all his insurance, and at the same time Ron started putting together a financial plan and asset allocation model based on all the information he had already gathered.

"Thirty days into this process, he said, 'Ron, I have never felt so good about all the parts of my financial life. Everything is coming together.' "

MEASURING SUCCESS

Ron applies the same strict quantitative measures that he uses to evaluate portfolios when he is evaluating how members of his team are performing qualitatively. He has translated those set parameters into an index, and staff members are measured against that index every quarter. "Our current customer Satisfaction Index is 10.85, our highest ever," Ron says of his system that is based on a scale of one through ten, with extra credit given by clients, who can vote up to 11.

"You know the difference between someone just showing up and doing enough to keep their job versus what they are capable of? I call that 'discretionary effort,' because it is. It's up to them whether they give it to you or not," Ron explains.

But, if you can harness that discretionary effort, you help individuals increase and enhance their own standard of living while giving that effort to the organization, creating a win-win for the employees and the boss.

Ron has made discretionary effort 20 percent of each employee's income, and he measures that effort through client feedback in the form of an annual survey that each client receives. If they don't send it back, then they fill it out during one of their one-on-one meetings. It is a simple survey designed to measure how well "love-affair" marketing is working in the eyes of the client.

"We may think that we are doing a great job, but the perception of the client is the reality of our life," Ron says.

The questions vary from year to year, and respondents are asked to rank their experience or the service they received on a scale of 1 to 10. If any of the questions gets a score of 7 or less, the person in charge of that area calls the client to ask where they felt let down and what changes the team could make to improve their experience.

Then there is a bonus question—the same question that gets asked every year: "It is the goal of Carson Wealth to provide the highest level of service you've ever received on a consistent basis. Are we doing that?" If the answer is yes, then a perfect survey score is 11, and 20 percent of that year's bonus pool is tied to that survey staying above 10.

Another 20 percent of the bonus is based on whether the team met the goals they established on the previous year's team retreat. The entire team has to have an 80 percent success rate for that 20 percent to kick in. The final 60 percent of the bonus is tied to three different value drivers based on which department they work in.

"For instance, in the trading area. People make trading errors—it's going to happen. So we allow a nominal amount of trading errors. If they stay in that range, they get an additional bonus," Ron explains. Another piece is linked to the volume of the work they are doing. So 60 percent of the bonus is tied to three value drivers where they go above and beyond and add additional value to their position.

The bonuses are tacked onto very competitive salaries. Ron closely monitors salary trends in the industry to make sure his people are always at the top.

"In salary, I want my entire staff in the seventieth percentile," he explains. "But if they maximize their bonus, I want them to be the top paid people in their area."

SYSTEMS MANAGING THE SYSTEM

It may sound like a complicated system, but everything Ron does is carefully designed to give both his staff and his clients every opportunity to succeed. Even when mistakes are made, all Ron focuses on is the initiative that the team member took upon discovering the mistake and how the entire team can learn from it. That is part of the team's core value system.

"Making a mistake is not a system breakdown," Ron emphasizes. "If we have to make a mistake, then let's develop a system to keep from making that mistake again so that we don't keep making the mistake over and over again. If you learn something from that mistake, you are now more valuable to me."

That is how he has developed the precision systems that keep the operation running smoothly, delivering seamless proactive service.

"Every single thing that we do here has a written system behind it," he says. "From the way you are greeted when you walk through the door to the protocol we go through when someone calls the office. Even though we call it 'random acts,' there is nothing random about it."

There is a system for the way the office is opened every morning. There is a system for how the office is shut down at night. There is a system for time management that everyone follows to make sure things get done in a certain order. There is a system for how outgoing voice mail messages are recorded.

When a client walks in the door, an extremely regimented system kicks in based on the level of that client. Who sees them first, who sees them second, who sees them third. There's a system for where the advisors sits relative to the client. There is even a system for the color of the paper on which reports are printed.

The most critical pieces of system fall into place during the time a prospect is becoming a client. During that transition, he or she may be hearing from someone on the team as often as ten times a week.

"We want them to know every part of the process because that's when they are most vulnerable," Ron explains. "They begin to think whether or not they really want to make the move, and by that time they may be getting calls from existing advisors asking why they are leaving."

To ensure that new clients get to meet everyone on the team, every couple of months they shut down the office at 4 p.m. for the "Friday Afternoon Club." Clients, especially new ones, are invited to come in and get to know the staff.

"There is an office manual this big," Ron says, holding his thumb and forefinger several inches apart. "There's a system for every minute detail that this whole organization runs by."

Ron says that comes from his training as a pilot. No matter how well he knows his aircraft, he pulls out his systems checklist every single time he prepares for takeoff, every time he prepares for landing, before he starts his descent, and when he runs into bad weather.

"Do you know how many pilots with ten thousand hours of flying time still land with their landing gear up?" asks Ron, who pilots his own plane. "Obviously, missing a system here is not life or death but there's no reason to do it."

If someone does violate a written system, it costs him or her 5 percent of their quarterly bonus, but they can earn that 5 percent back by collecting "above-and-beyond" certificates. Just as their name indicates, these certificates are awarded randomly when a team member goes above and beyond the call of duty in either servicing a client or supporting a team member.

"I just gave Amanda, our tech person, a certificate because she came in on a Saturday to put together a very specific action plan that I had requested," Ron says. "That was clearly above and beyond."

LEARNING FROM THE PAST

When coaching other advisors on how to build their own systems for success, Ron's greatest lessons come from the mistakes he has made along the way.

"The key to my success is I've never been afraid to fail," he laughs. "And I have failed. I've tried more goofy things than anybody would ever care to try."

The biggest mistakes are the easiest to see in hindsight. One that he sees too many people making is looking for bargains when hiring people.

"I figured out early on that you are much better off paying up and getting good people," he says. "I also got way too concentrated. I broke my own discipline in 1998–1999 and allowed myself to get caught up in owning way too much technology in the funds. Those are the two big mistakes I would say I made."

Other advice that he offers is to set up an account minimum right out of the chute and stick to it. Without that discipline, it is too easy to rack up small accounts that sap your energy and effort, making you reactive instead of proactive. And don't be afraid to hire staff, even when you don't think you can afford it.

"I tell advisors today that the quickest way to get to where you want to be is to get a really good righthand person who can take a lot of the pressure off you," he advises.

Finally, let technology do as much of the work for you as possible. Ron has two full-time people who do nothing but manage the proprietary systems that he has put in place. The right team and the right systems are critical in providing seamless proactive service.

A COMMUNITY LEADER

Between his commitment to clients and his commitment to family, it's hard to see where Ron finds the time or energy to give back to the community. Still, he has made community involvement a cornerstone of his business and family life. Last year, Ron and his wife cochaired a fundraising effort for the Salvation Army, raising a record amount of capital for a new facility for disadvantaged children in South Omaha. In addition, Ron and Jeanie raised money for the Child Saving Institute for a capital campaign. Jeanie sits on the board for the Elkhorn Foundation.

He gets his entire staff involved in "The Swing for Charity," an annual golf tournament that raises money for six local charities. The staff donates its time to organize the event, and as a team they decide which charities should receive the donations.

This year they began another community-wide event—the Carson Wealth Health Challenge, which has had extensive media involvement. Designed to bring attention to the alarming rise of obesity around the country, the Challenge has signed up 108 people to begin a healthy weight loss regime.

In what is left of his spare time, Ron is involved in both Angel Flights and the Flying Fez, both of which provide free flights to children who need medical care. Ron recently flew a mother and her little girl to St. Louis for an operation. He donates his time and the cost of the flights.

"My personal mission statement is to help other people find meaningful purpose in their life," Ron says. By taking the time to help his family, friends, staff, and clients do just that, Ron is able to fulfill that mission statement every single day.

CHAPTER 12: SALY GLASSMAN

Higher Levels

Merrill Lynch & Co., Inc.
Blue Bell, Pennsylvania

Photo credit: Eric F. Patent

THE NIGHT OF MY SECOND INTERVIEW WITH SALY GLASSMAN, I WAS *over an hour late. The usual heavy Philadelphia traffic was slowed to a near halt due to the fierce thunderstorms and showers left over from a hurricane. Instead of meeting at her horse farm, I joined Saly—pronounced Sally—and her family for dinner at their home. Saly had already worked a full day in the office, including a multihour interview with me. When I saw her that night, she was invigorated; she had ridden four horses in one of the biggest downpours I had ever witnessed.*

By the early hours of the following day—and a total of nearly nine hours of interviewing—it was clear to me what makes Saly a champion, whether for her clients, her family, or her community, and why she is one of the most outstanding financial advisors in the business.

Saly's competitiveness for showing horses (one of her horses is ranked eighth in the world) draws a close parallel to her success as an advisor. "I'm used to riding in the rain," she explains. When asked if training in the rain is typical in the equestrian industry, she said, "It's not ideal, but it's part of the game."

"If you're used to dealing with adversity and conditions that are difficult for others to contemplate, then everything else seems easy," she says, referring to the rejection she faced during the early years of her business and the down markets of the early 2000s. "That's why I believe expectations are so important in the securities industry. You have to expect tough times as a rookie. And in the markets, if you live through tough times and learn from them, then you can be more professional, because you will be better prepared in the future. When it rains, I have an edge; if others aren't used to it and didn't train for it, then I will be the one shining."

SALY'S BEGINNING

Saly grew up in a tight-knit family in Cheltenham, a suburb in Philadelphia. Saly's mother sent her three children off to college, and then earned her own bachelor's degree, plus two master's degrees. Then she became a music therapist, the ideal combination of her backgrounds in music and psychology. Saly's father was an accomplished civil engineer, and later became a successful self-made businessman. Saly credits her parents, who now have been married almost 50 years, for endowing her with a mind for psychology and music, an astuteness in business, and a dedicated work ethic. Saly's closeness with her parents extends to present day; in fact, Saly bought them property less than half a mile away from her home. She remembers a particular expression her father used to repeat throughout her childhood: "Forget about wishing, hoping, and praying; if you want something, make it happen." This became a code by which Saly would live her life.

At Cornell, Saly's parents paid mostly for her essentials. She maintained part-time jobs to cover other expenses. Saly compares one particular job, selling stereo equipment, to the beginnings of her financial advisory practice: "I didn't know anything about the equipment, I just had an understanding of how it fit together," she recalls. Almost immediately, Saly realized that her job was to understand the needs of the customers, and to rely on her own research and the local experts at the store to help find the right solutions. When she made a sale, she would go to the customer's house to set up the system. As the relationship developed, Saly would cross-sell, finding the right peripheral equipment and albums. In no time, even as a part-time employee, she became the leading salesperson in the New York region.

By the time Saly graduated with a degree in psychology, she realized it was too technical and impractical for her to pursue as a lifetime profession. She relied on advice from her father, who took time to understand her interests, goals, and aspirations. His recommendation: Become a stockbroker. In one vein, Saly was taken aback; she never took any business courses and didn't know the first thing about economics, let alone the stock market. On the other hand, she had an untapped—and undeveloped—gift for numbers, and knew she had the potential to make this aptitude work for her. "It all made sense to me," Saly says, explaining herself. "I am a linear thinker, goal-oriented, and a hefty left brainer, which complements my propensity for creativity, a right-brain activity."

During her interview with Merrill Lynch in 1980 in Elkins Park, Pennsylvania, branch manager Larry Forlenza recognized potential in the young woman. Saly told him she loved working with people and finding solutions for their needs, and she would work harder than anyone he'd ever seen before. He told her, "You have no experience and you never took any business classes." Then he paused, and said, "On the other hand, you're not going to cost me much money, so I'll take a chance on you."

Since Saly had no idea how to build a business, she let her instincts take control. Several hours a day she was a sales assistant for a group of brokers. During this time, she analyzed and determined, in her opinion, what the other brokers were doing right and what they were doing wrong. For example, she noticed they had inconsistent processes for servicing clients, developing business, opening new accounts, and even filing. In short, mistakes were made. Most striking to Saly, they typically waited for a client to call them. Then they would attempt to make a sale. "It was incredible that these professionals thought that speaking to twelve people constituted a successful day," Saly says in disbelief.

Because she was anxious to make a living, Saly describes her typical prospect at the time: "Anyone with a pulse. I needed the business and I had little confidence in my abilities, so it didn't seem right for me to pursue affluent individuals. It was a numbers game back then; the more calls you made, the more contacts you would make, which would result in new accounts."

Living a mile away from the office, Saly frequently walked to the office in the morning, arriving at 7 o'clock. Another trainee provided a collegial, yet competitive, spirit by working long hours, sharing ideas and knowledge, comparing goals, and seeking to reach goals first. For example, instead of focusing on how many times they dialed the phone, which Saly estimates was in the hundreds every day, they focused on how many daily conversations they had, which was around 60. Saly jokes that she wasn't able to feel the pain of rejection because her callused fingers and arm were sore from making calls. They took ten-minute breaks for lunch to eat peanut butter and jelly sandwiches. These routines became habits still practiced today, with the exception of the quality of food. "My motto has always been to be as efficient as possible at the office so I can get my work done and go home to be with my family," she says.

Not only did Saly overcome rejection, but she worked hard to raise her credibility. "I was worried that someone would look at me and say, 'You've never taken an economics course—you're a fraud!' Plus there was the added stress of being a female in a male-dominated industry." To offset these thoughts, Saly worked harder than ever to compensate.

One of the first, and easiest, areas to fix was her image. "I've always believed that you must project yourself in the most professional way possible to clients and prospects," she says. Living in an apartment, she and her husband, Allan, a fellow Cornell graduate and burgeoning architect, fought to make ends meet as both were launching their careers. One day, the couple was late with their $450 rent payment, and Saly refused to ask her parents, whom she felt had provided her with everything she needed to get started in the world, for the money. With nothing in savings, they placed an ad in the newspaper to sell their old but treasured Corvair convertible. A well-dressed man came by to look at the couple's car. Without looking at it a second time, he reached into his pocket and pulled out a thick wallet. Then he peeled five one hundred dollar bills from a stack, and handed the money to Saly. When the man drove away with the car, Saly and Allan took their rent payment to their landlord. Saly faced Allan and said, "We're never going to experience this again." Saly looks downward as she reflects, then looks up laughing and says, "At least I got the leftover Datsun—Allan took the train to work!" Still, to maintain an image in front of her clients and prospects, she parked the car a block away from the office.

"Incredibly, now that I'm successful, the material things aren't as important to me," she says. "Sure it's appropriate to present the right image for clients and prospective clients, but I love driving my diesel Ford 350 pickup, or even my farm vehicles."

She also believes that it was key to have a mentor, such as her branch manager. "I was always driven to succeed, I just needed someone to keep me pointed in the right direction and to answer my questions. Once he got me on the runway, I was able to take off independently."

KNOWING THE CLIENT

After being in the business 18 months, Saly came to a realization. She had been buying stocks without understanding her client's needs. "Something was inherently wrong with my business model," she begins. "To call people I didn't know, offering them solutions without knowing their problems and getting paid to do it was wrong. I felt like I couldn't live with myself. I did not want to benefit financially unless I believed in my heart the recommendation was absolutely right for the client."

Saly approached her manager, Larry, and told him: "This is all wrong. I don't feel I'm being true to my values. There has to be another way to build a business." She presented an idea to him. "I know it's going to sound disrespectful, but before I tell you, I need your assurance that you'll back me if you get pressure." Larry responded by saying, "If your idea is good for the clients, then it's good for the firm."

"I want to get to know people," she told him. "I want to ask them questions. I want to find out about their investment history. I want to know about their financial successes and their failures. I want to learn about their goals. And then I want to make a connection between what they are doing with their investments and how they are going to achieve their goals. I believe that if I can accomplish that, I am going to do a lot of business. I think people will be happy and I think I will have lasting relationships. And I will feel good about what I do for a living." Larry responded by saying, "I think you are discovering something that I believe in, but probably could not have taught you. You had to see this for yourself. I support your decision."

Saly's greatest barrier at this point was her incredible desire to succeed. "In the early days, I wouldn't take the time to educate my clients, or make sure they completely understood everything," Saly says. "Sometimes the best way to move forward is to move slower," she says. "This was very difficult for me to accept. It's still a very fine line in which I must always be aware. I'm always charging forward, but if clients aren't prepared, it may make them feel uneasy, and they could view me as being too persistent. I prefer people to perceive this energy as inspiration, and say 'she's very bright and she really puts everything she's got into helping me.'" Saly often feels she must slow down for others to catch up and appreciate that she is acting in their best interest.

Saly points to doctors as an example of the rationale behind her philosophy. "How would you feel if a doctor who knew nothing about you called you and said, 'This new erythromycin came in. It's completely state-of-the-art. I am going to give you this one chance to come over and try this drug.' How presumptuous! To me that would be complete incompetence. This may be an exaggeration, but it was refreshing to people that I was taking a different approach," Saly continues. "Most of all, my message was coming through strongly because of my conviction that I wanted to do the right thing for the clients."

Saly also called accountants and lawyers, saying, "My approach is different, but I think it's the right thing to do and I think I can really help your clients. Some of them may be getting misdirected because they may be buying products over the phone from people they don't know."

"The accountants and attorneys would respond, 'I love your approach—I am going to refer clients to you.'"

BUILDING A BRAND

Saly explains the importance of building a brand. "For me, it's the ability to perform financial planning at a very accurate and a very high level, with the ability to quickly assess people and their needs and their personality type," Saly says quickly, hardly thinking about it. "I integrate the financial plan with the personal profile I construct because there is a psychological awareness of where a client sits mentally, so I can integrate the two. It's like a combination of psychology and mathematics. I think I do that better than anyone I know. This has become my 'brand.' Someone starting in the securities business must determine what unique brand he or she can offer."

Saly is quick to point out her weaknesses. "If you ask me to develop an options strategy, I'll tell you that's not my expertise and I wouldn't even know where to start—sort of like me trying to cook. To determine a brand, first you've got to figure out what it is you do best. One suggestion is to ask a parent or sibling why you are special, what makes you great. What do you do that's better than anyone else? Another suggestion is to complete a personality assessment so you can get a better grasp on your talents, skills, and preferences. Finding your niche also might require some experimentation. It's important to pursue those areas in which you have a great interest, preferably a passion."

BUILDING A NETWORK

"Once you have branded yourself, then you can promote yourself. You can call an accountant and say, 'I've been working on financial planning for doctors who have been having a very difficult time with malpractice insurance and managed care; they are seeing their expenses go up and their income go down. I have a strategy to help these professionals cope with this particular circumstance. If you have clients that may be experiencing this problem, I would like to show you how I can help them," she says.

"You've got to leverage yourself by talking to other people who are in a position to promote you because you can only make one call at a time. But if you can call somebody who will then call five people on your behalf, you are getting leverage. Once you have a rapport with those accountants, you can say 'I am looking to develop another thirty million dollars in this sector of the market. Do you have any advice for me?' You would be amazed how many people will give you advice that don't ask anything in return. In general, people feel flattered to be asked for advice. It makes them feel good."

"You must, however, treat them with respect and delicacy since they are in a position to help you enormously. This is the same with attorneys, insurance agents, and actuaries. Call an actuary and ask him to run you through a pension analysis for a client with whom there is a mutual relationship. While you're there, ask, 'Do you have any other clients who are like this? This is the kind of client with whom I'd like to build my business. Can you make any suggestions as to how I might meet more of these people?"

One referral Saly received from a lawyer in the 1980s was a multigenerational family who was struggling to build a business out of their garage. They put most of their money into their business. Over the years, even though the family had little to invest with Saly, she provided them as much service and attention as she did any other client. In the early 1990s, a competing securities firm took the family's business public (the deal was too small for Merrill). The nearly $100 million in proceeds the family received was all entrusted to Saly, even though a competing firm worked with the family on the offering. Now, with a long-term financial plan in place and a well-diversified portfolio, Saly helps them with other financial needs, ranging from business advice and philanthropic planning, to large, complex loans and other family wealth planning issues.

Saly emphasizes the importance of "getting out there and swinging the bat, and not making any excuses. Sure you'll miss a few times but eventually you are going to connect. But if you never swing, how are you ever going to get ahead? I never spend one minute asking myself the question 'how do I get to the next level.' I just do it, and then it happens. People always ask me for my secret to getting to higher levels, and this is it. Unfortunately, they want a one-sentence proverb. They want a clear view of the path they should take, and only they can determine this."

In 1984 a member of Merrill's senior management introduced Saly to a Philadelphia-based accountant and attorney, Martin J. Satinsky, who was looking to grow his practice. While the two were opposites—Marty's quieter nature was a stark contrast to Saly's assertive and extroverted demeanor—they hit it off immediately. They admired each other's work standards, ethics, and reputations. Saly and Marty agreed to refer clients to each other with two goals in mind: to provide additional value to their clients by maintaining open lines of communication about their clients' finances, and to build their businesses. Clients were delighted that their accountant and financial advisor could work together toward their best interests.

Since then, Saly has aligned herself with dozens of CPAs, attorneys, and other professionals whom she respects. "Basically, if I can trust them with my personal business, then I can trust them with my clients' business," she says. "This has become a very big part of our practice."

"We're now deeply involved with many professionals that touch a variety of aspects of a client's financial life," she says. Saly points out that she's so focused on forging tight relationships with these professionals that she has their phone numbers and e-mail addresses memorized. "It also serves as a great time saver," she jokes of her zeal. It is, however, this diligence that enables Saly to proactively seek solutions that her clients don't recognize. For example, Saly is aware of tax issues that may affect clients, such as loss carry forwards, retirement plan contributions, and issues regarding trusts and estates. "The last thing I want is to find out that I could have done something proactive that would have been meaningful, but didn't do it. This way, we're one step ahead of the client."

BUILDING THE TEAM

At the beginning of her career, Saly urged her manager to provide her with additional sales support. As her business grew, she earned additional sales assistants who rotated around the office. Over time, she was able to determine exactly what her support needs were. She has learned that a small, intimate team—"that's extraordinarily efficient" she says—is the best way to maintain very deep relationships with clients, and grow a business.

Of course, a smaller team demands efficiencies. "I learned through my mistakes that you must focus on what is involved with the job," Saly continues. "If we have an opening, we take a good look at what is needed, then determine what type of person will suit that opening. Then we don't compromise until we get the exact person." Saly relies on her team for input on the decision to hire, since they are the ones who will be working with the person side by side. "Everyone here has a defined, written job description and a plan for backup when they are not here. And that backup person is completely skilled in the jobs of the individual they are supporting. This way, there's never a big gap in coverage."

Saly's obsession for perfection is found in the composition of her team. "It's a benevolent dictatorship," she says. "I realize that I am very driven, so a vertical team has evolved." Saly's fast pace, long hours, and ultracompetitive spirit understandably preclude her from pursuing partners or a horizontal team structure. "I'm not the type to meet a partner for coffee and sticky buns at 7 a.m. By then,

I'm already on my third activity." Saly then looks up at me and says sarcastically, "Besides, do you think I need coffee to give me energy?" (As an athlete and health nut, she doesn't drink coffee.) I take a great deal of responsibility for navigating this ship, and it's up to me to communicate my vision and lead the team in that direction. My team is fully capable of executing my plan."

Gail Dontonville joined Saly in 1989, though their relationship spans back to the early 1980s. Gail began her career at Merrill Lynch in the Philadelphia office in 1972, where she met Rose (whom you'll meet next). Gail remembers a time when everything had to be processed manually; even order entry was done on old-fashioned Teletype machines. With the added responsibilities of managing the care of her disabled daughter, Gail found the time to study for the necessary securities licenses. Gail has built an expertise in client transitions and she provides support in all phases of the client relationship.

Thirty-year Merrill Lynch veteran Rose Zavasky joined Saly in 1991. Saly met Rose in the Philadelphia Operations Center where Rose was the Supervisor of Customer Accounting. Saly was impressed with Rose's work ethic and ability to work through problems. "I told myself that one day, when I'm successful, I'm going to try to hire Rose," Saly recalls. Rose now serves as the team manager and coordinates all team efforts. "Rose makes such a huge contribution to our practice that I can't imagine one day without her."

Diane Cusick joined the team in 1994. She was originally an admissions officer and director of development at the high-end private school and collegiate levels. "Turns out she's a technical whiz in the retirement area," Saly says. "Other advisors in the firm call her for advice on retirement plans. She's knowledgeable about some of the most minute details, enabling us to provide a very high level of service."

Megan Bailey met Saly in 1994. Saly was riding a horse out of her barn and saw an 18-year-old girl standing at the end of her driveway. The girl asked Saly if she could ride one of her horses. After a few months of riding together, Saly asked Megan if she could type. The answer: "Ninety words a minute." Saly asked her to come in for interviews with the team, and the team hired her on the spot as a typist and a customer service assistant. Saly describes her as "a wonderful person, very dedicated and loyal, with a great work ethic." Megan now handles initial account analyses (such as spreadsheets and detailed reports) and the preparation of client recommendations.

Saly credits each individual on her team with being extremely detail-oriented, and being able to juggle multiple tasks simultaneously.

"We are extremely close. If someone leaves for vacation, she knows she can ask any one of us to care for her dogs, or even kids. The team regularly spends time at Rose's place at the Jersey shore, holds group parties, and even goes riding together. Outside of family members, I can't imagine any other team that is this close."

A WELL-OILED MACHINE

"Systems are also a great way to free your brain up," Saly adds. "I am frequently examining what works and what doesn't work in order to effectively evaluate my systems. I also heavily rely on my team to create efficiencies." Saly and her team used to meet regularly throughout the week. Finally, Saly's team told her that the team could accomplish what was important without her presence. "Their goal is for me to spend my time only on activities that are production-related. If I spend my time on operational matters, they would consider that a poor use of my time."

"When a client calls, the team answers the phone 'The Glassman Group.' They are an integral part of the business; for them to answer the phone 'Saly Glassman's office' would take away from what they are trying to accomplish. When a client calls, the first thing they try to do is help that person. This includes assessing whether it is an investment-related call, such as talking to me about their assets, or an operations or service matter, such as a wire transfer. They weed out all of the administrative components of the call in order to make my time more efficient. They also assess the client's mood and detect any undercurrent of dissatisfaction. Then they seek to solve the problem; if the problem requires my attention, they give me the facts before transferring the client to my line."

"My team is always on the lookout for assets. For example, if a client hints at assets that aren't managed by us, such as the proceeds from the sale of a property, my team notes that in a message or email for me to see." When Saly receives a message, it contains the person's name, phone number, time they called, when they prefer a callback, when they are likely to be home, the reason for the call, and if there are additional assets. "Every phone message looks like that. If the message doesn't include some of that information, then I would waste my time looking up the phone number, calling the client when he or she isn't there, or missing the assets." Saly emphasizes that the team's systems, even the detailed phone messages, are habitual. "We recognize that these habits benefit us all."

SETTING THE RIGHT COURSE

Saly seeks high net worth clients with substantial assets, and prospects' investment objectives must revolve around the preservation of wealth. Before Saly meets with a prospect for the first time, she requests all financial reports and statements. "I'll receive a very detailed report of all assets, and if it's from the CPA I may receive projections. Either way, I know everything the prospect owns," Saly says. With the data, Megan creates a spreadsheet that details all assets for Saly's review. Saly then speaks with the prospect on the phone to learn more about the person's needs and history. If Saly is willing to accept the individual as a client, they meet in person so that Saly can learn more about the individual's goals and objectives.

During the initial meeting, Saly spends much effort learning about the prospect's goals and objectives. "I don't expect prospective clients to call me up and say, 'Here, transfer my assets.' I'm willing to invest the time to show them how and why working with The Glassman Group would benefit them." Early in the discussion, Saly asks clients to focus on their true goals. Then she formulates a plan to meet the goals, including the future asset base needed and time frame. "Everyone basically should walk around with a number in his or her head," Saly says. "One may be thinking, for example, 'I need to get to ten million dollars by 2010.' "

Once Saly has a basic understanding of the prospects' goals, she determines the type of service the prospect would require and she promptly establishes expectations. "A major mistake financial advisors make is not discussing expectations." For example, an advisor could ask, 'What do you expect out of our relationship? What do you expect from Merrill? What portfolio returns are you expecting to receive?' If a client or prospect were expecting unrealistic returns, I wouldn't want him as a client because he will only be disappointed. If a client is expecting me to call him every day with market updates, it's not going to work out well for either one of us." Saly leans forward to emphasize her next point. "If you're not up front with expectations, you are being unfair to a prospect or client."

After the initial meeting, a written report is created that reviews all data that Saly has uncovered about the individual, based on the financial statements and their conversations. "We work in writing," Saly says. "That way, there's a record." The report includes a current assessment of risk, and rationale for why their current situation is likely or unlikely to help them achieve their goals. Next, Saly includes her recommendations, which may include simple adjustments to their portfolio or extensive alternatives. Lastly, the report includes all fees and expenses associated with working with Saly's group.

CONTROLLING RISK

"One of my main goals is to get my clients the highest return with the lowest degree of risk. A huge part of this involves preventing clients from making mistakes," Saly says. "For example, if you have an equity holding that is greater than five percent of the portfolio, then it may be trimmed or sold. If a stock goes down by twenty percent, it's analyzed further. If earnings aren't meeting a specified target, the company is examined. There is structure and we have disciplines. A client is less likely to wake up one morning and find that they lost half of their net worth because they had too much money in one asset class or stock."

Saly breaks risk down into simple, quantitative terms for clients. "Our role as advisors is to improve clients' probabilities," she continues. "That's really all we do. We tell clients, 'If you follow this strategy, the most probable result is X. Alternatively, if you take this strategy, the most probable result is Y.' When a client proposes that we buy a speculative stock, I explain: 'What if I told you that this stock has greater risk than the risk you already are taking? In other words, with this stock your expected return is, say, ten dollars, but you could lose ten dollars. Your current investment may return only seven dollars, but it might only lose three."

Saly feels that many advisors and investors don't pay enough attention to risk. She compares risk in the market to a child running in a parking lot. "The child runs between two parked cars and into the entrance of the parking lot. He says, 'See? I didn't get run over.' The fact that a car didn't hit him this time was an accident. The fact is, one day he will get hit. Of course, I can't make guarantees, but I can speak with conviction and confidence because I am aware of the strategy and can weigh the potential downsides with the upsides."

ALLOCATING ASSETS

"If the asset allocation is right for a client and a particular asset class is down, another asset class could make up the difference." For instance, up until year-end 2002, Saly's clients were holding a significant portion of their assets in bonds. "A client could have had stock losses of forty percent, but our huge gains in the bond market would have made up for a lot of the equity downside."

Saly believes too many people rely on a one-size-fits-all model for asset allocations. "I consider it far more personal, customizing a model that's right for each client," Saly says. While she studies experts' models, such as those of Merrill's strategist Richard Bernstein, she tweaks the models for each client's purposes. Saly compares customized asset allocations to diets and exercising, "which must be tailored precisely for each individual's goals and objectives, and based on their current situation. You don't want to just open a book or read an article and follow someone else's regimen—what works for one person may not work for another."

If Saly sets, say, a 60 percent equity allocation for a client, she'll establish a range of around 60 to 65 percent. "Many people don't realize that modifying asset allocations is like applying the breaks in your car; you don't immediately slow down, it takes time. When the allocation hits sixty percent, that sends a yellow flashing light to me, which gives me lead time to figure out the next move." Saly adds that when she was managing a transaction-based business, "it was almost impossible to handle five hundred or six hundred clients whose yellow lights were flashing simultaneously. The movement to managed money enables me to have more control and make the appropriate adjustments."

TRANSITION TO MANAGED MONEY

To maintain higher-level investing disciplines, service, and efficiencies, Saly converted her mostly transaction-based business to fee-based discretionary investment management. "My plan is to focus on each client's asset allocation, so that it is in accordance with their goals, their risk tolerance, and the expectations we establish for their portfolios. With a transaction-based business, my focus is diverted to other matters; for example, if we make the recommendation to sell a stock, I would have to call over five hundred individuals and sell over three hundred and fifty thousand shares. It's just not feasible. And how would I decide whom to call first? It would be unfair to the people at the end of the list."

After performing extensive research and informal interviews with her clients, Saly built a new business plan. Her primary mission was to elevate customer satisfaction to the highest level possible. She determined that transitioning her mostly transaction-based business into one primarily based on fees as a percentage of assets would solve several issues. Foremost, even though Saly would earn less money, her clients would pay lower fees, thus contributing to a higher return. Additionally, she would only earn higher fees if the accounts appreciated; when assets fell in value, she would share in the losses, as her fees would drop proportionately. "Simply put, I didn't want to make high commissions when clients were losing money," Saly adds. "With fees as a percentage of assets, my interests are clearly, and fairly, aligned with my clients. I have a responsibility to service the client and to concentrate on asset allocation."

Now that most of her equity business is with discretionary money managers, she says: "I'm not sure how most advisors are able to manage their clients' portfolios and still have time to run their businesses." Further, clients were thrilled about the new arrangement. "And most of all, my clients feel like they are in a better place, with a higher comfort level."

Saly points to the changing dynamics in the market as one of the biggest reasons for utilizing discretionary investment managers. "The average stock is three times more volatile now than it was ten years ago," she says. "This is statistically verifiable. However, the market as a whole is no more volatile. What does that tell you? It means you can't own just thirty-two stocks anymore, formerly the optimum number. The number of stocks you need to own now—to have the same level of volatility—is sixty-five. With sixty-five stock holdings, how are you able to keep on top of all those stocks? It just isn't possible to be both an analyst and portfolio manager, while servicing a book of clients. And what happens if a stock hits a threshold that you establish? Then you have to quickly call five hundred clients. The answer is to either cut your client base considerably, or hire experts—professional money managers with long-term performance records. This is the right thing to do for my clients."

THE RIGHT CLIENTS

In 2002, as Saly was still converting to a fee-based business, she concluded that another adjustment to her business model was necessary. Through the bear market, the clients who fared the best were those who followed Saly's investing disciplines. Additionally, certain clients were a classic fit for her service model, while others weren't. Saly decided to reduce the size of her client base by the number of clients that weren't an "ideal fit" for her areas of expertise. In time, she and the team identified approximately 10 percent of her clients who did not fit her client prototype. These clients represented only about 5 percent of the team's revenue, but they took up much of the team's valuable time.

Saly first learned the benefits of focusing on the "right" clients early in her career when one of her main goals was to create efficiencies. She conducted a thorough analysis of her clientele to determine which clients best fit into her advice and service model. That year, she began the first phase of streamlining her clientele by transitioning clients—whose needs or objectives had changed to the point that Saly felt she wasn't the right advisor—to another advisor who she felt was fully capable. Those assets totaled tens of millions of dollars. "As a businessperson it seemed odd at the time to give away business, but it was the right thing to do for the clients and my business," she says. Shortly after Saly helped the new advisor become comfortable with the clients, Saly's business surged. "As a result, we had time to work more closely with clients and further develop them." She broadened her platform to include virtually all financial services-related products and services, including providing trust and estate services, and offering credit services, such as mortgages. "Suddenly we had far deeper relationships with our clients." After that experience, she became acutely aware of the clients she wanted to work with.

Saly refers to her remaining clients as her "desert island" list; those she wants to be with indefinitely. "I am determined to take extraordinarily good care of these clients, including their children, grandchildren and—God willing—their great-grandchildren. I feel married to these clients, and in a marriage you don't walk when times get difficult—you work harder than ever to make things right. You can't please everybody all the time. My plan is to limit the size of my client base so I can please *most* of my clients *most* of the time."

COMMUNICATION

I tell my clients that if there's a problem, we must communicate. They must tell me when there is a problem in our relationship. For example, 'Is our communication faltering? Am I not meeting your expectations?' When clients confront me like this, I will genuinely say 'I'm really sorry if you feel that I let you down in any way. I never meant to. Our relationship is important to me.' "

Saly emphasizes that the industry seemed to lose its ability to communicate effectively with clients during the great bull market of the late 1990s. "Too many advisors just didn't communicate effectively with their clients," she says. "As a result, expectations were unrealistic, asset allocations weren't appropriate, and people lost sight of their real goals."

Saly establishes a communication schedule with each client. "I try to touch base with my larger clients every ninety days. I tell them, 'In January and July, I call you. In April and October, you call me. That means you have to pick up the phone twice a year, it's that simple. And if your situation changes for any reason, call me. If you can call a restaurant to make reservations, then you can call me to talk about something that's far more important.' This creates communication at least every quarter." The individuals that are called monthly, or even weekly, are those that are in a problem or situation that demands more frequent communication. "A parent may be sick, someone has passed away, or a client sold his home. If they need me, they have access to me. When no special situation arises, the client is back on the reliable, simple system."

"E-mail has proven to be extremely valuable as a communication tool. It enables us to be available 'twenty-four-seven.' Whether a client e-mails me at midnight or four in the morning, I know exactly when they sent it. It tends to speed up the time in which I can communicate with them. I try to return e-mails immediately, so if a client is still online, they really appreciate receiving a quick response. I use this mode of communication to enhance my service."

When speaking to clients, Saly doesn't end the conversation if she senses that the client has outstanding issues. "You can always tell by the way someone speaks, or doesn't speak, that something is on their mind. I proactively find out what this is; I try to get them to say how they feel." This may induce Saly to challenge them. " 'I can tell by your voice that something is bothering you and it would probably be better for both of us if you would just tell me how you are feeling,' They have to feel free to express themselves. By showing sensitivity to their emotions, they may respond with. 'I just feel really scared and alone' or 'I'm scared I'm going to die all by myself.' This discussion helps me sympathize with them and ultimately strengthens our relationship."

EMOTIONAL INVESTMENT

Saly emphasizes that, once you feel you're on top of your game, the best way to take your business to higher levels is to stop keeping score. Coming from a woman who loves to keep score—ask her how long it takes her to get to the post office and back (7.2 minutes)—she says she is able to move to higher levels because she no longer keeps score of the "little things." "Right now, as long as I have happy clients that are fulfilled, and my team and I are doing everything we're supposed to do for them, and I can come home and hug my children and my husband—Lauren and Janice and Allan—I'm happy."

"If you want to become a master, you must give up the scorecards and focus on your higher inner self." In her early years, if Saly was having a tough day and a client called to complain, she would think, "This is the last thing I need right now—he is getting in the way of my business." Nowadays, "I am emotionally there for them. I'm not going to say 'Well, I'm sorry your dog died, but I'm in the middle of my production.' Now I feel really happy and flattered that they felt comfortable enough to call me and talk to me about it. This has resulted in very positive personal growth. Of course it doesn't mean I'm off the hook; I still have a business to run and a responsibility to my firm and my team. I think it's important to set your priorities straight on what you are there to do."

She also jests that efficiencies help deepen relationships—even keeping her clients alive. One day a 78-year-old client told Saly that he was planning to sail his boat from Philadelphia to Maine, then back. The man was one of her first clients, starting with around $100,000. "I said, 'Who's going with you?' he replied, 'My wife is joining me for the trip there. Then I'll sail it back by myself.' I told him, 'You have millions of dollars. For goodness sakes, if you can't take a friend, *pay* somebody to go back with you.' He said, 'Why do you care?' I said, 'Because I cannot stand the thought of you sailing the boat in the Atlantic Ocean by yourself at the age of seventy-eight. You've been my client for twenty-three years, you are like a father to me, and I refuse to allow you to sail that boat by yourself.' I put my foot down and said, 'I want somebody else in that boat.' The man replied, 'It's funny, but other than my wife, there's probably nobody else who cares about me that way. I'll get somebody on the boat with me because you insist.' "

"This is what I mean by not scorekeeping. We should all be focusing on the quality of the relationships, and then the score won't be so important anymore. The revenue always seems to follow."

GETTING THROUGH DOWN MARKETS

Saly cites the benefits of right brain thinking during difficult times: "During the down markets, you need to listen to your clients and be empathetic. It's essential that you let the emotional side of your brain go to work and help clients express their feelings, then it's time for the left brain to determine how to keep them on track." Saly is thankful her clients were well diversified during the bear market, though she blames herself for not being more forceful with those who insisted on investing a large portion of their money in high-tech companies. For a few clients who insisted on doing so, Saly was frank, and told them: "I am not changing my principles. You'll have to find another advisor to handle that money."

"The markets of the early 2000s were a tremendous learning experience for everyone. Now that we've learned, we won't make the same mistakes again. I think when you go through that type of market, you owe it to your clients to do a little soul searching. Unfortunately, many advisors get so caught up in defending themselves that they don't use the opportunity to really look at their mistakes. If you don't, then you really can't grow from the experience. If you don't wring every drop out of that experience, then the whole thing has been wasted on you as a professional. This horrible experience provided an opportunity to completely reevaluate how I do things, so the next time this happens, I will be able to prevent people from making the same mistakes. I will have a stronger hand in enforcing our disciplines."

Part of that evaluation involves advisors taking responsibility for what role they may have played in contributing to what went wrong. This is hard for a lot of advisors because you have to admit that you made a mistake, but this is critical to reevaluate. "As advisors, we should be asking ourselves, where did we go wrong? Did we violate some basic rules of investing? Did we trim holdings that got overweighted? Did we reevaluate our asset allocation and ask ourselves, 'is seventy percent equities too high for this person's risk tolerance,' or were we too busy enjoying the ride? The fact is we *didn't* follow some of the basic rules because we *were* enjoying every moment. What a great feeling to look at your statement and have it be so much more money each month. It was difficult to take that away from people, and you don't want to disenchant clients by saying, 'Well, you know you're going to lose it all.' In reality, we should have been more grounded as advisors. We should have realized that this pace couldn't continue."

DEVELOPING BUSINESS NOW

Saly continues to be selective about whom she's willing to accept as a client. It's not surprising that her ideal client shares at least some of her characteristics: entrepreneurial, high net worth, tied into the Philadelphia business community, involved in philanthropy, and a horse lover. "I network like crazy," she says. "I'm basically seeking people like me. I'm skilled in handling high net worth financial issues for families, and all the complexities that are associated with them." Saly also has a niche catering to same-sex partners, most of which she developed in the equestrian industry, an industry that is convivial to same-sex relationships. "In general, people feel safe with us. With same-sex partners, there are tricky financial and estate planning issues because the law doesn't acknowledge those relationships. We have developed some terrific solutions for these clients, and as a result we've built a strong niche." The high profile Saly has established for herself is the result of her networking, her heavy involvement in the community, and her passion for horse showing. The relationships she develops within these venues are genuine; as a result, she is able to earn their trust. While these venues generate business for Saly, her client base remains her best source of referrals.

"Your clients will help you, but they are not mind readers," Saly explains. "You've got to tell them what you want. When I was first starting in the business, I would call people and say, 'I love doing business with you, and I'd like other doctors like you as clients. If you were in my position, what would you do?' And they would say, 'Well that's easy.' 'Who do you know?' I would ask them. After they gave me names, I would ask them to talk to these referrals in advance."

Saly's current goal is to reach $2 billion in client assets, up from close to $1 billion now, with around 80 percent of the assets in managed money. She's focusing on clients in the $5 million to $50 million range. "I want to do business with fewer clients who have more assets," she says.

COMMUNITY

It's little surprise Saly has firmly established herself within her community and her passions. She's the vice chairman of the Board of JJC, one of the largest child welfare agencies in the Mid-Atlantic region, and she's a board member of the Wissahickon Watershed Association, where for many years she has led conservation efforts in her local counties. She also actively mentors young women in need of positive female role models, and has continually had one at her side, in addition to her own daughters, for many years. "These young women have developed successful careers and relationships, and I am so proud." she says. "I am in touch with most of them regularly, and from time to time they reside with our family."

Then, of course, there are the horses. Saly and her oldest daughter Janice, along with her trainer, Kevin Babington, own, ride, and train show jumpers, including the famous Carling King, currently ranked eighth in the world. Saly's horses show under Kindle Hill Farm and compete for Ireland.

As our interview concludes after midnight, Saly glances at her watch. While she's willing to continue our conversation throughout the night, she calculates that she's been speaking approximately 8.3 hours, including our time in her office earlier in the day. She has also mentally sketched out a plan for her next day ahead, in spite of the late hour. "I like to create an edge," Saly says, describing herself in simple terms. "I like to shine when it rains."

CHAPTER 13: JOHN KULHAVI

Honor, Integrity, and Commitment

Merrill Lynch & Co, Inc.
Farmington Hills, Michigan

Pictured from left to right: Aaron Romain, Nicole Holmes, John Kronner, John Kulhavi, Dennis Cavanaugh, and Charles Kurrie

JOHN KULHAVI SHRUGS OFF THE WORD "HERO." HE IS CLEARLY UNCOMfortable talking about the medals he earned as a helicopter pilot in Vietnam, including two Distinguished Flying Crosses, "the ultimate for an aviator," he says. And only reluctantly does he talk about the truly heroic rescue mission he flew behind enemy lines to help retrieve five captured infantrymen being held as prisoners by the North Vietnamese.

But from the soldiers he served with in the military, to the team he has built at Merrill Lynch, to the clients who have trusted him through more than two decades of market advances and retreats, John personifies the basic concepts of "hero." The integrity, commitment, and honor that forged him in the military have become the hallmark of his work ethic today and the driving theme behind his business and his team. "Any success that I may have achieved in my life I attribute to the teamwork and goal-oriented nature of my experience on active duty and in Vietnam," John says resolutely.

THE BEGINNING

When he was enrolled in Central Michigan University, pursuing a double major in education and applied arts and sciences wasn't enough. He wanted to be more involved, so he joined the ROTC and then put in an extra year at the university just to be part of the program's new aviation training unit.

When he graduated in 1965, he had two degrees, a military commission as a second lieutenant in the U.S. Army, and orders to train with the armored division. After completing that training, though, John was ready to go back to his first love, flying. Since he already had his fixed-winged training from his time at college, he transitioned to helicopters and was sent to Vietnam the same day that his brother was flying out of Vietnam.

"My brother left Camron Bay the day I left San Francisco," he says. "We passed en route."

Once in Vietnam, John assumed the mantle of command quickly. He was promoted to flight leader after five months, leading ten helicopter crews with six infantrymen on each ship into each combat mission. He assembled each crew and planned every mission knowing that dozens of lives depended on every decision he made.

"I learned at a very young age how people acted under duress, under pressure," John says. " I knew when we were going into combat missions that there was always a possibility that not all of the crew was going to come back. That helped me put things into perspective, helped me appreciate the simple things in life, and it taught me how to utilize the maximum capability of all of the men that I work with."

Each of those lessons came into sharp focus when he was called out on a mission that left an indelible mark on John's life. He was stationed near the Cambodian border when word came that a unit on night patrol had been overrun by the North Vietnamese infantry. Most of the unit was killed execution-style, but five were missing in action. For the next two months his unit looked for the missing soldiers, chasing down leads and mounting assault missions into villages where they had been reported to be. There was never a thought of not rescuing these men.

"If you made no attempt to get men out that were captured, how would other infantrymen feel going into combat knowing that if they were captured, no one was going to make an attempt to rescue them?" he says.

Finally, a high-level unit commander received credible intelligence that the five men were alive and being held in a village across the Cambodian border. At the time, the U.S. military was still under strict orders not to cross into that neighboring country. Still, John was rousted in the middle of the night and told to get his best team together. Before dawn, he had his crew assembled. All U.S. insignia had been painted over, and the soldiers were instructed to remove all identifying symbols, including their dogtags. No one was told where they were going, and John carried one of only two maps on the mission.

"They gave me my coordinates, so I knew exactly where we were going," he says. At sunup, they stopped at the Cambodian border to refuel.

"I looked around, and I saw helicopters everywhere," he remembers. "It was unbelievable. It was like something you would see in a movie."

After refueling, he and the rest of the rescue mission flew into Cambodia and surrounded a small village. While the helicopters waited on the ground with their engines running at full speed, gunships were flying over the village providing cover fire for the infantrymen who stormed the town.

"We were very nervous sitting on the ground," John says. "It was the only combat mission I ever flew that we stayed on the ground, because once you have landed, you are a target."

Finally, he saw what he had come for. Five Americans in black coverings were running toward the helicopters.

"We recovered them," he says. "That dedication and loyalty made a huge impression on me. We risked fifty or sixty helicopter crews and all the infantry to save five men."

Once word got out about the daring mission, the colonel who put it together was chastised and relieved of his command. But eventually every infantryman in the country heard about it, boosting morale the way no speech ever could. When John's own orders came to leave Vietnam, he was reluctant to leave his team. At a time when most flyers waiting to go home were assigned less hazardous missions, he was still flying combat missions—up until the day he left the country.

"It was a very difficult decision for me to leave my unit, because they needed me as much as I needed them," he remembers.

By the time he rotated out of Vietnam, though, John had been shot down twice, awarded a purple heart, and realized that there had to be a safer way to make a living. Back in the states, the Army had put his leadership skills to work training the platform instructors and recruiting for flight school, which was no easy task. At the time, two out of three helicopter pilots were either being killed or wounded in action. He had 27 captains reporting to him, but as a captain himself, at the end of the month they were all drawing the same pay.

A NEW LIFE

When he and his wife had their first daughter, he knew it was time to start looking beyond the military for a career to support his family. He knew nothing about the brokerage business, but he did know that he wanted something that would reward his efforts.

"I wanted a job that would offer me the ability to excel or achieve some level of success, not just based upon the team or the organization, but based upon whatever effort I could put forth individually," he says. "This business offered not only that potential, but it was the closest thing I could find to owning your own business without having the capital required to start your own business."

He knew from his military training that the difference between success and failure was basically a matter of perseverance.

"My feeling was that if I could work twenty-five or thirty percent harder than the guy next to me, then over a certain period of time I would excel," he says. "I'm a true believer in that."

Hard work comes naturally for John. By the time he was 13, he was routinely logging in 60 hours a week going to school and helping his parents manage their grocery store in northern Michigan. If anything, life in the Army only reinforced that work ethic. John quickly applied that same work ethic to his new job. He consistently worked long hours, including Saturdays.

Instead of spinning his wheels trying to compete with the rest of the rookies working the same lists he had, John hit the road, traveling to towns anywhere from 50 miles to 200 miles away. It was wide-open territory in the farmlands around Port Huron and Algonac, Michigan.

"How many other brokers are going to drive a hundred and fifty miles to do a seminar or meet with a client?" John asks.

When he first landed in Port Huron, he went to the Chamber of Commerce and got a list of every business in the area. Then he started sending out mailers to every address he could get his hands on, both individuals and associations such as the Jaycees, the Landlord Association, and investment clubs.

"I would tell them that I was the Merrill Lynch account executive that services Port Huron," John says. "If you want a guest speaker, I'm the guy to call. I wanted the visibility"

Even within those smaller communities, John found another niche. Looking around, he saw that most brokers focused on individual accounts, while the banks were hitting on the big companies for their pension and profit sharing plans. He dug into the middle, focusing on managing retirement plans for professionals and medium-sized businesses.

Today, that market represents nearly 60 percent of his business.

TEAMWORK

Despite the tremendous success he was having going it alone, there was still something missing. In the military, John had learned the strength of teamwork, but in the 1970s, the brokerage industry was still a sales-driven, individual environment. John was convinced that, if he had a team of professionals working with him, together they could out service the competition.

"It wasn't because I was brighter or better educated than anyone else out there," he says. "Not by a long shot. It was because I had been in the military and was used to being on teams. Even though I was a rookie in the business, my limited experience already had showed me that specialists seemed to be more successful than general practitioners, whether they be physicians, dentists, or attorneys."

Being a professional himself, he thought the industry should be emulating that business model. He was convinced that a team of specialists working together could provide clients with better advice and better service than any individual.

First he went to his office manager with the idea. The manager wasn't crazy about the plan because it had never been tried at Merrill Lynch before, but he bought John a round-trip ticket to New York and scheduled an interview for him with Don Reagan, who was chairman of Merrill at the time. As luck would have it, Don had been a marine, so he could see the logic of the argument, if not a clear vision of how such a team would function in this industry.

Still, Don gave John the go-ahead, and with the manager's reluctant blessing, John began building the first team in Merrill Lynch's history, and one of the very first in the industry. He started recruiting other brokers in the office and then over the next few years learned several hard lessons about how *not* to build a brokerage team.

His first mistake was that everyone who came in received an equal share of the profits.

"While it may work for some teams, in this scenario it took away incentive," he says. "We had one individual on the team that was constantly having marital problems, and he couldn't work nights and wouldn't come in on weekends."

He was doing 25 or 30 percent less than the rest of the team but was still collecting an equal share of the compensation. The second hard lesson was learned when a major securities firm began heavily recruiting John's team to come over to their side. The rest of the team voted to jump ship, but John was torn between loyalty to his company and his office manager and loyalty to his team.

He chose the team, and spent the next four and a half years at that securities firm, but it was never a good fit.

"I was too structured for that firm," he says. "At Merrill Lynch you walk in wearing a business suit. Over there, guys were walking in with their shirts unbuttoned and t-shirts and big gold chains. It was just a loose, loose operation. It wasn't my cup of tea."

When the branch manager called and offered him his old position back, John jumped at the chance. He offered all his teammates the opportunity to come back with him, but they were all tied to closely to that firm. That was when John made his third and final mistake. He grossly overestimated the integrity and commitment of the men he had been working with for more than seven years.

"I made an agreement with my partners the day I left," he says. "I told them that I wouldn't prospect any of the accounts they serviced if they wouldn't prospect any of the accounts that I serviced."

They shook on it and parted ways. A week later, John was in Port Huron calling on a group of anesthesiologists that he had been servicing for years. When he walked into the office, though, two of his former partners were sitting there waiting to make their own pitch. John reminded them of their agreement, but the former partners made it clear that their first and only loyalty was to themselves, not to any agreement they had made with John.

"I said, 'So everything is fair in love and war,' and they said, 'Right.' "

Within six months, John had moved 27 of the 28 retirement plans his team had managed over to Merrill Lynch.

BUILDING A TEAM: A FOCUS ON SERVICE

John had been burned by his first hard lesson in team building, but he was still convinced that teams were the way to go and was determined to learn from his mistakes. This time he chose more carefully, not just the people he brought on board but how their responsibilities would be divided and shared.

The first order of business was to focus on service.

"Our whole platform has been based on outservicing the competition," he says. "We found out a long time ago that clients don't want their accounts up twenty percent and the next year down fifteen percent. They want consistency in their relationship and they want service."

First he needed someone to help him with the paperwork. That was when he first met John Kronner. At the time, John was majoring in finance at the University of Detroit and working in the Merrill Lynch back office. John Kulhavi offered him $5 an hour to help him out part-time. They clicked. Kulhavi liked his work ethic and his integrity, so he offered him a full-time job as his partner after graduation.

"I told him that if we are successful, he would be very well compensated and if we didn't make it, he could always go back to accounting," John Kulhavi says.

That was more than 20 years ago, and today neither of the Johns makes a move that isn't perfectly orchestrated with the other, rotating their vacations, their days off, even their holidays. That way, one of them is always in the office for client servicing.

With John Kronner's accounting background and John Kulhavi's commitment to client relationships, the two of them started building processes from scratch that have since become mission-critical to every advisor in the business.

The first was developing performance reviews for each client. At that time, brokerage clients only received static reports of their current holdings. There was no information about how they had actually been performing. So the partners began developing the same basic review that they are still using today; the only difference is that today the reviews are done on computers. Twenty years ago, they were calculated manually and typed up separately by a secretary.

"For every major client, at their fiscal year end, we would do a performance review and break everything in the portfolios down by category," John Kulhavi says. "Here's how much we have in equities, fixed income, and in international. Those were the three categories we measured. Then we would show them what the annualized rate of return was for the measured period and for their overall portfolio. We still do that today. We can show accounts that we started handling twenty-five years ago and what their net increase is today to the penny from the day they started with us."

The next step in building a team was to bring in a sales assistant. They weren't looking for just a secretary, though. They needed someone who was experienced, professional, and efficient. They found it in Mary Jo Nalezyty, who came to work with the new team and has been an integral part of the organization for over a couple decades.

"We would have great difficulty functioning without Mary Jo," John Kulhavi says. "She is as important as anyone else on this team, and she knows that."

The next gap to be filled was in fixed income. John Kulhavi had a good handle on the equities market, and had developed a covered call program for his equity clients to boost their overall rates of return. But neither he nor John Kronner specialized in the bond market. Charles Kurrie fit that bill. Charles had a business degree from Michigan State University and had spent two years in the Army, including one tour in Vietnam.

After leaving the service, Charles spent the next 14 years working in his father's mechanical contracting business, but when interest rates peaked in the early 1980s, construction ground to a halt, so Charles fell back onto his business degree. He started with Merrill Lynch in the mid-1980s, and immediately clicked with John Kulhavi's growing team.

"I took on the responsibility of the fixed-income portion for the team because the fact is, everybody was really in tune to what was going on in the stock market, and we needed to have someone concentrate on the interest rate–sensitive fixed-income portion of the accounts," Charles says.

Charles' job goes far beyond analyzing how much income each portfolio should be generating each quarter, though. He follows every aspect of the fixed-income market, and builds client portfolios from scratch, using a broad combination of investments to match income and liquidity needs with each client's risk profile.

It's an invaluable addition to the team because it is an expertise that few individual advisors can bring to the table. In fact, in 2003, that expertise alone helped close a new $10 million account for the team. The account came from an existing client who only had his individual account with them.

"He owns a business, and we asked him what he was doing with his corporate dollars," John Kulhavi says. "He was leaving it in a checking account at a local bank, and they were paying him a very low rate of return. So Charlie drafted a wonderful proposal and we showed him how he could have liquidity with triple his net after-tax rate of return."

The proposal focused on variable rate notes, made up of remarketed, preferred, triple A–rated and tax-exempt bonds. By blending a broad variety of bonds and laddering maturities, Charles was able to triple the rate of return the client was earning on the bank account, while maintaining liquidity.

Charles also acts as the personnel administrator for the team. He supervises and trains the new team members to ensure that everyone is moving in the same direction.

PRINCIPLES TO WORK BY

"We found out a long time ago that we spend more time together than we spend with our own families, so there has to be a tremendous amount of harmony," John Kulhavi says.

That harmony is built and maintained with a handful of very clear, very strict policies that each team member is expected to follow. First is the work ethic. The office is open from 8:30 a.m. to 8:00 p.m. every weekday. Everyone pulls his or her own weight by working the extra hours in turn. To keep the workload fair, Charles sits down with the team at the end of every year and passes around a calendar. Going by seniority, each person puts in one week for vacation or one holiday they want off, and the calendar goes around the table until all the slots are filled.

"Otherwise all the senior people would have all the holidays and the younger people wouldn't have much input," John Kulhavi says. "That wouldn't be good for morale."

Another policy is that anyone can talk to management at any time about anything. John Kulhavi maintains an open-door policy, and will go with any team member to senior management to discuss any issue.

"You will never find a team member of ours standing around the hallway complaining, gossiping, or whatever," he says.

Along those same lines, John has asked each team member not to be part of any office clique.

Finally, every team member is asked to support management in any way possible. The goal is that every individual on the team contributes to the overall welfare of the entire office. John Kulhavi and other senior members of the team routinely volunteer their time to help train rookies on everything from building financial plans to running asset allocation models. He even goes to other offices around the country giving speeches and doing training on team building.

"To me, that's a way of giving back," he says.

It's a discipline, though, that not everyone can thrive in. Recognizing that, John Kulhavi starts each new team member on a 12-month probation. That gives everyone a year to get comfortable in the situation and figure out where—or if—they fit.

"We had an individual that left the team at the end of last year," he says. "Our priorities and his priorities were considerably different. It's not saying either is right or wrong."

Even when it doesn't work out, John once again proves his loyalty by giving the departing team member enough assets to generate the same income that they were making as part of his group. The last member who left received $35 million in annuitized assets because that's what was needed to match his income as a team member.

One of the greatest strengths of the team is that everyone brings a different skill set to the group, and one of John's greatest strengths is knowing how to leverage each person to his maximum potential. While most brokerage teams working today are designed around a group of individuals all doing basically the same thing out of one office, each member of John's team has a specific responsibility that is fully integrated into the overall process.

"I found out with the military that the guys with the most sophisticated weapons win," he says. So continuing on that military theme,

John's goal has consistently been to develop the highest level of sophistication available within the group. One weapon he needed was a skilled estate and financial planning specialist, so he went after—and got—one of the top experts in the field. Dennis Cavanaugh (CLU, ChFC) joined John's team in 2000 after seven years as Michigan's estate and insurance planning specialist for Merrill Lynch and 24 years with his family's insurance planning firm.

"Denny has given us a planning capability that I think is unequaled throughout the firm, and that's a very broad statement," John says. "I don't know anyone who has the expertise he does."

COMPREHENSIVE FINANCIAL PLANNING

Denny does a financial plan for the Kulhavi team's clients and then he updates it annually. Each plan addresses estate tax consequences, estate planning, gifting to children, college funding, even mortgages. His role is to help the team understand exactly what that client's needs are, in terms of cash flow, risk tolerance, and personal long-term goals.

"The key thing I do is to empathize with the client's position," Denny says. "Whether they've lost two million dollars in the market or they've lost their husband, it's my job to find out what's important to them and then position the rest of the team for our initial meeting."

Everything is built on the financial plan, which is driven by each client's ongoing cash flow needs.

"Regardless of their net worth, I find that people don't know how much they are spending," Denny says.

In one recent case they were working with a client who had just lost her husband. She had no idea how much she had, what she needed, what to do with the proceeds of her insurance policy or the IRA she had inherited, or even the fact that at age 60 she was eligible to collect Social Security.

The first step was to find out how much income she needed every month. In this case, it came out to $4,735. With that income as the primary objective, they were able to develop an overall strategy that would generate the income she needed today and prepare her for the future.

"Denny has impressed not only clients, but accountants and attorneys that work with the clients with his level of expertise," John says. "That has led us to even more business through referrals.

Clients know that they can call Denny anytime and make an appointment. His job is not to sell them a product. His job is to give them the best advice possible."

Aaron Romaine and Nicole Holmes are two of the newest members of the team. Aaron started out as an administrator, and after four years of running portfolio analyses wanted to manage client accounts. He now provides great service for accounts that typically range in size from $100,000 to $500,000.

Nicole started working with the team nearly four years ago as an intern while she was a sophomore at the University of Michigan. She became a full-time team member after graduating in 2002. Her primary job is to help John manage his covered call accounts, but she also manages some of the second-generation clients.

The team manages more than 1,000 accounts, but this is just the beginning. With the core group in place and the malaise of the bear market behind them, John thinks his team is ready to take off.

"We have a tremendous amount of talent, and we have the drive and the ambition," he says. "In the past six months, we've gone back to what made us successful, which is being more assertive in asking for referrals. And we are getting them."

"Our niche business is the million to three million dollar account," he says. "We don't have a lot of turnover, and our clients are very loyal."

They are also all annuitized. Nearly 85 percent of the team's business is annuitized, well ahead of their peers. That has always been their focus.

A DISCIPLINED STRATEGY

That is a testament to John's keen commitment to discipline. This discipline is what helped sustain both the team and its clients through the three-year bear market because they stuck with those principles through the raging bull market.

"The two years before the crash were my two hardest years in the business," John Kronner remembers.

Clients who were earning 25 percent returns on their carefully designed, properly allocated financial portfolios were getting frustrated. There was almost a constant push from the clients to shift their portfolios into a more aggressive mode. The team held fast to the discipline of the plan, and despite all the turmoil of the market's rise and fall, they lost only one client.

The client wanted to be far more aggressive with his $2.7 million portfolio—more technology, more hot stocks. When John wouldn't budge, the client left.

"We told him we had our own reputations to think of," John says.

That client came back to the fold two years later, though, with less than $400,000 left of his original portfolio.

"We stuck to our discipline, and now he is back with our team," John says.

It is a discipline that has been forged and honed through nearly 25 years of sweeping market and industry changes, changes that John Kulhavi started implementing decades before. Asset allocation. Long-term financial planning. Teamwork. John Kulhavi was doing all these things long before they became industry buzzwords. For him, it was just the right way to do business.

"I am loyal, probably to an extreme," he says. "I look at the team as my extended family. I worry about each of them. I have great concern for them."

And that concern and loyalty is clearly reciprocated.

CHAPTER 14: RICHARD SAPERSTEIN

Corporate Cash Management and Individual Wealth Management Services

Bear Stearns & Co., Inc.
New York City, New York

OVER THE PAST TWO DECADES, RICHARD SAPERSTEIN HAS BUILT ONE of the most successful corporate cash management platforms on Wall Street, a platform that coexists alongside a thriving wealth management business. Working with a team of more than a dozen professionals, Rich is consistently ranked among the top tier of all advisors in the financial services industry.

When I first contacted Rich about my interest in interviewing him, he was reluctant, saying he preferred to maintain a low profile. However, when I suggested that others, especially those just entering the financial services industry, might benefit from the insights he's gained and the lessons he's learned over the course of his remarkable career, he agreed. I began by asking him to give me an overview of his business model.

"In many respects, what we're doing here [at Bear Stearns] is somewhat unique," Rich says. "We're actually running several platforms but there's a great deal of synergy among them and we're able to leverage that synergy in a very effective manner."

"On the cash management side, we offer a nonfee [transaction-based] compensation program for buy-and-hold clients and, through our associates in Bear Stearns Asset Management, we also offer a fee-based program for companies requiring more active trading. As a result of Bear Stearns' extensive industry relationships, we also maintain a very competitive position within the money market arena. Our clients have the opportunity to invest in approximately one hundred and fifty domestic and offshore institutional money market funds, which are denominated in U.S. dollars as well as in sterling and euros."

"Then we have a brokered transaction platform for companies managing their own cash; those clients have access to literally billions of dollars of auction rate securities. And, finally, there's our wealth advisory business. We provide portfolio management services to selected private investors, many of whom we've met as a result of our involvement in managing their corporate cash."

"One important reason our model works as well as it does is because we've been constantly refining it and our clients are directly responsible for many of those refinements. I've always believed that it's very important to talk to your clients and, more importantly, to listen to what they have to say. That's a point I often make to my team."

"You know, when I look back over the past twenty years," Rich continues, "what we've accomplished really amazes me. We've survived through very volatile market cycles, not to mention a great deal of adversity on the 'world stage.' And through all that, we've somehow managed to build a very viable business. I think what I find most rewarding are the exceptional client relationships we've developed along the way."

TEAM EFFORT

In his capacity as senior portfolio manager, Rich devotes much of his time to maintaining a watchful eye on the $6 billion in assets (as of this writing) over which he exercises discretion. Consequently, he relies heavily on his team, which he refers to as one of his "greatest assets."

"We handle quite a variety of assignments for our corporate and private clients," Rich says, "with capital preservation as the common denominator. Our cash management clients range from private companies to companies that have recently gone public to companies listed on the New York Stock Exchange. We've also established an 'Emerging Client Division' to focus on serving startups and the venture capital community."

"Although we draw on Bear Stearns' considerable resources in the due diligence area, we instituted our own formal procedures years ago for monitoring investment policy compliance and identifying credit-related issues," Rich says. "Those procedures afford us an important degree of confidence in our ability to protect our clients' interests. There's an old saying, 'the devil is in the details,' and I happen to subscribe to that philosophy.

"As far as our clients' policy statements are concerned, selected team members monitor our systems and meet on a regular basis to review client portfolios for compliance with those statements. In my opinion, that's one of the most important aspects of our client services."

"We also maintain an 'Approved Securities' list and produce a summary detailing the exposure to and credit rating of every issuer on the list every week. If an issuer has been placed on credit watch or has been downgraded, for example, we employ very specific protocols in communicating the situation, whatever it might be, to our clients. And, when it's appropriate to do so, we'll share our opinions as to what we believe to be the most expedient course of corrective action for the client to take."

"Other team members compile and issue our internal and external reports. They include the FASB 115 compliant reports we deliver to our cash management clients via a secure link on our web site."

"So, our team represents quite a range of professional disciplines. We currently have three accountants on staff as well as people who've either earned or are pursuing advanced degrees in finance, economics, and law. Other members of the team have expertise in trading, operations, systems, and administration.

Rich is so adamant about his internal procedures that every job function, "no matter how trivial," is redundant. "I'm determined never to have a break in client service." Rich acknowledges that providing this level of client service is expensive but says that, "In a world where it's increasingly difficult to draw a distinction between risk-adjusted returns, you can still control the levels of service you provide."

The importance of maintaining that "control" was especially apparent in the aftermath of September 11. At the time, he was with CIBC Oppenheimer and had no access to his offices, which were across the street from the World Trade Center. Within a matter of days, Rich moved his entire team to Boston. When everyone had gathered for the first time in the temporary offices, he thanked them for their willingness to accept the personal sacrifices associated with making the move and then said simply, "Recreate your operations."

"There was a bit of scrambling involved," Rich acknowledges, "but we were back in business by the time the markets reopened that following Monday. I'm proud to say that our third quarter FASB 115 reports were uploaded to our secure website right on schedule. We were in Boston for about three months and every single member of the team put forth a tremendous effort. All in all, it was quite an experience."

"Thanks to the exceptional talent I've surrounded myself with," he says, "we're well positioned to deliver a broad array of very sophisticated services, even under the most trying circumstances. That's just as true for our private clients as it is for our corporate clients."

WEALTH MANAGEMENT PLATFORM

Primary responsibility for the wealth management side of Rich's business falls to one of his senior associates, David D'Amico.

"David and I met at Oppenheimer in 1988 and, over the next dozen years or so, I came to have a tremendous amount of respect for him. Although I had kept a small book of high net worth clients from my days as a traditional broker, my focus at that time was on building the cash management business. Nevertheless, my wealth management business was expanding more or less on its own for a couple of reasons. Not only were many of my retail clients transferring additional assets to me, they were also providing referrals."

"In addition to that, some corporate clients were approaching me regarding their personal accounts. I had been telling my corporate clients for years that my area of expertise was in cash management but eventually I saw the light and realized I needed to ramp up my capabilities in the wealth management area. So, in 1999 I asked David to join my team.

"He's a consummate professional and we share a strategic, defensive investment philosophy," Rich says. "It's what he and I refer to as the 'get rich slowly' school of investing. These individuals have accumulated significant wealth, they've engaged us to deploy their assets in a very prudent manner, and that's precisely what we do."

BUSINESS MODEL SYNERGIES

"I think it's fair to say that we're all dedicated to providing exceptional levels of client service," Rich comments. "As I mentioned earlier, one critical component of our ability to meet that commitment is the synergies that exist among our corporate and retail platforms. In essence, we employ the same 'best practices' across the board and they're really central to our business model."

"More to the point, David and I leverage the same internal resources," Rich continues. "We both use our 'Approved Securities' list and both rely heavily on our compliance and credit monitoring procedures. Then there are the practical client benefits, especially with regard to our wealth management platform. When I'm buying a large block of bonds for our corporate accounts, for example, we have the opportunity to include our private clients in the transaction as well."

"Other best practices include our communication protocols, our research flow, and the manner in which we leverage the formal, highly detailed policy statements that capture our client's investment objectives and related requirements."

"The investment policy statement is really our road map," Rich explains. "It establishes the parameters by which we manage every portfolio and, importantly, it eliminates ambiguities. In many ways, the policy statement serves as a means of reassuring clients that their assets are being properly and carefully invested. Again, as I've said, wealth preservation is the common denominator in all this."

On the corporate side, the investment policy statement comprises four primary guidelines: approved securities, maximum and average maturities, minimum credit ratings, and concentration limits or the maximum exposure the portfolio can have to any single issuer. According to Rich, the private client policy statements might also reflect such details as risk tolerance, cash disbursement requirements, performance expectations, and long-term goals.

"At the end of the day," Rich says, "the investment policy statement creates a stronger, more effective relationship between our clients and us."

"Those are all illustrations of how we're able to leverage both our best practices and the synergies among our various platforms, and that ability has proven to be one of our greatest competitive advantages."

THE FORMATIVE YEARS

The story of how Richard Saperstein rose to the top of his profession has its beginnings not far from his offices in midtown Manhattan. He and his two older brothers were born in New York City and raised in New Jersey in what Rich describes as a blue-collar town. The Saperstein boys learned about fiscal responsibility from a very early age.

"My brothers and I always knew what it meant to have a good, solid work ethic. It was something our parents instilled in us through their own example," Rich says. "They both worked long, hard hours their entire lives."

"The same was true of my older brothers. They both had jobs during the school year and, in my family, there was no such thing as a summer vacation. Whether it was heavy construction, building maintenance, or running an elevator eight or ten hours a day somewhere in the city, my brothers always took it in stride. They were very hard workers, just like my parents."

"My dad ran a smoke and sundry shop in Manhattan and I went to work with him every chance I had. And I do mean 'work.' There was no sitting around reading magazines or people watching, but I really loved being with my dad and in the middle of the action. That's when I first began to understand what it takes to run a successful business. I'm still amazed by the amount of effort involved in running that little shop. It was a monumental undertaking on my dad's part."

"From the time I was just a kid, I might have been seven or eight, my dad always encouraged me to think like an entrepreneur. I'm sure he didn't use that word and I wouldn't have understood what he meant if he had, but that's what it was all about. He was always cooking up different ways for me to earn a few dollars."

"One time when I was really young, my dad and I drove to a local farm stand early one Saturday morning and we bought a bushel basket of tomatoes," Rich recalls. "We divided the tomatoes up on the kitchen table, put them in small paper bags, and off I went to sell them to our neighbors. That night, when my dad told me how much profit I'd made, I couldn't believe it. Obviously, it wasn't a huge amount but I was really impressed. That was one of the first lessons my dad ever taught me about the 'mechanics' of business."

Beginning in his early teens, Rich's chosen profession was landscaping. He learned the ropes working for a family friend and, when he was 14, he came up with a plan to launch his own business. Among other things, the plan involved investing his entire life savings, something on the order of $350, in a "professional quality" lawnmower. That was a considerable sum in those days, especially for a teenager, but Rich's business plan was solid. He had done his due diligence and he knew the lawnmower he had his eyes on was just what he needed to compete with the "big guys."

When his father found out what Rich had in mind, he offered to loan Rich the money. In return, Rich had to agree to take care of the family's yard free of charge. "The interest on my savings account didn't amount to much but my dad thought it was important for me to continue earning that interest," Rich explains.

As soon as the new lawnmower was parked in the Saperstein's garage, Rich began to market his services and, one by one, he built a customer base.

"But they had to be the right kinds of customers," Rich says. "That meant they had to live somewhere along my existing route; I didn't want to waste time traveling between jobs."

Consistent with his business plan, Rich offered a discount to anyone who lived next door to one of his current customers, but on one condition. "They had to let me give the lawn a horizontal cut in order to get the discount," Rich explains. "That way, I was able to mow the two lawns simultaneously."

The business blossomed and so did the services he provided. Within a matter of weeks, Rich had earned enough money to buy a leaf sweeper and other assorted garden tools. He wanted to enhance his earnings by providing more comprehensive services to his customers and, according to Rich, "the investment paid off."

That was an early example of what has become one of the hallmarks of his career. "I've always been a firm believer in reinvesting in my business," Rich says.

In short order, he was in a position to repay his father. "But, when I handed him the money, he refused to take it," Rich says. "All my dad really cared about was that I worked hard enough and smart enough to keep my end of the bargain. Anyway, I mowed our lawn once a week until I went away to college. I think my dad and I both got a good deal in the bargain; I know I did."

FIRST TASTE OF WALL STREET

Rich was still in high school when he set his sights on a career in financial services.

"One of my older brothers and I had always been involved in various ventures together. He had gone off to college and he called me one day. He said he was getting ready to do some investing in the stock market and suggested we pool our money. So we opened a joint brokerage account and began trading stocks. As it turned out, we had a run of good luck and when I saw how much money I had made and how much easier it had been compared to cutting grass and hauling leaves, I was hooked. That's when I first knew I wanted to be on Wall Street."

When Rich graduated with a degree in economics from the State University of New York in 1981, inflation was running in the low teens, interest rates were in the 20 percent range, and the job market was very tight, especially in the financial services industry. None of that mattered to Rich, however. One way or another, he was headed to Wall Street.

Every morning, he rode with his father and mother into Manhattan and they dropped him off in the Financial District. Wearing one of the only two suits he owned and carrying a briefcase full of resumes, Rich picked a building at random and took the elevator to the top floor. Then he worked his way down through the building and, whenever he spotted the words, "Member of the NYSE," he walked into that office, introduced himself, and left his resume.

After weeks of prospecting, Rich landed a job with E. F. Hutton. "They hired me as a financial planner at a starting salary of fifteen thousand dollars," he recalls. Richard Saperstein was on his way.

Along with several others, Rich prepared financial plans for high net worth clients and prospects. Determined to make his mark, Rich arrived in the office early, left late, and immersed himself in learning about taxes, insurance, estate planning, investing, and a host of other subjects. After 18 months, his determination paid dividends; he was promoted and assumed responsibility for managing a group of junior planners.

In 1984, Rich left Hutton and went to work for Janney Montgomery Scott. The firm intended to establish a financial planning practice in its New York office and Rich assumed responsibility for the project. One of his primary objectives was to automate the process and that, of course, was going to involve a relatively new technology: computers. "People were just beginning to migrate from IBM Selectric typewriters," Rich says, "and I realized I wasn't all that computer-literate. So, I took the initiative and started an internship program."

"I provided the details of what I wanted to accomplish and the intern handled the mechanics. Working together, we eventually created a program that automated the process and did so with a great deal of both customization and accuracy." That experience was the genesis of what would become Rich's longstanding reliance on and appreciation for technology, which has always played a significant role in his business.

A year or so later, Rich was finally ready to pursue his dream of becoming a stockbroker.

"The prospect of becoming a broker had always fascinated me," he says. "You can start your own business with no money down, the business has unlimited upside potential, and whether or not you succeed is entirely up to you and how you treat your clients. There's no other business quite like it."

Rich asked for his manager's support and a few days later, he was off and he was running. "I had just turned twenty-six and I was ready for the challenge," he says. "I continued on with my financial planning, but I began working the telephones. I had really struggled to earn this chance and I was determined to make it."

"Most rookies in this business work alongside other rookies," Rich says, "but I had an advantage. I had spent considerable time at both Hutton and Janney interacting with the most seasoned brokers in those offices and it was an invaluable learning experience."

Rich spent his "free time" cold calling, learning the products and services he was marketing, and forging relationships with his new clients. Over the following months, his business began to accelerate and Rich decided he was finally in a position to give up his financial planning responsibilities and become a full-fledged broker. That decision eventually led him to Oppenheimer & Company in May of 1987.

"Talk about timing," Rich says. "I don't think I'd been at Oppenheimer more than a few months when the market crashed." As Rich tells it, the weeks and months that followed served as a constant reminder of an important lesson his father had instilled in him.

"Throughout his entire adult life, my dad always had a healthy disdain for corporate America," Rich says, "and he told my brothers and me over and over again, 'Don't repeat the mistakes I made; you have to be in control of your own business.' I hadn't heeded his advice and I was in serious trouble all because my revenue stream was tied to circumstances far beyond my control. That's when I started to consider my options."

"It was 1988 and, after five long years of night school at NYU, I graduated with an MBA in finance. I was tired and I was discouraged but I wasn't about to give up," Rich says.

A DIFFERENT PERSPECTIVE

"The retail business was all about trading. That's how you made your money. That was especially true if you happened to be a broker but the clients had the same mentality; trading was the name of the game for everyone, including high net worth investors. I had known for months I didn't want to make my living that way and, if I needed any additional incentive to change the direction of my business, the crash tipped the scales."

"I was convinced the only way I was ever going to turn things around was to work with more sophisticated clients and, when I say 'sophisticated clients,' I'm talking about people who know about money and how it works, people like corporate financial officers. I knew they were responsible for large sums of money and that they had to have absolute confidence that the managers on Wall Street they entrusted that money to were extremely knowledgeable. The underlying challenge was capital preservation and that meant fixed-income product."

"The way I saw it, fixed income was the key to reducing the impact the market swings were having on my revenues, and the means to that end involved establishing relationships with senior executives at small and midsized companies and assisting them in managing their short-term, fixed-income portfolios."

In other words, Rich was about to enter the cash management arena. He was aware that this was a highly competitive business with thin margins. Nevertheless he was confident he'd be able to attract the right kinds of clients and produce the volume necessary to generate healthy cash flows.

"When I made my move into cash management, compensation typically was based on the numbers of days remaining to maturity," Rich says. "So, when a client bought seven-day paper, I'd get paid for seven days but I only had to work five days to earn the revenue. Translated, that meant twenty working days in each twenty-eight-day cycle and that gave me leverage."

"In some ways, I guess you might say it was like getting paid for cutting a lawn or two without actually having to haul the lawnmower out of the garage. I knew I was on the right track. It was just a matter of analyzing the upside benefits and putting them into play. What's more, I knew that cash management products were generally a whole lot safer than equities. Finally, I had the benefit of knowing the client was going to reinvest because the paper was going to mature. When you're building a business, few things are more critical than recurring revenues."

Rich was focused and he was determined.

"I sat down with my branch manager and I told him what I was planning to do. Things in the office were still in a bit of turmoil in the aftermath of the crash and I know he had his reservations, but he was a great guy and he wished me luck. When people in the office found out what I was up to, they thought I was crazy."

Toward the end of 1988, Rich began to transition his retail book to other brokers in the office he trusted and kept only a small core group of investors with whom he had an "especially good fit." Over the next several months, his revenues plummeted. "If my manager hadn't been so supportive," Rich says, "I'd have been in real danger of losing my job."

In addition to the dismal economic conditions, Rich quickly came to the realization that there wasn't much cash management product available at Oppenheimer, nor was there anyone to turn to for support or guidance. "Basically, I was on my own," Rich recalls.

As more and more of his associates questioned his decision, Rich became increasingly determined to prove them wrong. Ever the optimist, he says the fact that no one really believed in him was an advantage. "The cynics knew it was 'impossible' to make a living managing cash but, as far as I was concerned, that meant I had less competition and a great opportunity to build for the long term."

Due to his low revenues, Oppenheimer wasn't about to assign Rich a sales assistant and, because he continued to service his remaining retail accounts, the lack of administrative support was especially problematic. "I was constantly on the phone taking care of clients," Rich says, "and handling all the wires and check requests and the trading and doing my own research. At times, I felt more like a juggler than a financial advisor."

BUILDING FROM SCRATCH

So, there he is sitting at his desk bright and early one morning. His sleeves are rolled up and he's drinking a solitary cup of coffee. His hold on that desk is tenuous, he has no administrative support, he doesn't have much in the way of product to market, and he doesn't have anyone he can turn to for advice.

Along with all that, something else was missing: clients.

"I didn't have any cash management clients and I really didn't know how to go about getting them," Rich says. "So I did the one thing I knew had worked in the past. I picked up the telephone and started making cold calls. The problem was that I really didn't know what to say when I got someone on the other end."

Then Rich had a brainstorm, another one of those innovative ideas for which he has become so well known in the industry.

"I decided to 'go back to school' but this time I'd be both student and teacher," Rich explains. The plan was simple. I would offer prospects a weekly analysis of what was happening in the fixed-income markets. So, I rounded up all the financial newspapers, magazines, and research materials I could get my hands on and I read everything relating to the credit markets."

Armed with his newfound knowledge, Rich started calling prospects and asking if they were interested in knowing what he thought about what had transpired in the bond markets the previous week.

"I discovered that corporate executives were very interested in what interest rates were doing and why, how credit downgrades or upgrades might affect their companies, and how geopolitical events might impact future interest rates," Rich says. "I didn't realize it at the time, but I was gaining real insights and, after a while, I found I was actually able to answer the questions these people were asking me."

To this day, Rich continues to be a voracious reader and, as he says, he "learns something new about the markets every day."

It took Rich until sometime in 1989 to land his first cash management account. The client was a portfolio manager with a trust company in Poughkeepsie, New York. Rich had been maintaining an ongoing dialogue with the manager via his weekly market commentaries. One day, out of the blue, the phone rang. It was the portfolio manager and he told Rich he wanted to invest $100,000 in a 49-day auction rate security Rich had been talking to him about.

"I was so nervous, I almost didn't know what to do," Rich recalls. "I hung up the phone, wrote up the ticket, walked out of my office, rode the elevator to the trading floor, and handed the ticket to the head trader. I had been barraging her with questions for months and, when she saw the ticket, she gave me a big smile and said, 'It's about time.' It's one of those moments you never forget."

"Thinking back, what I really remember most about that first transaction is coming to the realization that I had provided the manager with a solution. I had solved a problem for him. It was a very small transaction but it's one of the most important transactions I've ever made. For the first time, I really had the sense I was beginning to make some progress."

More corporate clients followed over the balance of 1989 and Rich was working harder than ever. "I spent the entire year hoping I wasn't on the end of a burning rope," he says. Toward the end of 1990, his cash management business was on a steady upward track and his wealth management business was on a parallel course.

CHARGING FORWARD

As soon as his cash flow allowed, Rich wasted no time hiring a sales assistant out of his own pocket. "Money was tight, but I knew the only way I was going to maintain my momentum was to begin building a support staff," he says.

"Even though I needed more help, I just couldn't afford to assume any additional financial burden. So, leveraging what I had learned while I was at Janney Montgomery Scott, I established an internship program and it paid off, both for me and for the interns. They worked hard but they learned a lot. We still have an active internship program and many of the young people who've passed through the office have gone on to successful careers in the industry. It's been what you might call one of those 'win-win' situations."

In due course, Rich was in a position to invest more of his own money in building his permanent team. "It didn't make much sense to expand my client base if I wasn't able to provide adequate, or I should say more than adequate, levels of service," he says.

Again, from the time he purchased that lawnmower, Rich has been a firm believer in the merits of reinvesting in his business.

"I know people in this business tend rely on their senior management for seed capital, and I take that route myself from time to time. On the other hand, investing my own resources gives me a degree of control I might not otherwise have. And, of course, sometimes it can take months to get approvals and, when it's time to implement a new initiative, I believe in doing whatever I have to do to make it happen."

"So, more often than not, I take care of my own agenda and trust senior management to reimburse me down the road once I've proven that the investment was worthwhile. I've really adhered to that philosophy over the years and have never stopped investing, or I should say reinvesting, in people, training, equipment, and technology. It's all very much an ongoing process with me," Rich says.

By 1993, Rich had assembled a small team of professionals to support what he describes as a "very strong, very viable" corporate cash management business.

RECOGNIZING AN OPPORTUNITY

"Our model was consistent with the way cash management was handled in those days," Rich says. "Companies either outsourced the management responsibilities and paid a fee for services rendered or they had their own internal treasury staff and purchased securities on a strictly transactional basis. There was no such thing as a 'nonfee'-based program."

Then something happened that eventually would earn Richard Saperstein a place in the annals of the cash management business. That "something" was the infamous savings and loan scandal. In response to the public outcry that followed, the Financial Accounting Standards Board introduced a new corporate accounting standard, known as FASB 115. This ruling took effect in early 1994.

"In essence, as long as they don't actively trade their portfolio, FASB 115 enables companies to isolate market value fluctuations in their cash investments from their profit and loss statements," Rich explains.

"As I saw it, the FASB legislation created an incredibly strong incentive for companies all across the country to opt for passive portfolio management. I was convinced that, in relatively short order, companies would either be investing through transactional brokers or they'd outsource the responsibility to fixed-income portfolio managers on a buy-and-hold basis. Either way, I knew the cash management landscape was about to change forever."

"What I recognized was the opportunity to develop a new business model based on a nonfee approach to cash management," Rich says. "At the time, cash managers charged clients a management fee for services rendered and the fee was calculated as a percentage of the assets in the portfolio. The managers also executed their trades through institutional salespeople who collected the transaction charge or 'spread' that the salespeople built into the price of the security."

"After FASB 115 was introduced, managers continued to charge clients a fee even when there wasn't any active trading in the portfolio. And in those instances where trading did take place, in addition to the fee, clients incurred the spread when the institutional salespeople had included it in the price of the security or securities. It wasn't what I considered an equitable arrangement for the client," Rich says. "But that's how it was done and everyone just accepted it. I saw no reason to charge fees for managing a buy-and-hold portfolio when I knew I'd earn fair compensation simply by earning the spread when I executed transactions."

Although they had reservations, senior management at Oppenheimer approved Rich's proposal to offer a nonfee-based cash management compensation program. Similar programs are now commonplace but Richard Saperstein retains the distinction of being the first, as he puts it, "to do the right thing for my clients."

PROVIDING SOLUTIONS

While Richard Saperstein may be best known among his peers for his pioneering efforts on the compensation front, that achievement is only one example of any number of innovations he has introduced in the cash management industry. In fact, there's a tagline that features prominently on many of Rich's marketing materials. It reads, "Providing Innovative Cash Management Solutions Since 1988."

Those "solutions" include the following:

In the mid-1990s, Rich saw an opportunity to address an inconsistency in the way the financial industry and most corporations maintain their books. More specifically, although corporate America operates on an accrual accounting basis, Wall Street operates on a cash basis.

As a result, clients had little choice but to transcribe account data from traditional spreadsheets to their general ledgers—that is, until Rich took the initiative to hire accounting and software consultants to design and implement a new system. When all was said and done,

Rich was able to provide his clients with very comprehensive accrual-based reports.

Rich was also the first in his industry to deliver FASB 115 accounting reports via the Internet. Prior to this innovation, which he introduced in late 1999, these reports were generated in hard copy and clients subsequently keypunched the data into their general ledgers. Once again, Rich invested his own capital in developing this innovative electronic delivery system, which is now more or less standard throughout the industry.

TURNKEY OPERATION

"As my business grew, I continued to expand my team and hand over more and more of my routine responsibilities," Rich says. "That gave me the time I needed to pay closer attention to the overall direction of the business and to think about fundamental strategies relating to portfolio management, compliance issues, and other critical client services."

"I spent a great deal of time talking to clients and prospects about what their requirements were and how they saw them evolving," Rich explains. "Based on that ongoing due diligence process, we were constantly refining and expanding our infrastructure. It was hard work and I was reinvesting significant amounts of capital in new staff and technology, but we were clearly reaping the rewards."

"In 1996, I hired Jerry Klein to work with me on both the client service and short-term trading sides of the cash management business. As I've just said, we had a lot going on at the time. We were beginning to shift our focus from Fortune 500 companies to those in the small to midcap range. It was a strategic move on my part and, fortunately, it proved to be a good decision for our business."

"In any event, our asset base continued to grow on a steady upward curve and Jerry was absolutely instrumental in enhancing our efforts in the client services area. He's now responsible for our short-term, fixed-income trading and for corporate client communications."

"Things really began to accelerate when the 'New Economy' took hold," Rich continues. "During the technology revolution in the late nineties, companies were investing in 'technologists,' engineers, and scientists but not in accounting and finance professionals. Although these companies obviously had cash management requirements, they weren't especially interested in ramping up their treasury operations. In other words, there were increasing numbers of companies that wanted to outsource their cash management requirements to a turnkey operation."

And Rich and his team were prepared to meet that demand.

IN SEARCH OF THE BEST PLATFORM

In 1997, CIBC World Markets, a New York–based division of the Canadian Imperial Bank of Commerce, had purchased Oppenheimer. Five years later, the bank decided to exit the retail business in the United States and soon sold Oppenheimer to another brokerage. That left Rich with a difficult decision.

"I had been with Oppenheimer for sixteen years and initially resisted making a move but the writing was on the wall," he says. "After a tremendous amount of due diligence, and it was an incredibly exhausting process, there was no question in my mind about what I was going to do. I had found the absolute best opportunity on Wall Street for myself and, perhaps more importantly, for my clients."

Rich and his entire team arrived at Bear Stearns in May 2003.

"This firm has an excellent reputation and it's well deserved. In conducting my due diligence, one of the things about Bear that I found most persuasive is the firm's incredibly strong position in the fixed-income area. Obviously, that's an extremely valuable component as far as my business platform is concerned."

"Along with that, senior management here is perfectly amenable to my continuing to source bonds through the contacts I've developed over the years with traders around the world. I think that translates to the best possible situation for our clients. Although we do a considerable volume with the Bear traders, we also execute with traders at other firms both here and abroad."

"Another important factor that weighed heavily in my decision was that Bear Stearns Asset Management offers several fee-based options for companies whose cash management requirements dictate more active trading within their portfolios. Obviously, there's a significant advantage to us in being in a position to offer our clients both fee-based and nonfee-based alternatives. Everyone in Asset Management has been especially supportive and we have an excellent working relationship with that area of the firm."

"Then there's the technology platform. In my opinion, Bear has one of the most advanced technology infrastructures in the industry. Coupled with that, senior management has assigned a number of very competent technologists to support our ongoing initiatives."

"The last point I'd make about the merits of being here has to do with the culture within the company. Bear Stearns is what I'd describe as very 'client-oriented' and that's due in large part to the fact that the firm is more than forty percent employee-owned.

"In any event, as a result of our alignment with Bear, our clients now have the option of electing either a nonfee- [transaction-] or a fee-based compensation program and, as I just said, we give all our clients access to an exceptional money market platform."

GOING FORWARD

Although it has evolved over time, Rich's original business model continues to serve as the foundation for what many regard as one of the most successful cash management operations in the industry. But Richard Saperstein is not one to rest on his laurels and he continues to actively plan for the future.

"We have a number of things in the works," he says. "Right now, we're focusing on various enhancements to our technology infrastructure, including some minor and several major initiatives. Bear has one of the most advanced technology platforms on the Street and we're taking full advantage of that platform."

"Essentially, we're committed to staying in the forefront of our business as far as the breadth and quality of our client services are concerned. That involves everything from communications to reporting systems to facilitating trading opportunities. Whatever we're working on, it generally tends to be 'client-centric' in one way or another. And that's the key to whatever successes the future holds in store for us."

LESSONS LEARNED

When asked to sum up the most important lessons he's learned on his way to the top, here's what Richard Saperstein volunteered:

"That's a tough question but I'll do the best I can to answer it. The first thing I'd say, especially to those in the early stages of their careers, is to let your entrepreneurial instincts rise to the top and let those instincts guide your decisions."

"Be innovative. Think ahead and think smart. Find a better, more efficient, more productive approach to what you're doing. You have to anticipate the opportunities the industry is going to present as it evolves and you have to anticipate the opportunities that are going to be lost if you don't seize them."

"Don't attempt to be all things to all clients. Become a recognized expert and the 'go-to' person in a specific area. That might involve product or a geographical area or a segment of the population. Whatever it is, focus on it and see what you can do to gain a competitive edge. And, once you've got that edge, keep it."

"Invest in your business and keep right on investing. Go on out and buy that 'leaf sweeper' or new computer or hire a marketing consultant. Invest in whatever it is you need to drive your business to the next level. The returns will be there."

"Take risks. Whoever said, 'nothing ventured, nothing gained' knew what he was talking about. Don't be afraid to make mistakes. I've made a million of them and I've learned something valuable every single time. Have the courage of your convictions. It's not always easy but, if you want people to believe in you, you have to believe in yourself."

"Surround yourself with good people, let them make their own decisions and encourage them to be both innovators and risk takers."

"Don't ever think you know it all. Take my word for it, you don't. Go to night school, read everything you can get your hands on. Get to know the most successful, most ethical people in your business, pay attention to what they have to say and learn from them."

"And finally, and I know I'm repeating myself, always, and I mean always, act in the best interests of your clients."

CHAPTER 15: CARRIE COGHILL

She Wrote the Book on Financial Planning

D.B. Root & Co. (Commonwealth Advisors)
Pittsburgh, Pennsylvania

CARRIE COGHILL'S PASSION FOR EDUCATION HAS LED TO NATIONAL TV *appearances and two books, but her focus remains on the client.*

A few years ago one of Carrie's clients, a widow in her sixties, passed away. Carrie was there to hold her hand during her remaining days. She has also been there for her client's family. Carrie still helps the client's daughters manage their finances. She has been there to help the daughters make important decisions, such as what college to attend or what career path to take. They even spend some holidays together. More importantly, Carrie helps to instill the client's values and philosophies to her daughters. "This is the most important part of my job," Carrie says.

CLIENTS FIRST, BUSINESS SECOND

Carrie had her Series 7 license for seven years before she made her first sale, and she wears that feat as a badge of honor. As a licensed assistant to a top-producing advisor, Carrie learned the industry by working with people, rather than with products, and that has forever molded her perspective on client-centered financial advice.

"That time I spent as an assistant taught me to listen, and that is what makes me good at what I do today," she says. "I know what the clients are thinking, and I know what is important to them. That makes all the difference in the world."

Today, as president and cofounder of D.B. Root & Company, that is the difference that she tries to instill in everyone who joins the firm. Instead of recruiting hot brokers from national firms, Carrie and her partner David Root, Jr. prefer to find people who match their commitment and work ethic, and then bring them in as assistants to learn and grow with the firm. By the time they are ready to start producing, advisors at D.B. Root understand their role as their clients' trusted partners, not as just another revenue center for the firm.

CLIENTS FIRST

"One of the first things I learned when I was working for Dave was that, if you do the right thing for the client, you are never going to have to worry about making money or getting new clients. It just happens," Carrie says. While her firm's penthouse office sits atop one of Pittsburgh's skyscrapers, one might believe they offer white-glove service only to the wealthiest. In fact, they also cater to mainstream America.

For Carrie, the clients' needs take priority over making money. That commitment became a calling at the turn of the millennium, when the market started to plummet, and clients began to panic. When other advisors were using the duck-and-cover technique to protect themselves from the fallout, Carrie and her crew were on the frontlines, reaching out to clients every day, calming their fears and talking them through the crisis.

One woman needed even more than that. In the middle of the market chaos, Carrie received paperwork from a longtime client, requesting that her account be transferred. The client was ready to dump her entire diversified portfolio and push everything into bonds. When Carrie asked why she would consider such a drastic move, the client told her that she had talked to another advisor who had said she was crazy to be paying a fee to an advisor while her portfolio was losing money.

"I told her that I wasn't going to let a fee cause her to make a mistake with her money," Carrie says. Instead, Carrie prepared a comprehensive review of the woman's account, and screened it against market history.

"I showed her that if she got out now, she would not be able to recover her losses, and I used the chart to give her the confidence that the market will recover," Carrie says. "It was more of an educational meeting than anything else, but that was really all she needed. She just needed to know that the fee was not a good reason to make a change."

EDUCATION IS KEY

Education is a theme that runs through every aspect of Carrie's life. Reaching beyond her own client base to a national audience, Carrie has written two highly acclaimed books on financial planning and regularly appears on CNBC's *Power Lunch.* She also takes time to educate individuals during book signings.

"I truly believe people need to be educated about their money," she says. "My approach has been to help people understand what I am doing and not just following my recommendations. A better educated client makes a better client. That way you are in it together, and there is never a question as to whether you are doing the right thing."

Carrie began her own education early in life. Raised by her grandparents, Carrie's grandfather dropped out of high school to start what would become a very successful bakery. Although he was retired by the time Carrie and her sister came to live with them, business was still a major topic of conversation.

She discovered her love for numbers in a high school accounting class and had planned to get a business degree in college and then her CPA. But plans change. Carrie's grandmother died just weeks before Carrie graduated from high school, and, facing the loss of the woman she still refers to as her mother, Carrie decided to enroll in a junior college to stay closer to home during that difficult time.

When it came time to transfer to a four-year college, Carrie hit another snag. Her grandfather, who made a successful life for his family without a high school diploma, wasn't a big believer in college; he didn't want to support her continuing education.

"The deal I made with him was that, if he would help me out, I would get a job and go to school at night," Carrie remembers.

She got a job working as a secretary at a major regional brokerage firm, supporting two advisors. One was Dave Root. That's when her real education began.

"I realized that, no matter what level you were working at within a brokerage firm, you need to know everything because it is really the assistants that implement everything," she says.

And she means "everything." The two advisors she was working with at the time were trying to start up the firm's first comprehensive financial planning practice. This was 1986, so the whole idea was pretty cutting-edge—but it was a philosophy and a business plan that made sense to Carrie. As soon as she turned 21, she took her Series 7 exam to be a better resource for both her bosses and their clients. Then she studied to become a Certified Financial Planner; not because she wanted to be an advisor herself, but so that she could help take her team—and her clients—to the next level of service.

When her partners changed firms, she followed, supporting their business and working closely with their clients. Unfortunately, the new firm wasn't supportive of the financial planning initiative. It was much more sales-oriented, and Carrie wasn't comfortable in that environment. Fortunately, neither was Dave Root.

"I told him at the time that if he ever started his own firm to let me know," she remembers. A year later, that's exactly what he did, joining another advisor's independent financial planning business.

"Dave and I were working together and really focused on the idea of working as a team for our clients," she says. "We weren't acting as a traditional broker-assistant team. It was both of us working to cover all aspects of whatever the client needed."

MOVING OUT OF THE COMFORT ZONE

That was a comfortable role for Carrie, as she was still reluctant to strike out on her own as an independent producer within the firm.

"I never had a desire to sell investments," she says. "That was way too scary for me. But finally I hit a crossroads where I understood that it's not about selling investments. It's about helping these people. That really hit home for me."

The issue came to a head when Dave was promoted to president of the firm. He wouldn't be producing anymore, so she had to decide what she was going to do with her career. The owner of the firm gave Carrie a choice—a choice of which advisor she wanted to go work for next. She gave him another option.

"I told the owner that I was going to work for myself or I was leaving," she says.

She was met with the predictable resistance. She was young—still in her twenties. More importantly, though, she was a woman. He told her that if she were a man or at least had some gray hair and wrinkles, she might stand a chance in this business. Thankfully, she didn't listen.

"I'll never forget sitting there just shaking and thinking how inappropriate that comment was," she remembers. But she knew what she wanted, and now she had something to prove. Her first year on her own she was so successful that she won a top advisor's trip and the owner of the firm had to eat his words.

"That was great," she laughs.

Great until she was pushed out of her comfort zone—again. After working as a producer for only a year, Carrie had to take one of the biggest gambles of her career. Dave and the owner of the firm were coming to loggerheads over management issues, and the dam broke when Carrie was taking a well-earned long weekend on the Jersey shore.

"The phone rang at 10 a.m. on Good Friday, and it was Dave," Carrie remembers. "He told me that, due to management differences, he had decided to start his own firm. Did I want to come?"

Carrie was recently divorced and facing life as the single mother of her daughter Kelli, then still a toddler. But relaxing on the beach with a Bloody Mary that morning, she told him "yes" without even hesitating.

"I owed my whole career to him, in terms of who I was and what I had learned," she says. "But when I hung up I thought, 'What did I just do?' "

MARKETING MAGIC

What she did was help found one of the most successful independent financial advisor firms in the country, but starting from scratch turned out to be an entirely different ballgame than working with established firms.

"I walked into the firm the first day and said, 'Where are the leads,'" she says. "All of a sudden we went from never having to worry about generating leads to having nothing."

For Carrie and Dave, that meant marketing.

"That was probably the scariest part," Carrie remembers. "I had never done it. I was afraid of it. But they tell you that you have to get out of your comfort zone."

She was already very familiar with that challenge, so she began marketing with the same zeal that she used to break through all the other barriers that she had faced along the way. Ironically, she says it was being a woman that probably helped her the most during those first few weeks when the business was just getting off the ground.

"I was trying to figure out what to do to create new business for the firm and thought, 'Well, you just have ask other successful professionals what they would do,'" she says.

Anytime a new client would come in, Carrie would ask them for the names of his or her accountant and attorney. Then she would call up those professionals and ask them to lunch. She would begin each conversation talking about the firm and its philosophy; but by the end of each meal she would be asking their advice on how to prospect for new business.

"I think asking for help like that was easier for me because I'm a woman," she says. "I don't think it would be as easy for Dave to sit across from the table from another guy and say, 'I need your help.'" As it turns out, those other professionals turned into terrific lead sources for the new firm. Working with clients' attorneys and accountants allowed Carrie to showcase the broad array of financial planning services she was providing and by bringing these other centers of influence into the mix, Carrie was able to establish her role as quarterback for the team, providing service and support to both the client and the rest of the advisory team.

"Some of my best clients have come from those early meetings," Carrie says.

Word-of-mouth marketing brought in quality leads, but it's a very slow way to build a business, and an almost impossible way to build a new brand in the highly competitive world of financial advice. That was especially true in the late 1990s when the market was booming and major firms were cranking out new brokers and starting up new offices at a record clip.

Carrie and Dave cut through all that market chatter by taking a cue from their previous employer, who had a radio show. But this time it was TV. They bought a prime time slot—8 to 9 p.m. on Thursdays on a local cable channel—and began a two-year run as a call-in show.

"It was a blast," Carrie says. "It was very interactive because people were calling in, and it gave people a chance to see what we were all about."

That cable gig led to a half-hour show on the local NBC affiliate. The heightened visibility from television was effective, but incredibly expensive. By the time they were on the network, D.B. Root was spending significant capital each month on television marketing alone. It wasn't a great resource for referrals, but the investment built credibility and recognition that have proved invaluable.

"The real value was in the branding," Carrie says. "When clients would give us referrals, they knew who we were because of the show. I think that established and set us apart. Plus, it opened the door to CNBC and some of the other television we do."

Today, the only airtime the firm buys is for ad spots on Fox, CNN, and CNBC, but Carrie still gets plenty of time on the air. She is a regular on CNBC's *Power Lunch,* and has appeared as a guest on *Bloomberg Television, Simplify Your Life, The Ananda Lewis Show,* and other national and local programs.

LEADING THE CAUSE OF EDUCATION

But her focus today isn't on drumming up new business. It is on educating consumers about financial planning, and she has become a true evangelist on the subject.

"The marketing effort for me is driven out of being very passionate about what I do," Carrie explains. "Over the last five years I have seen a lot in this industry that I don't like, and it underscores the importance of having a thorough understanding of the market."

The light went off for her when the Internet bubble started expanding beyond reason. Looking for answers to what she thought was a troubling market phenomenon, she read the book, *The Internet Bubble.* The book talked about how all these companies were eventually going to burst, recreating the same boom-bust scenario that derailed the railroads nearly a century before.

Hooked on the history lesson, Carrie decided to dig deeper into these market cycles of booms and busts. Her research led her to a library in New York were she tracked down a copy of *How to Value a Railroad Security,* first published in the early 1900s. The book had been long out of print, but its message was as immediate as the Nasdaq at 4,000.

"It freaked me out," she remembers. "I wanted to go up to strangers and say, 'Do you see this?' "

But the fact was that nobody wanted to look. Everybody was caught up in the market euphoria, so Carrie launched her own crusade, organizing an entire seminar series on the dangers of the "new economy" based on the book and the lessons it held.

"It even talked about financial statements and about how, regardless of what auditors and financial statements you have, management will always conceal what it wants," she says.

Carrie hit the road with what she thought was a smoking gun, putting on seminars around the country about the dangers of the Internet bubble.

"It wasn't that easy," she says. "I was sitting there in an office in Pittsburgh watching people that went to Harvard and Yale talk about the Dow at thirty thousand and the Nasdaq at five thousand. I kept asking myself, 'What am I missing? I must be missing something, because these people should be smarter than I am.' "

She didn't have to wonder for long. With the collapse of the dot.coms and corporate scandals like Enron still shaking the market nearly four years later, Carrie is a more fervent believer than ever that the most important thing any advisor can give to their clients is education.

By that time, Carrie knew she had a lot to say and wanted to find a larger audience for her message. She was particularly concerned about the less sophisticated investors, the ones who are most vulnerable to market hype and overly aggressive salespeople. As a single mother herself, she felt a true calling to reach out to that market with a how-to book on basic financial planning.

She found an agent and started pitching the idea to publishers, but that wasn't the market the publishers wanted her to hit. They suggested she try her hand at a couple of other projects first, so she wrote *The Newlyweds' Guide to Investing and Personal Finance.*

"I loved writing that book because it was about so much more than finances," she says. "I meet with couples everyday, and we deal with all the different dynamics that are nonfinancial, such as who's the spender, who's the saver, what works best in terms of checking accounts and managing the money and budgeting and trade-offs. The book was a lot more conceptual than it was financial, and I think that information is invaluable."

The second book was also targeted at education. *What's Your Investing I.Q.?* is designed to be a fun, interactive way to teach financial basics through multiple-choice questions about investing, finance, and economics. Points are awarded for each correct answer.

"I wrote the book in 2002, after 9/11 and after the technology bubble burst," she says. "So my commitment to writing it was a lot greater because I really felt that there was information there that people needed to know."

Educating herself and her clients is what continues to drive her today. Her marketing emphasis is still on education, but the message has changed with the times. For example, when the markets are soaring, she keeps investors grounded—and when the markets tank, Carrie is there to hold their hands and reinforce the long-term outlook.

CREATIVE DIFFERENCES

Carrie's passion for teaching and marketing provides the perfect counterbalance to Dave's primary focus, which is bringing in new business and managing money. Since they started working together nearly 20 years ago, Carrie and Dave have developed a synergy that feeds off their different yet highly compatible strengths. A simple explanation is that Dave provides the vision and Carrie fills in the details, but there is nothing simple about the relationship that has developed over the years.

Starting out with just one assistant that they shared, Carrie and Dave grew D.B. Root to a regional powerhouse, with 25 employees, including five full-time advisors working out of two offices. Riding the wave of the bull market, that growth was almost inevitable and the firm pretty much expanded using its own steam. Carrie and Dave were each running their own books of business, and no one was paying much attention to running the company.

That came to a screeching halt when the market collapsed in the early 2000s. Suddenly everyone shifted into consolidation mode. They had to close one of the offices, and the headcount dropped to 14.

"The focus was exclusively on the client," Carrie remembers. "It was all about dealing with the market and about making the right decisions and providing the right advice for your clients. What we didn't realize was that no one was managing the firm."

There was no time to think about corporate structures when days and nights are filled with calls from panicked clients. When the dust finally settled, though, Carrie discovered two things: first, that successful businesses don't run themselves, and, second, that she had changed.

"I think for a lot of advisors, especially advisors who are very serious about what they do, those three years were very trying, and they can really wear you down," she explains. "I came out of that period very proud of the fact that I didn't lose any clients over it, but my focus had changed."

She discovered that what she loves the most about what she does is working with existing clients while continuing to teach the world about the market and investing. That falls squarely on the marketing side of the equation, which consumes an increasing part of her life and her business.

"I never thought I would be saying this, but getting out there and speaking to groups and doing the TV is fun," she says. "The problem is that I don't have that drive anymore to turn those people into leads."

The common model in this grow-or-die business is to be constantly recruiting and closing new business, and then passing those clients off to a string of able assistants. But that was the last thing Carrie wanted to do.

"I just didn't want to do that because I love the clients I have," she says. "They grow to rely on you, and that is what being a financial planner is all about. If my doctor suddenly told me that the nurse would be taking care of me from now on, I'd find a new doctor."

Still, there are only so many hours in a day, and between running the business, marketing, and managing her clients, there wasn't anything left over for closing new sales. Thankfully, that realization plays directly to Dave's strengths. When Carrie realized that she was, in a word, bored with her career, they restructured their roles within the firm. Dave, who had built his career as one of the top advisors with every firm he worked for, was strapped to the desk instead of doing what he does best—generating prospects and closing new clients.

"Dave is a typical entrepreneur," Carrie explains. "He is a visionary and the driving force behind this firm. He is also the best closer in the business. He could get money out of a rock."

That's when the partners traded hats. Carrie assumed the title and responsibilities of president, managing the day-to-day operations of the business while working with her existing clients and, of course, marketing. Now when she collects new leads, though, she passes them off to one of the three other advisors in the firm under a unique compensation package that lets her benefit in the new business without actually having to make the sale.

"I told Dave that my sales goal this year was to make him the number one producer in the company," she laughs.

She's not bored anymore, either. She juggles her three roles in the firm with almost seamless effort—and a lot of support from two full-time assistants. Of course, that means that she has time management down to a fine art. Mondays are firm days, where she catches up on and oversees the operations. Tuesdays, Wednesdays, and Thursdays are client days. Fridays are marketing days.

"I am always there if my clients need me," she says. "But they know the structure. I tell them from day one that when they call they will get Stacy. If they need to speak with me, leave a message with her and I will return the call within twenty-four hours."

Evenings and weekends are off-limits for work. That is time that she has committed to spending with her now teenage daughter.

"I always thought that, as your children got older, your time commitment to them became less," she says. "But it's just the opposite. When they are teenagers is when they need you around the most, and you need to know where they are every minute of every day."

REBUILDING

Under her new role within the company, Carrie is now facing her biggest challenge to date—building a team based on the client service model that she and Dave have perfected. That is a particularly difficult assignment working in the niche they have carved out between a one-person independent shop and a full-service wirehouse. Experienced advisors either want to go out on their own or stick with the big firms that can offer all the bells and whistles.

Carrie feels that the firm's broker/dealer, Commonwealth Financial Network, has been indispensable, not only in her business efforts, but also her own personal growth. "Typically, a broker/dealer is an organization that helps you transact business," she explains. "Commonwealth is different. They provide support to help you with literally every aspect of your business." She has relied on their practice management division to help create a solid structure for the firm. However, when asked about the real essence of Commonwealth, Carrie feels that it is all about the people. "The management team at Commonwealth has created an environment that cares about not only their rep force, but also their employees. This is the kind of firm Dave and I want to create. We know, through our observations of Commonwealth's CEO, Joe Deitch, that strong leadership is the key to creating a firm that has a culture we can be proud of."

"The biggest challenge in managing this business is finding the right people," she says. "The problem that we faced in the past is that we either hired people with no experience and really didn't know what they were getting into or hired experienced people who really wanted to be out on their own."

Today, she focuses on finding people with the values and character that fit the firm philosophy and have the ability and the desire to learn.

"We have had people in the past complain when things were changing," she says. "My answer now is that, 'Yes, things are changing and they always will. If you can't deal with change, you shouldn't be here.' "

When she took over leadership of the firm a year ago, Carrie sat down with each of the employees and asked them where he or she saw the firm and himself or herself three years from now. She didn't always like the answers she got, but she got a good feel for where everyone was, and how each fit into the future of the firm.

For instance, one of her assistants was finishing up his Chartered Financial Analyst certification. That was good for him, but the team didn't need an analyst. It needed someone who can work with clients. He was honest, though, and told her that he didn't see himself with D.B. Root three years down the road.

"That put us in a bad position because now we knew we had someone who really isn't in the boat with us," Carrie says. "But we respected his honesty, so we worked through it and it's worked out great."

Together, they worked out a deadline for him to find a new job, and Carrie had ample time to find and train a high-quality replacement. He is now working for a major securities firm in New York City as an analyst. "It feels wonderful to know that D.B. Root & Company played a productive role in his personal and professional development, even though he is not working at our firm," Carrie explains.

That exercise also helped Carrie identify some weaknesses in the organizational structure. There were some really great people in the office doing absolutely the wrong job based on their individual interests and skill sets. To find better job matches for her employees, Carrie put the whole staff through a "predictive index" survey, which highlights personality traits and lets you measure such intangibles as how someone is motivated and whether or not they are demanding or impatient.

"I have the honor of being the most impatient person in the office," Carrie laughs.

But the results are no joke. With a good feel for her staff and a clear understanding of how each person is motivated, Carrie says she has the team in place now that can move the firm to the next level of excellence and growth.

"Managing people is the most difficult thing I've ever done," Carrie says. "But it is also the most satisfying because we want to create an environment here where everyone can feel great about what they do. This is not just a job, it's a career."

Getting the right people in the right jobs is just the first step, though. Building and maintaining a real sense of teamwork and ownership in the firm requires constant nurturing, particularly in an office structure built around so many concentric circles. There are four advisors in the firm managing their own books, and each advisor has at least one assistant. On top of that are the administration staff and the tech people who manage all of the software and computers.

"It is easy to feel isolated," Carrie admits.

She battles that isolation by giving every member of the staff at least one job that entails some responsibility to the firm. For instance, one assistant was a great employee for the advisor she worked with, but was clearly not feeling connected to the rest of the firm. Carrie put her in charge of managing the entire contact management system, and now she is one of the strongest players on the team.

Then the entire staff meets once a week to check in and go over firm-wide issues.

"That is how we have been able to develop professional respect for each other," Carrie says.

That is also how Carrie and Dave have been able to maintain a consistent quality of client service throughout the market ups and downs.

IT TAKES A TEAM

While advisors manage their own individual books of business, they work together as a team to provide the best advice and service possible for each client. From the moment a new lead comes into the office, the team functions as a cohesive unit to ensure the best possible service and experience.

When a call comes in, it is transferred to an advisor, who doesn't let them off the phone until a meeting is scheduled. Once the first meeting is on the calendar, the real work begins. First, each prospect is sent a questionnaire that goes far beyond the standard financial questions. Going through it forces potential clients to begin quantifying their financial objectives and start thinking about what they really want in an advisory relationship.

The goal here is two-fold. It helps shape the direction of the first meeting, and it screens out the people that Carrie and her team really can't help.

"It works as a prescreening process, because some people will get the questionnaire and decide that this really isn't what they need," she says.

By the time the advisor and the client sit down to go over the questionnaire together, they are already moving in the same direction. During that first meeting, the advisor can start filling in the blanks by developing an understanding of each client's risk tolerances and personal goals.

From the information gathered there, Carrie and her teamwork form a combination of asset allocation models developed by Commonwealth Financial Network and their own research and experience to begin creating a plan for each client. A week or so before the second scheduled meeting, that plan is formalized with specific recommendations and sent to the client to review.

"A lot of advisors aren't comfortable sending out the recommendations before the second meeting, but we find it makes the process go a lot more smoothly," Carrie says.

The prospects have a chance to really analyze the recommendations being made and can be prepared with any questions and concerns they might have in the second meeting.

"Because we take a comprehensive financial planning approach, the timing of that second meeting could be excessive if they haven't had a chance to review the plan beforehand," Carrie explains.

It also helps to make the focus of the second meeting about educating the client instead of making a sale, because unless clients fully understand what the advisor is doing, they will never be fully committed to the process. By the end of the second meeting, it is no longer a question of whether the plan should be implemented, but how quickly the plan can be put into place.

Once the financial plan is in place, Carrie and her team meet with each client every six months to make sure it stays on track.

"No one leaves the office without the next appointment scheduled," she says. "It's kind of like going to the dentist. When you leave they give you a card. I think that policy has been very important in terms of client retention."

When it comes to making specific investment recommendations, the firm primarily uses retail mutual funds, individual securities, and even alternative investments, such as private placements, to fill in the asset allocation sectors. The goal is broad diversification through a select group of mutual fund managers and investment strategies that employ individual securities. Dave heads up the firm's investment policy committee with input from the rest of the advisors. Carrie assists in providing global market views to help set general direction, and Dave fills in the details.

"We don't do automatic rebalancing because our belief is that investment management is an art and a science," Carrie explains. "We are not market timers."

Still, you can't ignore the market completely, so the investment policy committee stays on top of business trends and market cycles, taking advantage of shifts where they can. For instance, after the growth sector made big gains through the first half of 2004, they started pulling some of that money off the table and moving it into value funds. They also avoid sector funds whenever possible.

"We are not taking huge risks with sector-specific funds because most of our clients have already made their money, and our goal is just to help them protect what they have," she says.

On the fixed-income side, for example, the team took a decidedly defensive posture in 2004 when the Federal Reserve began its much anticipated move on interest rates.

"Because of where interest rates were, we were very cautious about where we were putting money in that sector," she says. "To avoid making big interest rate bets, we used preferred stocks or private real estate investment trusts wherever possible."

CUSTOMIZED CLIENT SERVICE

That is exactly the protection and guidance that Carrie's clients have come to expect. While most advisors measure their professional success against the S&P 500 or some other market benchmark, Carrie measurers hers by her 95 percent client retention rate. That mark can be reached only through service, and Carrie makes sure everything that she and her team do centers on the specific needs of each client.

That attention to detail is best seen in the reports they put together for each client. These are never churned out by some standardized piece of software because a quarterly performance report means nothing without the proper context of where clients have been and what those numbers mean to them personally.

"For instance, I would never make a recommendation without understanding the tax implications for that client," Carrie explains.

One of Carrie's clients owns dozens of individual stocks that he either inherited or accumulated over the years. So showing him where his General Electric is today compared to five years ago doesn't tell him anything about their real value to him. For that, he also has to understand the cost basis of those stocks and what those shares are worth after taxes if he were to sell them.

So one of Carrie's assistants went to the client's home and spent three evenings going through all his paperwork, sorting through information and reconstructing his entire portfolio from a cost basis perspective. From that, Carrie has been able to develop a customized spreadsheet that reflects the true value and performance of his portfolio.

"The people that we are dealing with have spent their lives focused on their careers and their families," she says. "They are not used to dealing with these kinds of things. So the customization of this report is part of the reason they are with us. They are so appreciative, because they have never been able to understand their own finances in this way."

She even takes those reports one step further by incorporating all a client's assets into one understandable spreadsheet, even the assets that Carrie doesn't manage. Everything from savings accounts to 401(k) plans are included in each semiannual quarterly review.

"That is the most time-consuming element of our business, but the process is critical for all of us," she says. "I need to know everything to make sure we are accomplishing their overall goals. I don't know how to do that any other way."

And it creates a peace of mind for clients that money can't buy. Carrie vividly remembers a referral she received from one of her best clients. The prospect was in a panic and wanted her to drive 40 minutes to his home to help him make sense of his finances. He had $1 million in a 401(k) plan, with money stashed away in accounts all over the place—an annuity here, a certificate of deposit there.

"He was just so afraid and so disorganized," Carrie remembers. "He had no idea what he had and no concept of how to get his hands around it."

Carrie was able to consolidate everything into one statement for him and pull together a comprehensive, and comprehensible, financial plan for him.

"He is so appreciative," she says. "And that's really what it's all about."

Carrie applies that holistic view not only to how the money is managed, but where that money is going. As a result, she is a big believer in organizing family meetings and making sure there is proper intergenerational planning built into the process. Then she wants to make sure that the children and grandchildren understand what to do with the money once they inherit it.

"I have a client that lives in my neighborhood, and over Christmas one year his kids were coming into town," Carrie remembers. "He was going to be gifting to them that year, so I suggested that, since I had to meet with him to get some paperwork signed, that we all get together so that I can talk to them about investing and what they might want to do with that money."

Even if the kids don't have much money yet, she wants to get them started off on the right foot. She is helping one client's 24-year-old son map out his first 401(k) plan.

"He still lives at home and doesn't know what to do," Carrie says. "It's fun, and it's just so encouraging to know that this person is going to be so much further ahead. Also, from a business perspective, it helps create longevity by keeping that intergenerational wealth flowing into the firm."

That is typical of how Carrie approaches any new client, regardless of how much money they have to start out with. In fact, one of her most satisfying relationships was one that started early in her career. A young couple came to her with exactly $1,000 to invest.

"They had kids and they were both working and they decided that they wanted to start investing a thousand dollars a month," Carrie says. "We set them up with a plan, and they were so thrilled to get started."

As it turns out, a few years later they inherited a large sum of money, and, of course, they trusted Carrie to invest it.

"When that sort of thing happens, you sit back and say, 'Okay, that is how it's supposed to work,'" she says.

Once clients become part of Carrie's family, she becomes fiercely protective of them, willing to join a fight if she believes they have been wronged. One client came to her after taking a beating in the tech bubble. He was 72 years old, and his wirehouse broker put his entire portfolio into technology stocks. His $6 million portfolio was cut in half.

"It was truly a case of terrible mismanagement, and they really felt that they needed to pursue legal action," Carrie remembers. "We helped facilitate that by getting him organized and meeting with his attorney. Normally, I wouldn't get involved in something like that, but it was just wrong. It was really wrong."

THE SECRET OF SUCCESS

Looking back at her 20 years of success, Carrie admits that she never would have pictured herself where she is today. But now she can't picture living her life any other way.

"The secret is I love what I do," she says. "I love the feeling of a client walking out the door and saying, 'I feel better.' I think everyone gets to a point in his or her life where they don't have direction and are wondering what their purpose is. And the conclusion that I came to is that, from a professional perspective anyway, I am here to help people with their money. It's a huge responsibility."

She thinks about how much her clients trust her and depend on her, and is often amazed at how willing they are to sign anything she puts in front of them without even reading it or checking her numbers. It is a good reminder of how easy it is for these types of people to be taken advantage of by less than honest advisors. That is where she gets her motivation to keep pounding the table about education.

That helps keep her and the firm focused on the long-term view. For the firm, the number one goal is to make sure they are creating and perpetuating intergenerational wealth for their clients, and then making sure their assets are there when it is time to pass them on to their kids.

"If they don't do that, then what was all of their hard work for?" she asks. "There is a lot that goes into helping people to understand that, so, for the firm, that's really the direction we are moving in."

Carrie's personal goals weave into that message.

"My goal is to be the spokesperson for the firm," she says. "To let the public know that there is a place that they can go and get customized service."

And she admits to having at least one more book in her, but right now she's waiting for her daughter to head off to college before undertaking such a huge time commitment.

"I don't really know how that will develop yet. If I am going to be speaking to the public or to other advisors or to groups like single moms or newlyweds," Carrie says. "But there is definitely a desire to do it. I love doing the research, and I want people to walk away and say, 'Wow, I didn't know that.' "

Today her primary focus is creating balance so that every part of her life gets the most she has to offer. About the same time that she agreed to take over management of the firm, she sat down and wrote down five goals. One of those was to create balance in her life.

"As a single mom and as a businesswoman, you do what you have to do," she says.

And it just becomes too easy to do too much. To create that balance, she has laid out a formal structure for her days and her weeks, paying particular attention to planning her free time.

"That's where it becomes critical," she says. "I don't take client meetings on Mondays and Fridays anymore. I have my workouts on Tuesday and Friday mornings. You have to learn when to say, 'No.' And you have to figure out when enough is enough."

Carrie admits that she could probably make a lot more money working a different way, but then she would miss out on the things she cares most about—her clients, her daughter, and some of the community projects in which she is deeply involved.

Even in her free time, Carrie enjoys educating others—in this case, children. She's the vice chairperson of an organization called Economic Pennsylvania. "We educate kids, kindergarten through twelfth grade, about economics," she says enthusiastically, adding, "We're the most successful state in terms of kids participating." Our organization sponsors a stock market game in the state, where kids compete against others in a business plan competition and investing a mock portfolio for the best portfolio performance. "Every year we have an awards ceremony where we honor the kids, and the winners of each competition present to all the attendees. In addition to educating and helping to plan the annual event, Carrie is in charge of fundraising.

Carrie also contributes time and money to Pittsburgh Social Venture Partners, which links donors with nonprofits; the organization matches donors to a nonprofit. Each donor contributes money and time in a meaningful way, whereby the donors' talents are leveraged to maximize their effectiveness in the community. "Instead of handing off money to a charitable organization and not having any say in where it goes, we actually get in front of organizations and give grants and get involved," she says.

Given her current breakneck pace, Carrie contributes as much time as she can to her community. But again, it's all about balance. For now, she's doing exactly what she wants and living her life on her own terms. And she spends as much time as she can with her daughter, Kelli.

Carrie says she got the clearest picture of her life a few years ago through her daughter Kelli's eyes. It was "bring-your-daughter-to-work-day," so Kelli followed her through her entire day, sitting in on meetings and listening to her work with clients.

At the end of the day, Kelli accused Carrie of having lied to her.

"I said, 'What are you talking about?' " she remembers. "She said, 'You told me that you spend all day talking about people's money, and that's a lie. You spend all day talking about their lives.' "

"It was just so profound of her to realize that," Carrie says. "I said, 'That's exactly right. That's exactly what I do.' "

CHAPTER 16: JOHN OLSON

The Financial Guide

Merrill Lynch & Co., Inc.
New York City, New York

ONE OF JOHN OLSON'S GREATEST CHILDHOOD MEMORIES IS OF HIS first visit to Wall Street. As a seventh grader, he traveled with his mother, a New Jersey homemaker, to the New York Stock Exchange. "The energy and frenzied pace on the floor of the exchange had a real impact on me." John was singled out, and his name was prominently displayed on the legendary ticker tape, which read: "Welcome John Olson to the New York Stock Exchange." A representative handed John a copy of that ticker tape. To this day John keeps this tape as a precious keepsake.

John's father, a certified public accountant with a major accounting firm, sparked John's interest in finance. With his father as a role model, John majored in accounting at Ithaca College. He insists, however, that his father never actively pushed the accounting profession. "He was terrific," John recalls of his father. "He never pushed me anywhere. He just kind of suggested that accounting—the language of business—was probably better than a general business administration major and I really appreciated that advice."

Straight out of college, John was hired by Price Waterhouse, which was then one of the Big Eight accounting firms. Price Waterhouse actively recruited future employees from Ithaca College, which was known for its strong accounting program. Impressed with John, the on-campus recruiter invited him to New York for an interview at Price Waterhouse headquarters. The interview was a success and John was offered a job on the audit staff. As such, he spent three and a half years as an auditor at the accounting firm's offices in the Wall Street district of Lower Manhattan. He later spent time in the firm's tax department, a work environment that provided him with exposure to corporate and individual tax returns. "This was all great background—it taught me to pay attention to the details as well as incorporate a macro view of client needs," John recalls.

But despite that early success in the accounting world, John never really developed a passion for accounting. The profession, with its focus on historical numbers, lacked the creative or proactive spark that John sought.

Fortunately, through a good friend employed on Wall Street, John pursued his interest in the investment world. Ultimately, he interviewed at Merrill Lynch and in January of 1980, he was hired to join the firm's training program. As a new Merrill Lynch employee, John built a career on an early foundation of cold calling. To develop a data bank, John collected lists from reference books housed at different libraries, especially the Brooklyn Business Library, where John discovered "a tremendous set of lists."

"I would find lists of associations—different kinds of organizations that were not called as much—as well as corporate executives. I would get lists and I would make call after call," John says of his early career as a stockbroker. "I was working six days a week—working extremely hard."

"My entire investment career has been at Merrill," John says. "I really have seen absolutely no reason to change. I love the firm. I admire the integrity of the firm. I have been fortunate over the years to get to know senior management in different roles."

During the early 1980s interest rates were high, the Hunt Silver crisis was in full force, and the price of gold had peaked at $830 an ounce. With money market rates at 14 percent or higher, John's initial cold calling efforts centered on offering products tied to the high interest rate environment such as Cash Management Account® (CMA®) services and municipal bonds. The high interest rate environment facilitated his efforts to sell comprehensive cash management services. But selling—especially through cold calling—was not an easy undertaking, he recalls.

"I was not really trying to sell anything as much as offer a great service," John says, looking back on his early career. "It was hard. I was always successful, but I wasn't generating a lot of commissions. My payoff was in terms of gathering assets; I was able to build relationships, develop trust, and ultimately manage clients' assets and liabilities."

He used a plain vanilla formula to attract new accounts. Customer education was his calling card and John focused on getting people comfortable with the CMA service. And over the years, he has consistently viewed his role as that of "advisory planning."

"I used to call it being a problem solver, a financial person, or a financial guide," he says.

THE FINANCIAL GUIDE

Indeed, as a financial guide John began to work closely with his clients and their trusted advisors, primarily their accountants and attorneys. He describes his role as that of a third "leg of the stool." With that approach, John was slightly ahead of his time. Given his background as an accountant, John naturally migrated toward a comprehensive review of a customer's financial outlook. As a result, his attention was devoted to the overall financial health of each client, rather than buying and selling a particular investment.

"Rather than selling a product, I have always believed in positioning a process with clients. I will never consider myself a salesperson. It is more important to talk about the whole picture. I would ask about their assets in 401(k)s and IRAs, as well as mortgage details, college savings plans for their children, and their estate plans. These are areas in most people's lives that tend to be overlooked. My aim is to pull all aspects of a client's financial picture together and to advise as to the most appropriate path for the individual client to achieve the overall objective."

"Pretty early on, I became extremely goal-oriented with clients," John says. "My duty is to move toward a specific objective in the most appropriate and tax-efficient manner possible."

Of course, with that approach John did not lead his peers in transaction fees and never thought in those terms, but he was successful in building a steady flow of incoming assets. And he continued to develop new ways of increasing his portfolio of assets under management. For example, during that era, Merrill Lynch operated an information booth at Grand Central Station. John found a novel way to build business relationships. "I used to go there from six in the morning to eight o'clock at night, speak to commuters going up to Westchester and Connecticut, and build relationships that way," John says.

His networking efforts at Grand Central Station, combined with his early rigorous cold calling program, represent key developments in John's evolving as a financial adviser. What's more, with a paper-and-pencil approach to financial planning, as well as utilizing several analysis tools, John maintained a highly disciplined approach to client management.

A GOAL-ORIENTED APPROACH

For instance, he quantified a customer's financial goals. In this role, John helped his clients identify how much capital they needed to finance major life milestones such as tuition bills, retirement, and other life events.

Goals are important, John says, "whether it's running a marathon, earning money, or losing weight. Therefore we are very specific on quantifying a retirement lifestyle and so forth." As part of his quantitative approach to financial planning, John provides clients with sophisticated tools in estate planning, capital preservation, and investing, which are provided by Merrill Lynch through the firm's broad menu of product and services. "Our firm offers a breadth and depth of services that we are continually improving upon to keep in line with clients needs and to take advantage of improving technology."

Of course, like any novice, John made mistakes during those early years of his career. "I certainly have made some mistakes in the securities I have selected. We never went overboard, but some of those didn't work out as well as I would have hoped. We all make mistakes. And hopefully, we learn from them. That's the whole key," John says.

"And I would say my business today, in a many respects, is a lot simpler than it was years ago. I make sure that I totally understand all investments and all the structures, whether it is a fund or any kind of partnership. I have streamlined the process and the investment platform that I utilize with my clients."

MOVING FORWARD

John's career was fueled higher by client successes, a steady stream of referrals, and his association with a great mentor, Mark Pollard (also a *Winner's Circle* advisor). John met Mark through Merrill Lynch's Right Stuff Program, which was started in the late 1970s. With three years of experience in the investment business, John entered the program in 1984, and was paired with Mark, a long-time veteran in the field. Along with three other younger investment professionals, John met in Mark's office at 4:30 on a weekday afternoon. The meeting was followed by dinner. "Then we spent the next day in a hotel suite and we just talked and talked about what we do. He talked about his day, his philosophy of the business. And that was a significant event," John says. "I still have the notes from that meeting and I look at them from time to time. He's been a great mentor, as have been quite a few others in the firm."

While observing Mark Pollard and other successful professionals at Merrill Lynch, John compiled a list of traits shared by top performers in the business. He noticed, for example, that successful professionals typically arrived at the office very early. Not surprisingly, John believes that an early start is an important ingredient for success—he reports for work by 7:15 a.m. at the latest. "This is not a nine-to-five job." When asked what he attributes his success to, John answers, "Hard work and always taking care of clients."

Client referrals and relationships have also fueled John's career. One key relationship began on a golf course, where John met the chief executive officer of a very successful company. The two met when they were placed in the same foursome. "We became friends before we did any business," John recalls. As the friendship evolved, John learned that his new golfing buddy was unhappy with his current money management team. What's more, the game plan lacked long-term financial planning. John agreed to take on the assignment, but with one request. "I did have the nerve to tell him that I wouldn't do it unless he committed to sit down with me and put into place a financial plan. And I think he appreciated that. I know his wife appreciated it," John says. "I believe that it is imperative for both spouses to have an understanding of the family's financial health. If a primary wage earner passes away, the spouse is left to not only handle the death, but also to take on what can be an overwhelming task of beginning an education of his or her financial situation."

Attention to short-term and long-term details helped to fuel the long-term investment relationship that ultimately developed between John and his new golfing buddy. As part of the game plan, John spent months gathering information, analyzing data, and meeting with the prospective client in an effort to create a comprehensive financial plan. The financial strategy included estate planning and nearly every other aspect of financial planning, including tax and retirement strategies.

"He valued my advice," John recalls, adding that his client was very vocal in expressing gratitude. "He's been terrific in referring people to me. The highest compliment that a client can bestow upon me is to have the confidence to refer a friend, family member, or colleague."

The success of that relationship validated John's business strategy and provided a "watershed" moment in his career development. As a result, he tweaked his business plan by hiring additional staff and applying a team approach to asset management and client development. His new team approach included two assistants: one to help John in the area of financial planning and the other assistance devoted to administrative tasks.

"Since then, I've always had somebody on my team dedicated to gathering the information and doing the planning. It takes an awful lot of time to do it right. You need a detail-oriented individual who enjoys uncovering all of the necessary components," John says about his team approach.

Over the years, John has continued to build his own investment team within the firm. His group is vertically structured, with each team member providing specific services and talents to the mix. The staff has evolved to include a planning professional and an employee responsible for tracking performance figures and preparing client reports on a quarterly or monthly basis. "For most of our clients, we provide a complete package of asset allocation summaries," John says.

Another team member handles stock and bond market transactions, including activities in the municipal bond area, a responsibility that includes working with the Merrill Lynch bond trading desk on a constant basis. Altogether, his team currently includes a total of four individuals.

"We do use a lot of the Merrill tools, but then we tailor them. We are able to elevate planning to the next level. Within Merrill, we will use the custom planning tools for ultrahigh net worth clients." John says.

As the financial services industry has evolved, John has become especially focused on quality service. He takes pride in making sure a client's entire professional services team, including accountants and attorneys, are providing high-quality service and meeting key financial objectives. And in addition to the big-picture outlook, he makes sure that his administrative staff is sensitive to the details that matter most to his clients.

"I've always been fanatical about service. We deliver an experience that is one of the best in the industry," John says.

A SECONDARY BUSINESS-BUILDING STRATEGY

In addition to long-term financial planning for high net worth individuals and corporate executives, John developed a second strategy that was crucial to his expanding business. He began to court the accounts of corporate clients and cultivated a diverse portfolio of institutional clients. In that niche, a major turning point took place during the mid-1980s, when John developed an investment advising relationship with an individual who was also general counsel at a telecommunications company.

"We had a good relationship, and therefore he felt comfortable recommending me to manage the company's assets in that same way."

His client's company had previously invested its short-term cash with a firm and was losing money through that investment relationship. Consequently, executives at the telecom company were anxious to find a new investment team and the general counsel—pleased with the progress and the quality of advice for his personal account—recommended John as the person to take over the professional management of the corporate account.

The corporate account initially consisted primarily of about $500,000 to $600,000 that was invested in short-term cash with maturities ranging from 30 to 90 days, including a combination of money market funds and short-term commercial paper. When the company launched an initial public offering a few years later, the company turned to John to handle its proceeds of $1.2 billion.

What's more, while implementing the corporate investment strategy and providing other financial services to the company, John nurtured key relationships with the top 13 executives at the telecom company and he ultimately began to manage their personal financial accounts as well. "The company has since been sold. But I still have the individual accounts for all those clients," he says.

Additionally, he learned the importance of offering a wide menu of services to corporate clients, including short-term cash management, commercial paper, and variable rate preferred stock, stock repurchase plans, stock option plans, deferred compensation plans, and 401(k) plans.

"We get involved in all aspects of corporate services for the company," John says.

How did one relationship with a company executive blossom into different strategic alliances? Equal doses of creativity and hard work yielded such dividends, John says. Relationships are nurtured with constant dialogue with his clients and house calls. And even now as an established professional, John goes the distance to meet his clients—at their convenience—during early morning hours or after the U.S. markets close.

"I get out of the office a fair amount," he says. "A lot of my clients are right around the [New York] metropolitan area. I would go to see them during the day and talk to them and just explain some of the services that we have."

THE PERSONAL TOUCH

After the initial consultations, John typically invites his clients to meet the various specialists from Merrill to discuss the firm's vast range of capabilities and services. The face-to-face visits facilitate the flow of conversation and enhance the developing relationship.

What's more, meetings in clients' offices can also generate additional referrals. For example, in a client's office, other executives are likely to walk into an office, thereby providing additional introductions and networking opportunities. And once the introductions are made, it's not uncommon for the original client to make a referral right on the spot. "It happens a lot, actually," John says. "I'll be introduced, and the client will say, 'Maybe you should talk to John.'"

He began building his base of business during the mid-1980s, just as the retirement market was undergoing massive change due to the introduction of the 401(k) plan and other forms of retirement accounts. As the playing field shifted, John quickly became educated on the new services and worked closely to align his clients with Merrill Lynch specialists from various corners of the financial marketplace.

Clients have praised John and his staff for their attention to detail. For instance, one client recently commented that John's staff seemed to anticipate events before they happened. That client was a recent widow, who was discussing her investment accounts and assets with John and his team of professionals. During those conversations, she called their services "extraordinary" and praised their collective abilities to anticipate her needs.

"That made me feel great," John says. "That's exactly what I want to hear. And whether it's pension plans that have to be amended or making mandatory distributions, we just want to be on top of any kind of issue."

Toward that end, John and his staff scrutinize client statements to make sure all client accounts are properly linked. The team also carefully tracks bill payment services, the client's ability to view accounts online, and other nuts-and-bolts chores on the administrative side of the ledger. As such, John has trained his team to be "proactive" rather than "reactive."

In assembling a team, John seeks "like-minded" individuals who share his passion about service. He seeks team players that take the initiative and make outgoing calls to clients. His staff is willing to handle various client requests, including inquiries about online services and computer installations. "We go to the clients' homes and apartments and hook up computer systems as well."

"My team is constantly looking for ways to improve the level of service that we provide to our clients." For instance, in the early 2000s when Merrill Lynch introduced a service called "Beyond Banking," which reduced transaction fees for various bank services, John's team was one of the most successful teams throughout Merrill Lynch's national network in terms of offering the service to clients. John says his team was successful because, "... we positioned the product as a 'value to the client' and a way for them to save money." With the new service, John calculated that clients could potentially save on such items as ATM fees, bill payment charges, and account fees. "We figured, on average, we saved our clients around $250 per year. That is a value, and it helps to build trust—especially when clients aren't expecting it. So we just did a terrific job on that. We proactively called, explained the new service and how it would work, and made sure clients were taking advantage of it," John says. "It is essential that clients know we will continually strive to ensure that all of their service needs are satisfied."

Offering advice is the foundation of his business. John seeks to create an environment in which clients seek his advice when faced with financial decisions, whether they are selling a home or other lifestyle changes. His role as advisor features four key elements: risk analysis, organization, asset allocation, and discipline.

As part of the goal-setting process, John creates a comprehensive profile of his client and reviews tax statements, balance sheets, benefits statements, and other important financial documents. Assembling this paper trail can take weeks or longer depending on his client's schedule. What's more, during initial consultations, John provides a detailed outlook about his professional background and his approach to financial planning and asset management. And, although he has assembled an impressive support team, he remains directly involved in each client relationship. "My clients have put their trust in me; this responsibility I do not take lightly," John says firmly. "If a client receives a call from anyone on my team, they can have the confidence to know that the information and advice have come directly from me."

After the initial consultation, follow-up meetings may involve both spouses, if the client is married. John subsequently provides specific recommendations and an action plan for handling asset allocation, investing, disability, life insurance, estate planning, and other key aspects of financial planning. Once the investment program has been created and implemented, quarterly meetings, in person or via telephone, are "a very important part of the whole process," John says.

He's strict about holding quarterly meetings with clients, who receive a package of reports that summarize the distribution and performance of their assets, including those managed by third-party money managers. These quarterly meetings are a very valuable component of the relationship, he says.

"It gives me a chance to talk about performance and asset allocation, but it also gives the client the chance to talk about what's changed in his or her life," John says, adding that quarter-to-quarter lifestyle changes are not unusual. "So it's very important that we have this strict quarterly agenda where they can say that they are thinking about a job change, a bigger house, a plan to retire earlier or whatever. It's really important to try to talk about the whole process."

This type of dialogue has been especially welcome by high-level corporate executives, who typically work with many people but speak in depth with very few. In such a situation the senior executives on his client list value John's listening skills.

"They can't talk to their colleagues or support staff. It's just not that kind of relationship. So I try to be a very good listener and ask a lot of questions about their goals and their dreams, so to speak. And they like to talk about it; so I think we get to know our clients that way—by just asking the questions."

Of course, there have been many challenges in his career, including the turmoil following the stock market crash of 1987 and the minicrash of 1989. More recently, the stock market difficulties from 2000 to 2003, including the events surrounded the tragedy of September 11, have also created a challenging environment for financial professionals.

"We fortunately got through that period quite well because we were well diversified," John says. "But equity performance was still down and it was a challenge to keep clients invested when things were so bad." In that environment, John embarked on a program to frequently educate and reassure clients. During meetings he reiterated the long-term goals and explained his strategy.

"It's a challenge but it's what we do and that's what we get paid for. Patience and discipline have worked in the past and will continue to work in the future," John says. "It's not always easy when the performance is down, like in the early 2000s. But you have the conversations: Clients want communication and they want to know what's going on and so you always want to keep them informed on everything going on in their portfolio."

Looking back over his career, there have been other challenges along the way, including his early start from day one, with just a desk, a phone, and no clients. In those days, his simple goal was to bring in new assets. "Once I brought in a hundred million dollars in assets, I kind of plateaued there for a while. And then I broke through it."

He moved to the next level by adhering to his business plan and developing his network of referrals. Even today, he asks for clients to make referrals and finds it especially "gratifying when they come without even asking for them, which is usually the case." Additionally, he continues to network in social and professional settings. "People will approach me to help them with their planning and their assets and liabilities. But a lot of it is through referrals, both solicited and unsolicited," John says.

That basic plan continues to drive his business today, even as he continues to fine-tune his strategy and make adjustments to the structure of his team. But, above all, he is not a mere stock picker. Merrill Lynch offers its clients a full buffet of financial products and services, including home mortgages. With an eye on that menu, John makes it his business to provide the most appropriate financial services to clients.

"I'm not calling clients to buy a particular investment because we put it on our focus list and sell another stock or something like that. It's not a short-term business. I think when you have a short-term business, you are too caught up in the transactions," says John, who allocates individual stock-picking and trading duties to carefully screened money managers and fund managers. He employs a range of fund managers, representing a variety of portfolio sizes, trading strategies, and investment styles.

"We do our own research on different funds," John says. "We track the ones we work with very closely. So we are familiar with their holdings and what they are doing and what their performance is."

THE COMMUNITY

John's business development is enhanced by his participation in various community and cultural activities. He sits on the board of a school foundation and several nonprofit associations. His involvement extends to Ithaca College, where he attended school.

John targets a few significant causes and focuses on those organizations. He derives extra pleasure by getting his preteen daughters involved in worthwhile causes. For instance, with his daughters, John helped to paint a recreation center and playground in Harlem.

"The secret, though, is not allowing yourself to be spread too thin, so you are not going in too many different directions," John says.

"My focus is always on the client, and doing what's right for them given their specific objectives. "

Chapter 17: Mary Deatherage

Above and Beyond

Smith Barney
Little Falls, New Jersey

ONE OF MARY DEATHERAGE'S CLIENTS, A 41-YEAR-OLD SINGLE woman, was a 9/11 victim; she worked in one of the high floors of WTC 1. The woman left her $4 million estate to her brother.

The brother, whom Mary had never met, transferred the accounts to his advisor.

Once the accounts were transferred, he took a close look at the comprehensive financial plan Mary had constructed for his sister. He asked Mary to create a plan for him. After they met and Mary had a clear understanding of his financial situation, she presented him with a plan. Impressed, the man transferred back the $4 million accounts, plus his $2 million in assets. "I've never seen anything like this," he told her. "No one has ever understood me so well."

That attention to personal relationships is part of Mary's character, and her desire to truly look after the welfare of her clients.

"When you become this close with a client, you'll do anything for him or her, and he or she becomes very loyal," she says. When issues surface, Mary gets involved: "I help in any way I can."

A PLANNING ORIENTATION

Without a plan, what's the point? That's the question Mary Deatherage has been asking herself and her clients since she started her career in 1986, with what is now Smith Barney.

"At that time, Wall Street's culture was very sales-oriented," she says, referring to the stockbrokers stock-pushing mentality back then. "From the beginning, I had more of a planning aspect. Things like asset allocation just made more sense to me. It's much more time-intensive to approach each client from that direction, but I don't feel like I can make a responsible suggestion unless I understand the whole thing."

And she means, "The whole thing." Before she will take a check from a prospect, she wants it all—all of their tax statements, all of their bank statements, all of their financial statements. She tops it all off with an extensive understanding of their personal goals, private ambitions, and lifetime concerns. From that, she expects to gather all their assets, but it's a long process that can take months, sometimes years to achieve.

That's a business model that most advisors would shy away from. It is not only time-consuming, it is also incredibly labor-intensive, requiring painstaking attention to detail. Still, Mary Deatherage wouldn't have it any other way. She wouldn't make a move in her own life without carefully analyzing every factor and weighing every move, so why would she do any less for her clients?

That philosophy has enabled Mary to build more than a simple clientele; she has built lifelong relationships with the families she serves. These days, the relationships all start with a phone call to her. All of her business is from referrals, and, when that prospect calls, the first thing Mary wants to know is, "Why?"

"We'll chat for a little while, but then I'll say to them, 'What's the issue you want to thrash? Why are you calling me?' " she says. "There must be something that's really forcing them to make the decision in the midst of their busy day to call me up and start interviewing me."

Usually the answer is something vague, such as the client isn't happy with the market. Mary digs deeper, asking about their experience with the market. What has worked in the past? What isn't working now? From there, she schedules their first appointment.

"Many times—I would say the majority of the times—I say to these people, total strangers, 'You know what? Can you send me all your statements? Can you send me pages one and two of your tax return from last year so that I can really understand you before we meet so that I can be more intelligent when we talk,' " Mary says.

Invariably, she gets the information she asks for, but when the prospects come in for that initial meeting, it can be an hour or more before they actually get down to talking about money. Instead, Mary opens up the conversation with a few well-selected "magic questions." Questions such as, "Can you tell me about your family?"

"You don't want to ask, 'Do you have kids?' " she says. "That can be offensive if he or she doesn't have kids."

When they do have kids, though, parents love to talk about them—both the good and the bad. Sometimes Mary finds out more than she ever wanted to know about the children, but for the most part it is an opening to begin discussing the broad outlines of a financial plan. For instance, asking questions about how they are doing in school opens the route to discussing education planning.

Then she hits them with the big one: "Tell me about your parents."

"We are talking to adults, so asking about their parents can open a huge can of worms," she says.

That's because parents are always an issue. Sometimes the prospect is worried that they are going to have to support them. Sometimes they are concerned about their own inheritance and don't know how to broach the subject with their parents. That leads the conversation back to the prospect's own situation. Do they have an estate plan? Do they have a will? Do they have a plan for their children if something should happen to them?

"Those types of questions really open up the conversation," she says. "People like to talk about themselves. I think it's interesting, and it helps me understand them. By the time that they are done, I've always identified four or five specific things that they could do that are kind of unique to their situation, and we haven't even talked about money."

It isn't until after that first meeting that Mary and her team really start to work. Armed with all the prospect's financial information and personal history, Mary begins building a customized financial plan that incorporates every aspect of the prospect's financial life. Depending on the size of the client's portfolio, these plans can run dozens of pages, with a two-page executive summary at the beginning.

"If you are a two million dollar prospect, then you deserve to have somebody who really kicks the tires on your financial plan," she says.

Mary starts each plan from the ground up, looking at everything from a client's tax bracket to his goals and objectives. To illustrate, Mary pulls out a 50-page plan she recently put together for a prospect who, at age 56 and with about $2.6 million in assets, wants to retire.

The first step is to review his current asset allocation. He has nothing in large-cap value and is overweighted in small and midcap stocks, along with a heavy allocation in bonds. Using what she knows about his risk tolerance and Monte Carlo-type analytical software, she begins the process of building a sample retirement portfolio by plugging in various asset allocation models and illustrating how each is projected to perform against a set series of variables. To keep on the conservative side, she assumes 4 percent annual inflation and a 7 percent annualized return on the portfolio.

"If the early 2000s have taught us anything, it is to slow your assumptions down," she says.

Setting a goal of achieving $91,000 in pretax income, she runs an optimization report that illustrates the best asset allocation possible to meet those goals within his personal risk tolerance parameters. Then she compares that allocation to the current portfolio mix.

"That way we can show him how his current plan doesn't correlate to his long-term goals," she says. "I won't dwell on this too much. Usually, the fact that we've done it makes the prospect confident that I understand it. Then I can explain it to him without going into every single page of my proposal."

With a clearer understanding of what the prospect needs to do to achieve his goals, Mary starts building a portfolio recommendation, using hand-selected private money managers for each piece of the investment mix. She compares each recommended manager's performance against their benchmark index and screens that against the risk he assumed to achieve that return.

"If I am recommending a fifteen percent international allocation and I like a particular money manager in the international space, then I am going to compare their results to the international index," she explains. "My analysis will show them what the managers did versus the blended index. Did the managers outperform the indexes, and did they do it with less risk? That becomes my overall thesis. If we blend it out, then we'll end up with less risk and higher performance."

That final portfolio recommendation is where most proposals end, but for Mary it is just the beginning. From there she does a complete net worth analysis, discussing everything from paying down the mortgage to buying insurance. The proposal even includes spreadsheets on what estate taxes will look like under various scenarios. Mary discovered in her earlier conversations with this prospect that he had a son with AIDS. She knew that he hadn't talked to his attorney about it, so she discussed setting up a special needs trust. She also knew that he was interested in charitable giving, so she included a plan to accomplish that with some appreciated stock that he owned. After Mary arranged a meeting with the lawyer, she accompanied her client. Mary was willing to broach the tough topics, delicately describing only the information the lawyer needed.

"Then we always end each proposal with our commitment, what we promise we will do for you," Mary says. "From that point, we have set the stage."

The executive summary clearly outlines each goal, and she explains to the prospect exactly how he is going to achieve his goals and monitor progress along the way. Along with her commitment, she makes certain that he is making the same commitment to her. Financial plans are not static documents. People change. Situations change. She needs to be fully involved in all those changes to make sure the client stays on track.

When one of her clients, a corporate executive, lost his job, Mary was one of the first people he called. With that one phone call, everything changed—the investment strategy, the retirement plan, and the strategy to pay for the kids' college.

"We had to redo the whole thing because now the situation that we were assuming was completely gone," she told him.

A WOMAN'S ADVANTAGE

Before Mary had children, she typically worked until 8 p.m.—including the night before she gave birth. While many would consider childraising a diversion when building a business, Mary describes it as balancing her two lives: "Nothing in life is easy. But, if you love what you do—for me, it's being with my kids and going to work—you adapt." Mary describes her husband, Bill, and their sons Mike and Matt, as "the most important people in the world."

Bill is an investment banker, who works long hours in New York City. Without full-time help, Mary never misses a beat—or an event. Whether it's a school play or an ice hockey game, Mary's there. When traveling out of town, she'll walk her kids to the bus, take a flight, and then return in time to help them with their homework. "Most of the time they never know I'm traveling," Mary says.

While many believe men have an advantage in the business simply because they can spend more time working, Mary considers it a disadvantage. "First, they miss out on part of their children's lives. Secondly, my family life brings me closer to my clients." After the birth of each son, Mary sent an "initial public offering birth announcement" to each client and some prospects. Now that her sons have grown, she feels her clients have been a part of her family. "My clients remember Mike as a baby. Now he's six foot two. My clients look forward to receiving a picture of my family every year during the holiday season."

Besides a family connection, Mary believes there are other reasons prospects seek her out—and it helps that she's a woman. "When you meet a prospective client, there's always a reason that they are coming to you. They don't wake up in the morning and say, 'I think I need a new financial advisor.' There has to be some problem that's prompting them to think outside of their comfort zone. When they come to me, I know there's something going on. Often, they confide in me, sharing information that they never shared with their former male advisor. This is an advantage many women have over men."

"Because I'm absorbing information about them, investments are almost never part of the first meeting." Mary always asks individuals to bring their financial statements with them during the first meeting. "It doesn't make sense to analyze an individual's financial situation before I've met them. First I get to know them to better understand their needs. Only then can I match their investments with who they are. If their investments already match perfectly, then we'll talk about some of their other issues."

"To many people, talking about money is incredibly personal. You can go to a cocktail party and a stranger will tell you about his or her problems, whether a health problem or an issue with a child. But they'll never tell you about their money." Mary explains it another way: "Think about your friends and neighbors. You may know very personal information about them, but you may not know anything about their money. For somebody to open up about his or her money, a major barrier has been overcome."

MARY'S BEGINNING

That attention to detail was probably engrained in Mary's previous life as a Certified Public Accountant. Her original goal had been to become a teacher, but her husband was in the Army, and life on the road as a military wife wasn't very conducive to building a career.

"I was scared I wouldn't be able to get a decent job because we were always going to be moving," she says. "But I realized if I got a business degree, I could always get a job."

With her degree and her CPA, she went to work for a major accounting firm, staying focused on working hard and earning that next promotion. She was on track for partnership, putting in the requisite 18-hour days when everything changed for her.

"It was the night of the Fourth of July, and I was in a closed conference room with three partners working on an acquisition report for CBS," Mary remembers. "We had spent the entire week working twenty-four-seven on this acquisition report, and it's eleven p.m. on the Fourth of July."

She knew her clients were out enjoying barbeques and fireworks, while she was cranking away on dry numbers. She also knew that, even if everything went well at the next day's meeting, when all was said and done, she was still the outsider. She would simply leave and move on to the next assignment. Not only was there no lasting relationship in her line of work, in many cases as the CPA she was the enemy the moment she walked in the door.

"That night I realized that I could take the technical side of the CPA training and the people side of the teaching and pull it all together," she says.

She began the long process of interviewing with financial services firms in the area, but her conversation with the branch manager at the former Shearson (predecessor to Smith Barney) office really struck a chord.

"He was leaning back, listening to my story. Then he said, 'Well, it's clearly a case of a square peg in a round hole. You'll fit in that round hole, but you will never be comfortable there,' " Mary remembers. "It was like this light bulb went off."

She went to work at that office and never looked back. She absorbed every piece of training she could get. Thanks to her accounting background, she was familiar with the number crunching side of things and wasn't afraid to tackle the more technical aspects, such as retirement and estate planning. But what struck her most was something one of the trainers told the class her first day there.

"The sales manager of the whole firm got up and told us, 'I promise you, if you put your head down for two years and work hard and don't get distracted by office politics and don't get distracted by what's going on around you or by what you think of the market or by anything else—if you just work hard and do a good job, you will never have to work that hard again," she says.

So Mary rolled up her sleeves and got to work, following her rookie training to the letter. She pulled out the local business directory and started cold calling the executives. If she couldn't get through to the boss, she talked to the secretary about an IRA account—anything to get a piece of business on the books by the end of the day. That strategy didn't last very long.

"You get a bunch of those little two thousand dollar accounts, and you really regret that pretty quickly," she says.

So she hit the seminar circuit, picking broad topics and sending out invitations to everyone in that zip code. That just led her down another dead end.

"Attracting the wrong crowd can be really expensive; and if it rains, they just don't show up," she says. "I once had a seminar, the worst one I ever had, and only two people came."

That was when she began formulating her first business plan. She realized she needed to do two things—set herself apart from the rest of the folks calling that same tired prospect list *and* get herself in front of the people with money. Mary zeroed in on the realtors. If they didn't have money themselves, they knew who did because they were in the unique position of following money in motion. She pulled together a quick seminar on financial planning for realtors and started knocking on doors.

"I promised them that I was going to talk about tax law changes as they related to realtors or retirement planning for realtors," Mary says. "Really, it's the same thing for any self-employed person, but I just called it for realtors and I always included a relevant case study."

It worked. She reached the point where she was doing three of these a day and starting to build some momentum, but the real turning point didn't come for Mary until she was offered the biggest accounts of her budding career. The owner of the real estate office where she was giving a seminar offered to open an account that day for $25,000.

She turned him down.

"Here I am, three months in the business; and at the end of my presentation, he stands up and tells his group, 'I like Mary, and you know what? I am going to open an account with her right now. You know why? Because she's here. She's selling,'" Mary remembers. "Of course, at that time I would take anything that walked in the door. But then he tells me he's going to give me $25,000 to see what I can do for him."

"I said, 'No, if we can't talk about your real money, I don't want to deal with it,'" she remembers.

It's hard to say who was more surprised by that interaction, Mary or the prospect whom she had just turned down. But it got everyone's attention. In that moment, Mary was able to clarify for herself and for the prospect exactly the kind of relationship she wanted. And she was able to convince herself and that prospect that neither of them should ever settle for anything less.

"It was interesting because I fascinated him somehow," she says. "We kept in touch because I wasn't going to let him go and he was interested enough in me that within a couple of years he gave me what is now twenty million dollars, and there's more coming."

Today, he doesn't make a business decision without passing it by her first, and she is the one who orchestrates all his personal and financial business by working directly with his attorneys and accountants.

"I am the one that will pull together his estate attorneys, his accountants," she says. "I am the one that will organize all the different issues in his financial life, which is really interesting."

That is her goal with every client.

THE EXTRA MILES

"If you are in a big, stressful divorce, I will go to court with you," she says. "I will go to every lawyer meeting with you. And a lot of times, the lawyers end up working directly with me because I can be the intermediary for the client because the client is often distraught."

While the client deals with the emotional aspect, Mary can deal with the legal and financial issues. Whether it's a business acquisition, a divorce or estate planning work, she usually understands the family dynamic better than the attorney ever could.

"They are like deer in the headlights," she says. "They don't know what to do, so I will follow through. That's really satisfying because you know you've made a big difference and you know they really needed you."

Earning that trust, though, entails assuming a tremendous amount of responsibility for each client.

"You have got to make sure that you are worthy of their trust and that you really do understand them on an ongoing basis," she says. "You can't go back from there."

MARY'S BIGGEST INVESTMENT

You also have to make sure that you have all the support people in place before you can even begin offering that level of service for your clients. Mary realized early on that she couldn't possibly build the business that she wanted without making a personal investment in herself and her clients.

"In the beginning, I didn't have any money," she says. "I was making whatever the minimum was, around twenty-four thousand a year."

She was sharing an assistant with four other new brokers in the office, and the branch manager was not going to fork over an entire salary just because Mary had a plan. So she engaged that assistant in her business, making her a partner in the operation.

"I delegated things that nobody would," she says. "I wasn't giving her filing and typing—anyone could do that—but I wanted her to learn, so everyday I taught her something. And at the end of the month, I gave her $75."

Guess who got the most attention from that assistant?

"When I got to the point where I felt like I was out of control, I couldn't breathe because there was just too much work to do, I realized that I had to step up and make a compromise with the branch manager," she says.

She realized that she wasn't going to create the kind of business she wanted unless and until she was ready to make that investment in it herself. Today, she manages a full-time staff of five, two of whom are registered financial consultants.

"My overhead is huge," she acknowledges. "But I think most advisors are very shortsighted about growing their support structure to allow their businesses to grow. I am the only one in the office that does that. People look at my business today and say, 'Well, she can afford it.' But I couldn't afford it then. It was an investment in my own business."

She doesn't have a set formula on how much income she needs to be generating per staff member, and she doesn't run the math on how much each additional team player should contribute to her own commission stream. Mary fills positions based on the services that her clients require, and she pays her employees based on the value they bring to the team, not just on what the market can bear. For example, her operations manager, Sandy Shen, is the one team member whom the practice can't manage without.

"Sandy is amazing," Mary says. "I have accountants and attorneys who won't deal with anyone but her because she is so organized. She can handle an estate that needs to be distributed to eight different individuals. She keeps all the individuals calm and they understand that everything is being done fairly, and that it will be right the first time."

That's the kind of service that goes beyond a price tag, which is why Sandy makes more than most sales assistants. The rest of the team includes Mary's office manager Jay Dewan, Claudine Callison (who is also a financial consultant), Lauren Saxton, and Lisa Manders (who has been with Mary since 1995).

The secret to building a successful team, Mary says, is finding the right people and then giving them the autonomy they need to create personal ownership of the business. For instance, Jay started with the firm in 1999, but was clearly getting antsy just being Mary's sales assistant. She helped him get a job in the firm's mutual fund division in New York, but kept in close contact with him. In 2001, when her business grew to the point that she needed someone to manage it, she offered him the job.

"He's much happier here now," she says. "He lives locally, and he has a lot more autonomy. He has relationships with the clients that are unique to him."

And that support system frees Mary up to provide the intense level of professional service that her clients have come to expect. For instance, her realtor client brought Mary in on a business deal that actually had nothing to do with his personal investments. Still, she worked with his team of attorneys on each step of the process, all the way down to taking home the legal documents at night and proofreading them.

"A lot of advisors don't appreciate the influence they can have with a client," she says. "You may wonder why in the world I'm sitting in on these meetings when I'm not an attorney, but I can add a lot of value because I really understand the client and his business."

Of course, it doesn't hurt her business either. The attorneys on the other side of the table get to know her and respect the way she does business, so it's not uncommon for them to call her when they need a financial advisor. In fact, one of the attorneys working on the deal with the realtor called her in the middle of those negotiations. He wanted to talk to her about his own finances and wanted to refer one of his clients to her.

"I don't do this for the purpose of generating additional business," she says. "I do it because I want to add value to my client. But that's the kind of stuff that happens."

She also gets a lot of referrals from her clients' accountants, thanks again to her attention to detail. One result of her being proactive with all her clients' finances is that their accountants get a full report every quarter on any tax issues, such as capital gains. Accountants also get copies of each proposal.

"That may sound like it's no big deal, but it is time-consuming, and that is how you get referrals," she says.

Probably the greatest secret to Mary's success, though, is that no detail is too small for either her or her staff.

"We will do things like go out to a client's home and set up Internet access for our site," she says. Again, that may sound like a minor thing, but for many clients, it's the extra step that keeps them loyal.

For Mary, solving clients' problems is the bottom line.

THE COMMUNITY

Mary also helps to find solutions in her community. She describes her involvement with Mountainside Hospital as her second job. Spending ten hours or more per month on various committees, ranging from vice chairman of the advisory board to the investment committee for the foundation, when asked, Mary jumps at the chance to help out. "They gave me the best presents in the world," she says with a warm smile, "my children."

She's passionate about helping the hospital maintain its high-touch and high-tech standards. "This is a community hospital that really cares about every patient," she says. "Most people don't realize how difficult it is for a hospital to break even, let alone turn a profit. Without this great institution, patients would have to go into New York City for specialized care. This high-quality medical care and personal attention must be preserved.

"I really care about my community. I really care about my team. And I really care about the clients I am working with; and frankly, if it doesn't click, I will refer them to another advisor because life is too short," she says. "I like dealing with nice people, with people who really need me, and people to whom I can provide outstanding value. Hopefully, I'm providing a real value, and if I can't, then I won't take the business."

"Our clients' financial problems are our problems, and we don't stop till we find the right solutions. They're like family, and each one is a tremendous responsibility."

CHAPTER 18: PHIL SCOTT

The Bulletproof Strategy

Merrill Lynch & Co., Inc.
Bellevue, Washington

SEVERAL YEARS AGO, A MAN IN HIS FORTIES SOLD HIS OIL COMPANY AND netted $20 million. He had met with a several financial advisors and received proposals that he felt didn't meet his needs. Then his brother told him to speak to his advisor, Phil Scott, who was perhaps "the best in the business."

When Phil first met with the prospective client, he took the time to listen to the businessman's needs, including his entire financial situation. The prospect told Phil, "People in your industry all basically do the same thing, so to me it's a matter of the fee you charge."

Phil responded, "I take a different approach than most advisors. My goal is first to understand your current and/or future income needs and then to position your portfolio to ensure your income stream will grow every year so that you and your family can maintain your standard of living. I call this making you 'bulletproof.' I want to first position you so you never have to worry about income again. This is my specialty and my primary focus."

"You're the first advisor who truly understood what I was looking for and had a solution for my need," the businessman told Phil.

Phil Scott has honed a service and investing strategy that has earned him clients for life, as well as a spot on *The Winner's Circle* list. He says it's all about taking care of clients and a lot of hard work.

HARD WORK

Phil learned long ago that there are no shortcuts to success, and he never looks for any. Since he started his career with Merrill Lynch more than 20 years ago, Phil has ground out his success one client at a time by being the first one in the office every morning and the last one there every night.

"My view is that most people don't work that hard, and they work in spurts," he says. "I think you are much better off working at a pace you can consistently handle. And if you can find someone who works hard consistently, you have someone who is going to knock the cover off the ball over the long term and build a great practice."

When he is asked to speak to new recruits about being successful in this business, Phil always gives them the same advice: Make the coffee every morning. The first person in the office every morning makes the first pot of coffee, and Phil tells the rookies that they should be competing to make that pot.

You never know when that effort is going to pay off. Phil landed one of his largest accounts just sitting in the office one Monday morning. The Monday was a holiday and his wife was sleeping in, so he thought he'd go in early and catch up on some paperwork when someone came strolling through the office. He walked up to Phil's desk—because Phil was the only one there—and announced that he wanted to open an account.

"I thought that was my lucky day, but it turns out there was no luck involved," Phil says. "He came in on that Monday morning because he knew the markets were closed and he wanted to see who was working that morning. That was the person he wanted to work with."

Working hard is only half the battle, though. You also have to work smart, Phil says.

"In order to pay the price, you have to understand the benefit of that work," he argues. "And you have to understand that if you really want to be good, the only way you are going to do that is if you make your clients money with integrity and professionalism. And the only way you are going to make money for clients is if you really are a student of the markets—a student of investing—and if you understand the role that discipline plays in both building your business and in managing your clients' money."

DISCIPLINE ALWAYS PAYS OFF

Discipline and hard work come naturally to Phil. After high school, he went to the U.S. Naval Academy in Annapolis and spent his Navy career flying A-6 fighter jets off the *U.S. Constellation* aircraft carrier. After seven years in the service, though, Phil wanted to find a career that would compensate him for his effort, not just his longevity. He was accepted into Merrill Lynch's training program, and he never looked back.

As if the rigors of advisor training and life in the bullpen aren't hard enough, Phil found a way to set the bar even higher for himself. As a rookie, he quickly discovered the Catch-22 of the brokerage business.

"Everyone comes into this business wanting to be a money manager. The problem is, you don't have any money to manage," he laughs.

Without a book of business as your benchmark, there is no way to keep score on how well you are doing. So Phil made up his own scorecard. He wrote down a list of the activities that he knew eventually would lead him to success, and he gave a point value to each of those items. For example, he gave himself two points for a cold call, four points for a follow-up call, forty points for an appointment.

"My goal was to get to two hundred points a day," he says. "Of course, you don't make every goal every day, but my goal for the week was to have a thousand points. So, if I had a bad Monday or Tuesday, I had to really get after it on a Wednesday or Thursday. And I did that for a long time."

At the beginning, it would take long hours in the office and on the weekends to rack up those 1,000 points. Still, Phil never let any setback send him off course, and he had plenty of setbacks. His very first introduction to marketing was a resounding failure. He was set to blast out of the starting gates in his new career, so he put together a direct mail piece on certificates of deposit and mailed off 500 of them before heading off to New York for his first training session. CDs were yielding better than 14 percent; and, after all, this was Merrill Lynch.

"I figured I would get at least three hundred back," he says.

The first Friday of his training session he called his wife, Lesli, to see how many responses had come in. None. He called the next week, and got the same answer. In the third week, one came in. Then one more arrived.

"It was terrible," Phil remembers. But he made it work.

He converted one of those first responses into a long-time client. Then another response came from a local accountant. The accountant also became a client, a good friend—and a great referral source. Over their years together, that one accountant has referred more than $75 million worth of business to Phil, including $20 million over the past year alone.

"I'm thinking that mailer is a complete disaster, but I ended up developing a great relationship out of it," Phil says.

If possible, his second attempt at marketing was an even bigger failure. At the time, he and his wife were living in an upscale condominium complex in Bellevue, Washington. He decided that was a perfect venue for his first seminar, so he put one together and sent out 120 invitations to his neighbors. Ever the optimist, he was expecting a turnout of at least 40. Since he didn't have any business yet, they were doing this on a shoestring, with Lesli baking cookies and making pots of coffee.

They waited. And waited. Nobody showed up. At one point, Lesli went back to their condo to see if they had put the wrong date on the invitation.

"We just sat there, eating cookies and drinking decaf coffee thinking, 'Boy, this is going to be a tough business,'" Phil says.

But it couldn't be tougher than landing a jet on an aircraft carrier, so Phil kept at it. His big break came when he finally got an appointment with the head of a major industrial company. Again, it was his tenacity that finally paid off. After leaving message after message with the top guy, Phil left his final message. He told the prospect that, if he would just return his call and talk to him for two minutes, Phil would never call him again. When the prospect called him back 10 minutes later, Phil had another offer.

"I told him that if he would just meet with me once, I'd leave him alone forever," he says. "No more mailings, nothing."

Phil got his meeting, and within a few weeks he was conducting his first seminar at the company. That was when he really began building his base.

Early in his career, Phil's wife Lesli played a key role in his success. At the time Lesli was a high school business teacher. After school she would go to Phil's office and spend many hours doing whatever she could to help. She fixed computer problems, developed marketing materials and strategies, and helped with administrative tasks. This enabled Phil to spend more of his time developing investment strategies and tactics.

A DIFFERENT MODEL FOR A CHANGING WORLD

While he was busy knocking on doors and making cold calls, Phil was also taking a good, long look at what was going on in the market. Interest rates were sky-high and bonds were yielding 15 percent or more, while the Dow Jones Industrial Average had languished in the 1,000 range for over a decade. Nobody wanted to even hear the word "stocks," but Phil could see the writing on the wall.

"My view is that this whole asset allocation process that we go through, allocating between cash, stocks, and bonds, may be appropriate for institutions; but that is inappropriate for individuals most of the time. At some point an individual's or a family's first priority will be the need to generate a 'safe' cash flow from investments. A 'safe' cash flow, in my view, grows over time so that you can protect your purchasing power. I think bonds carry a lot more risk than most people think," he says. "People invest in bonds for either safety or income, but bonds won't protect your purchasing power, especially if interest rates go down."

That was just starting to happen when Phil started developing his own investment strategy. It didn't take him long to find an audience for his message. Clients were seeing their 14 percent CDs mature and were rolling them over at 8 percent.

"They were experiencing a 40–60 percent cut in pay in an investment that was supposed to be safe," he says. "They were very confused."

But they were also very willing to listen to Phil's seminars on "How to Retire on an Increasing Income." Stocks were still a four-letter word back then, so he was very careful not to use that term. Instead, he talked about dividends and how to invest in a way that generated a steadily increasing income stream. This was still more than a decade before the utility industry was deregulated, and good utility companies were enjoying strong monopolies and throwing off double-digit dividend yields.

"I used the analogy of an apartment building," he explains. "If you owned an apartment building that was generating fifty thousand dollars a year in rent, would you really care if an appraiser came along and just said, 'We appraised your building at twenty percent below what you paid for it.' You would say, 'I don't care, it's providing fifty grand a year rent, and I just raised the rent ten percent. So what? Value the apartment at whatever you want, as long as my rents keep coming in and I can occasionally raise them, I'll be happy.' "

At the same time, Merrill Lynch's chief investment strategist was running the same numbers as Phil and looking at the rising baby boom population, which was just beginning to have an impact on the economy. The message was clear. Interest rates were likely to continue to drop, and equities were going to climb because these boomers were starting to spend—and spend big. That message hit home with Phil.

"That was huge for me, but it took me a long time to figure out how to put together a portfolio that offered a competitive yield but still gave this generation of risk-adverse investors a sense of security," he says.

He knew the answer lay in dividend-paying stocks, and he knew he had to offer his client a lot more than just a fat portfolio of utilities. He carefully researched and developed a conservative strategy that produced a portfolio of quality stocks that paid good dividends and had a tendency to raise their dividends.

"In the marketplace there's a direct correlation, over long periods of time, between dividend growth and price appreciation if you buy things at a competitive yield," Phil says. "So, once I could connect the dots for people along that line of thinking, it was easy to reposition their portfolios."

He was still swimming upstream, though. Clients were hesitant to jump in quickly, but a few would let him put a small amount, maybe 10 percent, of their assets into his "unusual idea."

"After three years, I would say, 'Okay, the hundred thousand that we put in this idea of mine, is now worth a hundred and fifty thousand. The income stream from the dividends has gone up forty percent, the bonds that you own are still worth that original nine hundred thousand, and the income has gone down thirty percent; so maybe we should put more into my idea,' " Phil explains. Slowly but surely, the clients followed his lead.

A buying discipline, though, is only successful when there is a strong "sell" discipline attached at the other end. Phil knew that and developed parameters around when to get out of a holding.

BULLETPROOFING THE CLIENT

Every move Phil makes is based on protecting each client's cash flow needs. He figures that investment returns beyond that are pure gravy. So the first thing every prospect does is fill out a questionnaire that not only measures the client's tolerance for risk, but also generates a general measure of his or her cash flow needs, both now and into the future. Only when Phil understands exactly how much cash flow the client needs does he begin building an asset allocation model.

"If a client tells me that he's going to need $480,000 a year, then I know that he is going to need to put $8 million into my income portfolio yielding 6 percent to get that income," Phil says. "If that client has total assets of $20 million, the first thing I will do is take that $8 million and put it into his income portfolio."

In this scenario, the portfolio would generate the income the client needs, and that income would grow every year to keep up with inflation. Only after solving that critical income question does Phil invest the rest of the money based on that client's tolerance for risk.

Even if the client is still working and doesn't have a cash flow problem, that is still the first piece of the equation that Phil tackles. For example, if a client is eight years from retirement, Phil determines what his income needs will be eight years down the road. The asset allocation plan begins with solving 30 percent of that future cash flow issue today.

"I know that by funding thirty percent of their cash flow needs right now, they will not have a cash flow problem in the future because of the growth in my income portfolio," he explains. "So that's what I do first. I solve the cash flow problem. Once we solve that and they understand my thinking in terms of the importance of increasing income streams and how we do that, then I get into the asset allocation of the rest of the assets based on the individual's tolerance for risk."

It's a message that resonates with Phil's clients, most of whom have taken enough risk in their careers and now just want peace of mind. One client had been with a technology company for years, accumulating $20 million of his company stock. He was reluctant to sell any of those shares because he still thought they would increase in value until Phil painted the picture for him.

"I said, 'Look, you have enough money. If you just do this right, you don't have to worry about anything the rest of your life, so while it would be nice if the position went from twenty million to forty million, how would you feel if it fell in half?' " Phil says. "We talked about his lifestyle, and I showed him that while it might be nice if the stock doubled in price, it would be a disaster if the value was cut in half."

The client ended up liquidating the entire stock position, netting about $14 million after taxes. After determining that the client needed to earn $300,000 a year in pretax income, Phil carved out $5 million for the income allocation.

Another client came to Phil as a referral. He had just sold his oil company for about $20 million. He knew that this was a once-in-a-lifetime event for him, but didn't know much outside the oil industry. By the time Phil met with him, the prospect had already met with several advisers pitching for his account and proposals were stacked all over the office. The last thing he wanted to do was talk to another advisor, but his brother was working with Phil, so the referral took the interview as a favor more than anything.

"The first thing I told him was that I approach investing a little differently," Phil says. "I told him I wanted to make him 'bulletproof.' "

Then Phil walked him through his philosophy and how he would approach managing this man's financial future. The client was on board before the first investment plan was even developed.

"He told me that he had met with several other advisors, and that I was the only one who really listened to what he needed and what he wanted," Phil says. "Everyone sat down and just started talking about asset allocation models and efficient frontiers, and all this guy wanted to know was where was his income going to come from and how his portfolio would be positioned so that he didn't have to worry about it."

AVOIDING THE HERD MENTALITY

Since the beginning of his career, Phil has always been a student of the market. So before they start talking about asset allocation, Phil makes sure that every client understands—and agrees with—his view of the market. His philosophy is that, if clients understand why they are doing something, then they are going to be more willing to ride out the inevitable market fluctuations and be more comfortable with the final investment decisions.

Central to Phil's investment strategy is his belief that, just as when he started in this business, the current market is going through a sea change and his clients have to be ready for it. For the past two decades much of the growth in equities has been driven by expanding price-to-earnings (P/E) multiples, Phil says. Given the low inflationary environment, P/E ratios can't continue to expand as the have over the past 20 years, which means growth in equity values will have to be generated by growth in real earnings, not expanding P/E ratios.

"That reality is going to create a different investment environment going forward," he says. "So we need to rethink how we are going to allocate assets, and we need to be a little bit more strategic and tactical in our thinking."

In the industry today, most portfolios are divvied up based on the concept of "modern portfolio theory," which was developed in the late 1950s. Modern portfolio theory is based on the notion that you can get higher rates of return and take less risk by buying and holding different asset classes over long periods of time. Unfortunately just as this notion was becoming popular in the mid-1960s it stopped working for almost 17 years. From 1966 to 1982 inflation steadily rose, so interest rates went up, bond prices fell, P/E ratios collapsed, and stocks were flat. Investment returns, based on the theory of holding different asset classes (stocks, bonds, and cash) produced dismal results.

In the mid-1990s modern portfolio theory again became very popular on Wall Street because with declining inflation we had falling interest rates and expanding P/E ratios.

"Over the last twenty years, inflation went from around fourteen percent down to about one percent, and, because of that, price-earnings ratios went from eight to twenty-six," he says. "There is a direct correlation, over time, between P/E ratios and inflation. As the rate of inflation slows, P/E ratios expand and vice versa. Today we have very low inflation, so P/E ratios can't keep expanding. The best scenario is for inflation to stay low and P/E ratios to stay high, which is what I think will happen. But if inflation jumps up again, P/E ratios will likely come down, as will the returns on stocks."

"Modern portfolio theory, that is, holding different asset classes for a long period of time, may be a great concept for institutions; but it doesn't work well for individuals because individuals have very different needs. Individuals need to position their portfolios so that they can generate an increasing income stream, either now or in the future. In this way they can maintain current standards of living for themselves and their families. This is a very different need from most institutions, yet we try to treat them both the same. Individuals have a tendency to think, 'If it's good for the Stanford University endowment, then it must be good for me.' This is most often not the case."

"Given the current environment of low inflation and high P/E ratios, I think investors are going to have to be more opportunistic. We won't have the benefit of declining interest rates or the tailwind of expanding P/E ratios to give us the excessive rates of return in which we've become accustomed. For instance, instead of just buying General Electric and holding it forever because it is a great company, investors are going to have to be a little more opportunistic." Phil and his team are applying that today with all four portfolios they manage. One is a blue chip portfolio that mimics the S&P 500, but carries only 30 stocks. Their managed value and aggressive growth portfolios both focus on generating absolute returns rather than relative returns. And, of course, he manages the income portfolio based on the same dividend yield-growth formula he started developing 20 years ago.

Managing those portfolios is the heart and soul of Phil's business, and he does so through research developed primarily by Merrill, as well as outside sources. He then combines this with the proprietary analysis that he has developed over the years.

"We subscribe to a lot of outside research, but most of the people we subscribe to also manage money—so they have some skin in the game," he says. "If they are making recommendations, I want them to own what they are recommending."

Then he overlays his own criteria on top of that research, measuring such basics as cash flow growth, price-to-earnings, price-to-sales, etc. He follows a very strict discipline for buying and selling stocks. That discipline includes placing a stop loss on each holding to make sure his clients don't get trampled.

"With growth stocks, it is rare that you know something is wrong with the company before the stock goes down," he says. And after a big runup, he's not afraid to take a breather. Using this stop-loss system, he's gotten out of many technology issues before they had significant drops.

In 2003, after posting strong returns in his growth portfolios, Phil's market research started turning negative: So he pushed the pause button and hedged those gains with a partial position in an inversely correlated mutual fund.

"In my view, nobody can get it right all the time," he says. "But I want to avoid being in a situation where I could face significant downside. So when investor sentiment is exceptionally bullish, chances are most of that good news is already reflected in stock prices and it's time to get defensive. On the other hand when investors are overly pessimistic and stocks are being shunned, the downside risk is probably limited. I want to be in stocks as long as I can, but if investor sentiment is too optimistic, chances are the upside is limited and it's best to just step aside. You can always wait and get back in when investors are overly pessimistic. We have proprietary models that we developed that measure investor sentiment and give us a sense when those extremes have been reached. And since we manage only on the basis of an asset-based fee, the client has no worries about high transaction expenses."

For asset classes that they don't manage in-house, Phil uses the same strict guidelines for choosing money managers as he uses when he's picking stocks. First and foremost, he starts with the track record. He evaluates managers based on their 1-year, 3-year, 5-year, and 7-year performance records. "If they have outperformed over any one of those periods of time, I'm interested," he says. "For example, if they have outperformed one year, underperformed over three years, but then outperformed again over the next five years, I'll still take them; because I'm looking for consistency."

Once he finds the track record he's looking for, he starts looking at the people making the decisions. He wants to understand each person's investment philosophy and measure how strictly he adheres to it. He wants to make sure that the people responsible for those returns have been there the entire time and are still calling the shots. He also looks for people who have their own money in the fund. That makes for a very short list of outside money managers, but that's fine with Phil. If you have the right people, you don't need a lot of them.

"Most of these managers already have a great deal of diversification, and I don't want to overdo it," he says. "And I want to make sure that the people that we are working with are people that we know so that we can keep tabs on them. And again, there's not a lot of turnover with our managers because as long as they have outperformed over a one-, three-, five-, or seven-year period of time, I am not going to fire them."

SERVICE MODEL

Every quarter, Phil and the team discuss performance with each client. "Our clients are able to clearly articulate their performance numbers, why their portfolio performed that way, and what our views of the markets are," Phil says with pride. "There are many reasons why this is so important to us: First, we stand behind everything we do and we believe in full disclosure; second, if a client has an issue, we need to talk about it right away; third, we want to manage clients' expectations, which can become distorted due to media coverage or general conversations with their friends. And lastly, we want to make sure each client completely understands what we're doing and why. They must know where the performance is coming from—whether from the income side or the growth side."

Clients with more complex situations may receive monthly calls. Phil has found that the longer clients have been with him, the less they say they need to hear from him. "That's because they trust that we are properly executing their long-term, well-crafted plan, and there's not a lot of change," Phil explains. "They understand how we manage money. We keep them well educated, so they feel very comfortable with us."

In addition to the phone calls, the team sends emails to clients confirming changes to their portfolios and why the change was made. Additionally, "if there's something unusual happening in the marketplace, we send clients an email—or call them—so we can very thoroughly explain what's going on and why," Phil says.

BUILDING A SUPPORT SYSTEM

Phil manages his team the same way. He looks for smart people with staying power. He hired his first assistant, Kim Scharff, more than 15 years ago, long before he had the production to support a full-time staff member. But he had been appointed manager of the Bellevue, Washington office, and an assistant came with the job.

"She was such a hard charger, and incredibly dependable," he say. Naturally, they clicked and have worked together ever since. Together, they started posting strong enough growth that it was soon time to bring another assistant on board. That's when Karen Petersen joined the team. Shortly thereafter another assistant, Tanya Skillings, joined to manage the quarterly review process for our clients.

"I needed somebody who could help with the client relationships," Phil says. "And then as my business grew, I knew I needed somebody to help with the clients, getting the day-to-day stuff handled and answering their questions. I couldn't go out there and market myself and deal with managing all of this money at the same time. So, I brought in Joe Gazes."

As the business grew, so did the team, and so today Phil has three investment associates. Every time a new client comes on board, he's assigned to one of the associates, who works closely with Phil to develop that client's individual cash flow plan and asset allocation strategy.

"I'll meet with my associate and our new client. Together, we decide how to structure the strategy and in what order we're going to get things done. The investment associate is responsible for implementation, but under my direction," Phil explains.

Phil always brings in top talent. Joe Gazes is a former banker and a CPA. Larissa Thompson graduated from Stanford, and John Shork graduated from the Naval Academy.

"John was my boss in the Navy and a very smart guy," Phil says. The members of my team are very smart people, and they are great with the clients. I try to match up personalities so the day-to-day business of getting things done in portfolios and making sure clients are taken care of are done by them and our administrative assistants. That gives me time to work on our strategies and tactics. I can look at how we're positioned from an overall standpoint, decide how we want to be positioned—and then develop our investment view, strategy, and tactics going forward."

The system works. Kim has been with Phil for 16 years, Karen for 12, and Tanya for eight. In fact, only one person who joined the team has left.

"Everybody works hard, but I don't expect that they should work harder than me," Phil says.

Phil had an opportunity to prove his point at the end of 2002. The market was still in its relentless freefall after years of steady growth, and no one was happy—not the clients, and especially not the staff who had to work with the clients. Tensions were rising, and the friction started wearing down the team.

At the start of the New Year, Phil called a team meeting.

"I told them that they were each going to take a month off on top of their regular vacation," Phil says. "I didn't give them a choice. I told them I wanted them out of the office, and that I didn't want to see them."

That sent two messages. The first was that he cared about each of them personally. But the other message was that they couldn't operate as a team without each person there and working at one hundred and ten percent.

THE COMMUNITY

Phil and Leslie are also one hundred and ten percent dedicated to their community. In addition to raising three children (Andrew, Christopher, and Julia), they are active at St. Thomas School, Boy Scouts, and Bellevue's Children's Hospital.

"Whether in business, the community, or my family, I never stop giving one hundred and ten percent," Phil says with a smile.

CHAPTER 19: LARRY PALMER

Hard Work and Integrity

Smith Barney
Los Angeles, California

LARRY PALMER BELIEVES THAT 90 PERCENT OF BEING SUCCESSFUL IN this business comes from showing up every day and doing exactly the same thing you did yesterday, only doing it smarter and more efficiently. And most importantly—always proving your integrity and placing clients' interests first and foremost.

Larry Palmer ticks off the mistakes he has made during his 20 years as an advisor like badges of honor. He didn't listen to his clients. He hired the wrong people. He had the wrong business model in place. He chased the wrong type of business. He lacked both the discipline and maturity he needed to help his clients when they needed him the most.

"When I first talk to potential clients, I tell them that when they hire us they are getting twenty-two years worth of mistakes," he laughs. "And then I tell them that those are all mistakes that we are never going to make again."

It's a refreshing honesty that most people can relate to, whether they want to admit it or not, and one that most prospects can respect.

"I'm not the smartest guy on earth, and I'm not the best connected guy on earth, but my philosophy has always been that ninety percent of the success in this business is showing up everyday and doing the exact same thing you did yesterday, only doing it smarter and more effectively," he says.

One of Larry Palmer's early mentors once told him: "Clients will almost always forgive you when you make a mistake, but they will never forgive you for integrity violation." "Too many people believe that they'll be fired if they make a mistake," Larry says. "That's not true. It's how you respond to the mistake you make and how you look them straight in the eye and say, 'We made a mistake. We are going to fix it.' "

Even though he grew up in the San Fernando Valley in Southern California, Larry relates deeply with the Midwestern work ethic that his parents instilled in all his siblings from the very beginning. His father is from the South, and his mother is from the Midwest. Together, they raised their family with a set of values that places hard work and integrity above personal gain.

"I believe what has helped me more than anything else is just the wisdom my parents have given me in terms of dealing with people and making sure you stay grounded," Larry says. "You stay true to your values. I was raised with integrity, and if I haven't ripped somebody off by now I don't think it's going to happen."

FINDING A NICHE

By the time he was in high school, Larry was already being pushed toward the brokerage business. His father's best friend was a broker at one of the largest wirehouses in the country at the time, and he kept telling Larry that this was the career for him because he was good at math, he was outgoing, and he was good with people. But Larry was too busy playing sports and hanging out with his friends to listen.

He started paying attention, though, when he was looking for an internship while he worked his way through school at UCLA, majoring in economics. He went to the business school's career center, and was offered the opportunity to work as a cold caller at the same wirehouse where his father's friend worked. He was hooked.

"I saw all these young guys wearing nice suits," he remembers. "They were aggressive and kind of out there, trying to make things happen. It looked like they were having a ton of fun, and they were making money."

The ten-week internship turned into a permanent part-time job, and Larry stayed until he graduated from college. After graduation, Larry was convinced that he had found the right career; he just hadn't found the right business model.

"This was 1982," Larry says. "The bull market hadn't started yet, we were just coming out of the Reagan recession, and interest rates were at twenty-one percent. It wasn't vogue to be on Wall Street, but I thought, 'I know I like this, and I don't know what else I'm qualified to do.' "

He was cold calling and pitching stocks, making all those early mistakes that eventually gave him the focus and the footing he needed to define himself professionally and decide exactly what kind of broker and person he wanted to be. He knew cold calling and hyping stocks weren't for him, so he and a colleague moved over to a "white shoes" firm that focused on high net worth families and middle-market corporate accounts, long before corporate services was a popular business.

Larry had found his niche. Still a decade before most of the rest of the industry had discovered the lucrative world of stock options and insider sales, Larry discovered SEC Rule 144 block sales for corporate affiliates and control persons. This was still wide-open territory because these were complicated transactions that few brokers understood. What Larry understood, though, was that this was a expertise that would not only set him apart from the rest of the brokers cold calling these corporate executives, it would open the door to the rest of those insiders' assets. After all, he figured, "I can provide higher levels of services and advice if I understand a client's entire situation." He wanted to be a true financial advisor.

Every week, he would wait for the Vickers List to come in the mail, and he would pore over the names.

"Today, you can get this information in real time over the Internet," Larry says. "But back then, the reports came once a week; and the lists were three months old. You still called these guys, though, because no one else was."

Larry laughs when he remembers the very first call he made off the list. It was a tiny company—he doesn't even remember its name. But he does remember that the stock was only trading at 96 cents.

"I didn't have a lot of skills in this area yet, and I figured, well, if this one blows up, it's only $96 in stock," he says. "Then again, every client is important—as is every transaction."

While it was a mistake he figured he could afford to make, he didn't need to worry. That sale went smoothly, paving Larry's way into the world of corporate finance and high net worth clients. He followed that path into the upper echelons of his firm until 1994, when the writing was on the wall. The organization was in financial trouble, and it was about to be sold. Larry wanted to control his own destiny and so he began entertaining offers from most of the firms on the Street.

Smith Barney put together the package he couldn't refuse. The firm was just forming the nucleus of what would evolve into one of the most significant corporate services platform in the industry; plus, their platform for servicing high net worth individuals was top-notch. Larry wanted in on that ground floor.

"The managers looked me in the eye and told me that they were going to be investing a lot of capital in corporate services, which was a big part of the business that we were building," Larry says.

Smith Barney already had the best consulting managed account practice on the Street, Larry says, and it was just rolling out a new platform for doing stock options. Those two tools, combined with the new emphasis on corporate services, dovetailed completely with the practice Larry was already building. It was a perfect fit.

THE RIGHT PLATFORM FOR THE RIGHT MARKET

Since he started reading the Vicker's List, Larry has concentrated on providing executives with effective management of their 401(k) and stock plans. Today, nearly three-quarters of his book falls into Section 16 of the 1934 Securities Act. These are officers and directors who own either 10 percent of any equity security registered pursuant to Section 12 of the '34 Act. Section 16 insiders generally include the chief executive officer, president, chief financial officer, chief operation officer, or they are the major heads of independent business units or subsidiaries.

Interestingly, Larry didn't focus on these specific clients because their names were on a list, though. He targeted them because he felt these individuals could benefit from his knowledge and the extensive services offered by the firm's corporate services platform.

"These are the guys with the capital," Larry says. "These are the guys who need the financial, estate, and liability management planning—everything that we do from a private wealth management standpoint. The corporate services platform is a perfect entrée through the backdoor to handle those transactions and then do reinvestment planning for those individuals because they are holding large pools of liquid capital."

Many of these corporate executives, in fact, are holding large pools of investment with absolutely no idea of what to do with it. Especially during the bull market, multimillionaires were being churned out of the high-tech industry faster than the financial services industry could build products and services to handle their unique financial and personal needs.

Most of these new superwealthy clients came from middle-class backgrounds with no concept of sophisticated investment and estate planning. They were suddenly dealing with numbers they had never dreamt of and problems they had never imagined.

"That's the beauty of our platform," Larry says. "When we go into a company, I probably have thirteen points of entry from which I can create revenue and add value."

That makes it easy for him to compete with brokers who are out there selling a product or selling their firm's research. Those end up in yes-or-no conversations—which are nothing but deadends, as far as Larry is concerned.

"I don't want to hear 'yes' or 'no,' " he says. "I want to be able to educate them about all the things that we can do, and then have them tell us where there needs are and where we can add value."

The highest point of contact, generating the most profound impact on his client, is the Rule 144 sale, which is still Larry's "bread and butter." Attached to those lucrative stock options is a labyrinth of tax and legal issues that most of these entrepreneurs had never even heard of, much less understood. Larry made it his business to understand every one of the rules and regulations—and to figure out a way to explain it to clients and prospects in a way that wouldn't put them to sleep.

"This is the driest stuff you've ever heard of," Larry says. "But I have a quirky personality. I've read all of these regulations cover to cover, and I think it's interesting. Maybe I should get a social life or something."

During the raging bull market, from 1995 to 1999, it was a very easy sell. At the time, Smith Barney had the number one platform for handling stock options and Rule 144 trades.

"We could go in and sell our menu of corporate services without ever making a presentation to an officer," Larry says. "But because we were getting that captive order flow, we then had the perfect pool of assets from which to go out and deliver private wealth management and consulting services to that officer."

The strength of Smith Barney's stock option platform became one of Larry's most powerful prospecting tools. If the firm didn't already make a market in the prospective company's stock, Larry would work with the investment banking and capital markets trading side of the business to get that market-making platform in place. If Smith Barney agrees that making a market in a particular stock would be a good business decision, then it becomes a great piece of business for Larry.

"Most people competing for this business will call the CEO and tell him that they are the number one firm in handling Rule 144 transactions, and the CEO will tell him that he already has a twenty-year relationship with someone else," he says. "When we call him up, we say, 'We are a major trader of your stock, and we would like to come in and talk to you about your company.' That's a call they are going to take."

Everyone is selling essentially the same product, Larry says. It is the context in which you sell that product that determines whether you are successful or not.

AFTER THE FALL

With the crash of 2000, everything changed. The Rule 144 trades ground to a screeching halt because all the options were suddenly underwater and no one was going to exercise their options at those bargain-basement prices. So Larry just pulled out the same playbook he has always used and recommitted himself to his philosophy of working smarter and more effectively.

Corporate officers were no longer trading their options, but with quality stocks trading at depressed prices, corporate boards were suddenly in a buying mood. Corporate buyback plans increased. Meanwhile, when the market dried up for these stocks, their market makers disappeared along with it. That left Larry with a bigger playing field than ever.

"A lot of sponsorship for these stocks went away during the bear market," Larry says. "So we would go in and make a market in that stock. We could step up and tell the company, 'Look, we are here for you when nobody else is.' You can get into the door and talk about things like this."

In fact, creating an opportunity where most people can only see a crisis has always been the key to Larry's success. That's how, in the aftermath of the crash, he turned the tide of corporate scandals that swamped the market into his advantage. With Capitol Hill trying desperately to return investor confidence to the marketplace, Congress passed the Sarbanes-Oxley Bill, adding another layer of complex rules and regulations to an already confusing mix of laws surrounding options and compensation packages.

Corporate executives were paralyzed by the added confusion, so Larry, who has a penchant for these legal labyrinths, hit the road. He and partner Marty Erzinger had already put together a training video for their firm that explained the ins and outs of the new securities laws, so Larry started pitching the act to corporate clients and investment bankers.

"It was basically the Monday Night Football color version of the securities law," he says. "Normally what happens is that if a company is thinking about going public, some lawyer comes out and says, 'Here's the Securities Act of 1933. Here's the Securities Act of 1934. If there are twelve individuals on the board, six of them will be snoring."

Larry and Marty wake them up with an interactive introduction to securities law, taking listeners through the basics and intricacies of Rule 144 and the insider trading regulations, but spicing it up with real life examples of case laws and some of the people who violated the securities laws and ended up in the proxy statement.

"We give them actual cases, synthesized down about companies they have heard of," Larry says. "In fact, we have one company we did this for where one of the guys on the board said, 'I worked at that company, and I know the guy who went to jail.' "

Even though they aren't lawyers, Larry and Marty are able to bring clarity to the often opaque side of insider sales, creating tremendous credibility with both prospects and clients.

"To me, a Rule 144 transaction is a commodity transaction," Larry says. "All people think about is who can execute it the cheapest."

The only way to escape that mentality—and that sales trap—is to go out and sell the company, its counsel, and its directors on the fact that you can not only execute it better, but that you have the intellectual capital to protect them from having their name printed in the company proxy statement.

"We can show them that we can help to protect the corporation from a lawsuit because somebody didn't do something right, which happens all the time," Larry says. "We can also help to protect them from the downside risk in their stock and from being trapped in window periods because we know how to coordinate order flow."

It is such a powerful presentation that Larry was able to capture an account that not only had a longstanding relationship with another major firm but had a representative from that firm sitting on its board of directors. The other firm had been one of the company's venture capital investors, and for five years it had a corner on the firm's Rule 144 transactions.

"But the guy handling that account had only been an advisor for about five years," Larry says. "Someone just handed him the business, and he was just taking unsolicited orders. He wasn't adding value."

Larry saw an opportunity. Larry proposed that Smith Barney could possibly make a market in the stock. "Suddenly, they have credibility, and second-tier players will come in. That creates better liquidity, gives the officers more places to trade, and more sponsorship of their stock by default. Optically, that looks better and it will tighten up their spreads."

Larry and his team now manage all the company's cash, all the officers' equity compensation plans, and about $120 million in personal assets for the company's top four executives.

"That's a textbook example of how we spread our tentacles and get ensconced with the company," he says. "They aren't all like that, but that is how they are supposed to work."

DIGGING DEEP

That corporate business, is only the beginning of the story. Once Larry and his team are fully ensconced on the business side, they start working on the personal side, developing relationships with the senior executives, bringing the full power of their platform to the high net worth clients who need it.

The conversation—and the relationship—begins with a daunting 32-page questionnaire that every prospect has to fill out before Larry will consider working with them. It can take hours, but without it, Larry simply doesn't believe that he can provide the service the client needs, and the simple act of filling out the form shows Larry that the prospect is just as invested in the relationship as he is.

"Every firm on Wall Street has a planning profile," Larry says. "CPAs have one, attorneys have one they use for estate planning. But nobody ever, in my opinion, has put a planning profile together in a way in which someone that uses it can derive the right information and create a proper flow for a client to take them from A to Z."

Most client profiles begin and end with the client's assets. How much do they have, where do they have it, and how can the advisor get all those assets into his book? Larry believes that putting asset management first is like putting the caboose at the beginning of the train.

For Larry, the most important part of the process is figuring out whether the prospect has the right platform with his attorneys and CPAs, whether the accounts are titled properly, how liabilities are managed, and much more.

"Liability management for us is anything that you can insure—where you have to make the business decision to self-insure or to lay off that risk on someone else," Larry explains.

For instance, the form asks if the prospect sits on any corporate board, and, if so, when was the last time the prospect talked to an attorney about directors and officers insurance.

"The average D&O hit is seven million dollars," Larry says. "Most people don't realize that."

The form even asks if kids in college are driving family cars, or if they have the cars in the kids' name for liability purposes. After personally reviewing each 32-page questionnaire, Larry puts together an outline of action items—usually 10 or 15 items that the prospect should look at immediately.

"For example, we might suggest that they increase their homeowners liability insurance from one million to five million dollars," he says. "What we try to do is display our intellectual capital and create credibility by advising them on things that we don't get paid to do."

By the end of that process, Larry usually closes on at least 95 percent of the accounts that have gone through it. Of course, plenty of people don't want to be bothered with such an exhaustive report, but one of the things Larry has learned from his years in the business is that he probably doesn't want to do business with the people who won't do the profile, anyway.

"I can't do what I do for my clients without that information," Larry says.

In fact, he spent nine months preparing one prospect who resisted doing the profile. He was the CEO of a major public company and in all his years of working with financial advisors, he had never been asked for such a thorough examination of his finances. He finally sat down and started working his way through it, and by the time he and Larry finished the process, the client had already started moving all his assets from a long-term relationship at another major firm and consolidating them with Larry.

"He told me that through all of the planning profiles he did with his other advisors, we were the first people to actually read it," Larry says.

This 32-page document has become the crux of every move that Larry and a client make. Every year during a client review, they go over it again, point by point, making sure that everything is still on track and that the overall plan is still relevant to and reflective of the client's long-term goals and short-term needs.

"People's lives are a lot more dynamic than we think they are," Larry says. "We need something to benchmark where we started out so we can see where we are today, and not just from an investment return standpoint. I need something that says, 'Here's where you told me you were as a family or as an individual a year ago. What has changed and where do we go from here?' "

BUILDING A PARTNERSHIP

Every question on that planning profile came from the lessons Larry has learned in his two decades as a financial advisor. The most important of which is that high net worth clients don't need another broker. They need someone with a 30,000-foot view of their lives who can shepherd their wealth along. And that important realization came from listening to what their clients needed from them, not thinking about the business they can derive from that client.

"We started realizing what our clients wanted, and we created a way to take control and ownership of that process," Larry says.

But the process is only a roadmap to the target destination: a deep, long-term partnership between Larry and his clients.

"Once we have been through the process and focus on the action items that are generated, it shifts the focus," Larry says.

"They are no longer a prospect. It's 'Hey, we need to call up your homeowner's insurance guy and get this liability thing take care of.' All of a sudden, we are rolling up our sleeves together and taking care of these issues together. It just changes the whole nature of your relationship."

The planning profile has also had a profound impact on Larry and his entire team. Once they have gathered all that information from prospects and clients, they commit themselves to overseeing the client's investment strategies.

For example, one of the questions on the profile asks which discount broker the client or prospect uses, because it's a safe bet that anyone in a high net worth bracket has several brokerage relationships and an account on the side that they want to play around with.

"It's not that we want those assets," Larry says. "We don't. But we want to know what they are doing so that when we set up their platform we can factor in the fact that they want to trade ten percent of their assets themselves online."

A clear understanding of where all the assets are also creates an opportunity for Larry to add value by bringing a product or service to the table that the client may not have considered. One prospect, who had a longstanding relationship with another major wirehouse on the Street, went through Larry's planning questionnaire; Larry saw that the retired corporate executive had set himself up as his own private equity firm because he liked doing his own deals.

Larry found a perfect match between the prospect and one of his parent company's own investment initiatives, Citi Alternative Investments, which builds co-investment opportunities with sophisticated clients. Through Larry, the client is now investing a significant amount of capital in Citigroup's municipal arbitrage fund, an investment vehicle that the financial services firm originally created to hedge its own muni investments and leverage those returns.

Larry has also set him up with the head of Smith Barney's estate planning and philanthropic services. Together, they were able to identify some fiduciary liability issues inside the client's private foundation that he wasn't aware of. They were also able to advise him on raising capital for the foundation.

Needless to say, the client is now moving a significant portion of his assets over to Larry's team and consolidating his assets under the private wealth management umbrella.

"I think what's happening is that people are responding to the fact that we are trying to strategically advise them and take a much more active role in everything they do financially," Larry says. "We talk to their CPA. We talk to their attorney. We set up at least an annual conference call with their estate planning attorney. The process has worked very, very well for us."

And it has worked very well for the clients, too. With Larry and his team assuming the 30,000-foot view of the client's total financial picture, they know that someone is managing the entire process and keeping an eye on all the assets, even the ones that are still at other firms. Eventually, though, most clients see the value that Larry is bringing to the process and move all their assets over to him.

It took two years for one client to move all his assets over once he started working with Larry and his team. A year into the process he even acknowledged that he really needed to call his other advisor and move everything over, but because of a long-term relationship, he just couldn't seem to make the call.

"He looked at us and said, 'I know you guys are the A Team, but I am a loyal guy, and I just don't know how to call this guy up,'" Larry says. "We never pushed him; we just continued to give him great service. A year later he told us, 'I called him, and I feel great about the decision to work exclusively with you.'"

That is the kind of response that makes the added work filling out and then reviewing that massive questionnaire worth the effort—for both Larry and the client.

"The reason I know this planning profile works is because people actually take the time, in spite of all the complaints, to fill it out," Larry says. "That says to me that they really want someone to look at the whole picture. And to me, that is what financial planning is all about."

CLIENT-FOCUSED SUPPORT

Of course, Larry can't handle the demands of managing thousands of corporate accounts (about 150 high net-worth families and two offices) by himself. Besides Marty, who heads up a lot of the corporate and family business in the Denver, Colorado office, there is one technical analyst, a business manager, two people who do nothing but handle stock options transactions, and several assistants keeping things running smoothly.

In 1995, Larry was introduced to Sharon Moses Coleman. A former military brat, her ethical ways clashed with her former boss, a stockbroker at another firm who was practicing unscrupulous behavior. Her passion for the business led her to Larry, whom she'd heard about in the industry. While the two instantly clicked, Sharon rarely spoke a word during her first six months. When confronted by Larry, she finally admitted that she was reserved to ensure she was working with a team and an organization with only the highest standards and morals. Larry and team lived up to their reputation.

When asked to describe Sharon, Larry (the godfather to her daughter) responds: "She defies classification. She's smart, loyal, and a lot of my success is because she is really good at what she does."

Leann Dexter is the group administrator. She handles all the personal touches. She writes the letters, sends out the flowers, and mails the Christmas cards, and she balances his hectic travel and business schedule. "We hired Leann because she is great working with CEOs," says Larry. "This woman represents us very professionally on the front end and makes our quality of life better.

"Nobody can get on my calendar," he continues, "unless they go through Leann. Her primary role is to be the point person and have people who call in be satisfied that they were dealt with professionally and efficiently. She then funnels the calls to the team members."

That frees Larry up to do what he does best: working one on one with his top clients and coordinating the vast array of the firm's products and expertise with the people who need them. A busy day for him is meeting with six of his top clients, either in person or on a conference call. Between those calls he touches base with at least two prospects on his radar screen.

"I need to keep that part of the juggernaut moving forward," he laughs.

MOVING FORWARD

"I think you have to reinvent yourself every five years in this business," Larry says. "And I don't mean change your business model and fire all your clients. You have to take your skills up a notch. You have got to improve the way you present who you are and how you do what you do. You have to expand the depth of the products and services that you offer."

Larry then articulates the "CANEI—constant and never-ending improvement. That's the name of the game in this business. Do you know what we really sell? Integrity. We sell intellectual capital. Other than that, there's little differentiation from us or any formidable competitor. This is what we get paid for."

Clearly, Larry's reputation precedes him. He says it's the thrill of edging his competitors with superior service and integrity that gets him out of bed each morning at 4 o'clock, anxious to go to work. His relentless pursuit toward building his base of knowledge and skills extends to his personal life as well: He's a formidable Ironman competitor and competes globally. Larry strives toward his personal well-being and athletic goals the way he pursues his professional goals: with stamina and obstinate vigor.

Professionally, his goal is to build a book of around 200 high-quality families or individuals within the next five years, while steadily increasing the average assets of his clients. Financial goals? It never crosses his mind. "I never use dollar signs to measure success."

"The only specific goal I have in this business is that I get better at what I do and that my staff gets better at what they do," Larry says. "Another critical goal is that we have extremely low turnover amongst our clients because to me, the best litmus test for us in terms of how we are doing our job is not assets or revenues. It is that we have no liability. We are not getting sued or in arbitration with any clients, and we have low client turnover. I'm successful when my clients attain their financial goals. That is how our business will grow."

In fact, when the conversation turns to financial versus personal success, Larry gets very philosophical.

"I would rather maintain my small, intimate clientele and have clients that have been with me for twenty years who will tell people, 'Yes, I would trust this guy with my life,' " Larry says.

"I learned long ago that at the end of the day, once I had proven to myself I was worthy and good, and professional at what I was doing, that's when I think I became good at what I was doing," he says. "I think there are these phases you go through where you may put it out there that you are good, but you don't necessarily believe it."

And when he needs a reality check on how far he has come in personal growth, he only has to look as far as his father

"I always tell my dad, 'I'm not the man I want to be. I'm not the man I ought to be. But I'm a lot better than I used to be,' " Larry says. "To which he always replies, 'You let me know when you think you get there, and I'll let you know when you are not.' "

Chapter 20: Joe Montgomery

An All-Star Team

Wachovia Securities
Williamsburg, Virginia

THE OPTIMAL SERVICE GROUP'S VICTORIES COME FROM THEIR clients' *successes.*

A longtime client and his wife recently approached Joe Montgomery. They had just stepped off a 30-hour plane trip from China and were anxious to share with Joe the treasure they brought back: a 17-month-old adopted baby girl. Joe looked down at a smiling baby, who looked back with her big brown eyes. The couple looked at Joe and said, "Thank you. We couldn't have done this without your guidance over the years." Joe, a former professional football player, had tears welling in his eyes.

When building a team, Joe had in mind his old coach at The College of William & Mary: "He has always surrounded himself with the best talent he can find, always seeking to find someone better than himself," Joes says. Indeed, every member of Lou's coaching staff had become either assistant or head coach of either a college or professional team, including one who earned a national title.

Everything about Joe and his team is "best-of-breed," whether it's people, the service and products they offer, or the advice they provide. Everything Joe does is dedicated to his mission: "Our mission statement is simple," he says. "Our job is to help our clients achieve their preferred futures."

As an early adopter of the wealth management model of financial planning, Joe (through the Optimal Service Group that he founded) developed an open platform service model that provides what he figures is best-of-breed products and services for his high net worth and institutional clients. With his skilled team of professionals focused on that driving theme, Joe keeps their clients on course to meet that preferred future, factoring in the obstacles that may lie between today's plan and tomorrow's reality.

"We know it's not going to be a straight line along the way," Joe says. "Life just doesn't work that way. There are adjustments. Sometimes you get a little more wind than you had expected, and sometimes that wind is in your face. We make sure that we are always sitting on the same side of the table as the client, helping him adjust his sails as the winds shift to keep him on track to his preferred future."

That sailing analogy spoke volumes when one of Joe's clients was getting ready to retire. In the mid-1980s, when interest rates were high, the client was convinced that all he had to do was stash everything away in high-yielding bonds and he could put his future on autopilot.

"We had the hardest time convincing him that he needed to diversify," Joe remembers. "We needed to convince him that he needed some growth in there, too. There's just too much risk in a single-asset class portfolio."

Joe was finally able to talk the client into of a hybrid structure—with half his money going into conservative equity mutual funds and the other half laddered in corporate and government agency bonds of varying maturities. Every year, when one of those bonds matured, they would diversify the portfolio a little bit more. Over the next few years, they had built a nicely diversified portfolio that was giving him the income he needed, along with the growth that he didn't think he would need.

That was when his life blew into a strong headwind. His son was diagnosed as bipolar, and it was up to the client and his wife to take care of him. With Joe at the helm, though, guiding the client's financial plan, the couple was still able to enjoy their lifestyle with assets left over to cover their unforeseen expenses.

"He called me up later and said, 'I realize that I almost made a really bad mistake and that I wouldn't have been able to take care of my son,'" Joe remembers. "That's what gets me up in the morning."

PREPARING FOR LIFE

Joe learned early in life that designing an ideal future is a highly individualized process. Growing up as a star high school athlete in Lynchburg, Virginia, Joe was under tremendous pressure to continue his football career at the college level. College recruiters were tailing him, trying to get him to sign with them. It was Joe's parents who finally gave him a chance to sit down and really think about what he wanted.

"My parents sat me down in the living room and said, 'We think it's great if you want to play football in college, but if you don't want to, we'll figure out a way to pay for your college education without scholarships,'" Joe says. "That took off so much pressure. 'We want you to do what's right for you, what's right for your future,' my parents told me."

That was a message that would resonate throughout the rest of Joe's life. With that freedom to choose, Joe decided to give college football a try, and he signed with William & Mary so he could play for then coach Lou Holtz, now famous as Notre Dame's legendary former head coach. Four years later, after earning a business degree, being elected co-captain of the football team, winning a spot in the school's Hall of Fame, and making the All-American Team, Joe was off to the big leagues.

That's where he learned all about having his plans blown off course.

"When I got to the pros, I was good enough to play, but not so outstanding that every team was willing to sign me," he admits. He signed on with the Philadelphia Eagles, but was later cut. The next year he joined the Charlotte Hornets of the World Football League. He played only part of one season and hung up his helmet when the league folded.

By that time, he was already thinking ahead about what course adjustments he needed to be making to his own career. He headed home for Lynchburg, where he met Larry Phillips, the manager of Wheat First Securities, which has since evolved into Wachovia Securities, and applied for the training class. Once accepted, Joe established a new game plan.

"In professional sports, you can be your best and still lose your job," he says. "But if you work hard and smart in the securities business, it's hard not to be successful."

Joe was ready to work hard. He considered his first three years in the business as his training program—and began building his endurance and experience by cold calling, selling municipal bonds and stocks. Just as a head coach needs to know everything he can about playing every position on the field, a good financial advisor needs to learn—and then put into practice—everything he can about the business before he shoots for the big leagues. Eventually, he earned his Certified Financial Planning™ designation and was ready to start building the type of practice that he believed people needed.

"Our approach has always been to help anyone who wants our help," he says. "We find out what people need and try to help them fill that need."

It's a deceptively simple approach that conjures up images of down-home charm, but doesn't get lost in a homespun imagery. Joe has built a practice that consists of high net worth retail clients and multibillion-dollar institutions by building incredibly sophisticated systems and providing the diligent oversight necessary to make sure each client has the seamless service he or she has come to expect.

"We run the Indy 500 everyday," he says. "When you are going two hundred miles per hour, you take your eyes off the road, and you're dead. Those cars don't have rearview mirrors because if you look back, you're dead. We don't have time to look back."

The true skill isn't in racing around the track, though. It is in making that process appear effortless, so that all clients feel like they are the firm's number-one priority, receiving the same level of attention and the same positive experience, no matter what his goals or how much they have to invest. Even though one of Joe's largest institutional clients has more than $1 billion invested with the group, he prefers to talk about his experience with a woman who had just come through a bitter divorce with two young children that she needed to support and plan for.

"We analyzed her personal situation and placed her on a strict spending and savings regimen," he says. "We carefully allocated her assets and planned for many life events, including educating her children. She has remained disciplined about saving money on a monthly basis, taking full advantage of dollar-cost averaging, and she is now financially comfortable, with no problems paying for two college educations, her home, or her retirement. She has been an astute student, soaking up all the advice we've provided. In fact, since her father passed away she has been making some very sophisticated decisions about settling the estate."

IT'S A TEAM EFFORT

That is exactly the type of success story Joe was convinced he could write for all his clients when he started in this business. But he also knew from his football career that it takes a team of dedicated professionals to pull off that kind aggressive game plan. He started building that team nearly 25 years ago.

Returning to Williamsburg in 1979, Joe created the Optimal Service Group. His objectives were to meet the need of affluent individuals nationwide, and develop long-term relationships based on a high level of skill and service. Again, Joe turned to an important lesson that he learned from Coach Holtz: Never be afraid to hire people smarter than you are. Today, Joe has built a team of highly skilled, highly motivated professionals who pride themselves on three principles that they believe give them the competitive edge: sound financial advice, quality investments, and well-structured execution.

"Our comprehensive financial planning and wealth management process really sets us apart in helping our clients achieve their preferred future," he says. "When we consider our clients' accounts, we're not referring just to their investments with us. We consider everything they are involved in financially. For years, brokers have managed just the asset side of the balance sheet. We include the liability side, and our trust capabilities are second to none."

Of course, Joe gives tremendous credit to the broad selection of products and expertise that Wachovia Securities brings to the table, but having the right ingredients in the cupboard doesn't make you a great chef. He knew he needed a strong team around him to harness the power of those products to create best-of-class service for his clients.

"More and more affluent clients are looking for not only a comprehensive range of services, but for expert advice that can address their total financial needs," he explains. "Providing all of that—and doing it well—simply takes more time, energy, and knowledge than any one person can ever have."

Over the years, he has built a team of 11 professionals that can fulfill those lofty goals. The team's wealth management area, which includes Bill Muth, Judy Halstead, Sean Driscoll, and Pamela Sardeson, helps clients identify investment objectives, set asset allocations, monitor strategies, and review portfolio performance. It also provides expertise in investment and financial products, portfolio analysis, financial planning, trust and estate analysis, and administration.

Thomas "T.C." Wilson, previously the firm's Director of Institutional Consulting, joined the team in 2001 to coordinate its efforts with institutions, such as endowments and corporations, and to help with asset allocation and planning for high net worth clients. Robin Wilcox, former Director of Consulting Services for another securities firm, and Bryce Lee complete the institutional side.

"We are essentially treating our high net worth clients the same as our institutional clients, with similar tools and resources" Joe explains.

The client services group, which includes Pamela Malamphy, Ashley Parnell, and Christine Stiles, supervises operations and administrative projects, overseeing the myriad details that go into running a multibillion-dollar practice. Providing that next level of expertise to high net worth clients is critical to servicing this increasingly sophisticated market, and it is instrumental in separating Joe's business from other financial advisors' practices.

"We want to be our clients' CFO," he says. "You never give up control of your money, but like any good CEO, you need to have a good CFO. When you hire us, you don't have to go through all the details. We design our practice so that, as CEO, our clients hire us as they would a CFO."

BUILDING A BUSINESS, NOT A PRACTICE

When building a team in this industry, Joe notes that too many advisors partner for the wrong reasons, such as for the sole purpose of taking more time away from the office. "If that's your primary mission, then that's probably okay," Joe says. On the other hand, Joe compares his team to a law firm with numerous attorneys who cover many specialties. "If you're the only lawyer, then business is only operational when you're around, and you're limited to your particular specialty," he says. "But if a client walks in and you can provide comprehensive service and expert opinions on the spot, then you're really adding value and you can own that relationship. The relationship of each client must be extrapolated into the strengths of the entire team."

He also points out that his team provides continuity. "If I get hit by a car, clients know that they are still in great, caring hands, and I am assured that my family will be well taken care of. Additionally, clients also know that we'll still be here when their children, grandchildren and great-grandchildren are ready to open accounts. We're not just here day to day, we're here decade to decade, generation to generation."

Building a team, he believes, requires not just people, but depth. "Every team needs the credentials, backgrounds, and experience level required to really understand the growing complexities of clients' situations," he says.

Perhaps the most important element of building a team, Joe says, is ensuring that the right synergies are in place. "With synergies, instead of growing a team arithmetically, you can grow it exponentially. We can blend any two individuals on our team and there will be a synergy. We feed off each other, in terms of expertise, ideas, and personalities. We're not just a group of people showing up in the office to pick up a paycheck; we're all on the same mission, and we each know how the other fits into that mission and what our individual goals are. Each member of our team is a first-string starter."

THE ENVISION-ARY

The role of the CFO is to see everything—every asset, every income stream, every liability—then coordinate all those moving parts into a single, seamless financial plan with all the elements working together toward a single, identifiable goal. That job became a lot easier when, using Wachovia Securities' Envision program, Joe and his team implemented an entirely new process for managing their clients' total financial plans.

Envision is a sophisticated yet elegantly simple, client-friendly advisory process that drives a holistic and ongoing view of a client's entire financial life. The result is an investment strategy that provides confidence in meeting those goals while avoiding unnecessary investment risk. This program doesn't drive his wealth management process. It *is* the process.

The centerpiece of the Envision process is software developed by Financeware Inc., a powerful modeling program that works in real time, while the client is sitting in the office. The program allows Joe to model thousands of potential investing and economic scenarios with a client's unique personal and financial characteristics guiding each step of the process.

Joe can input such individualized data as cash flow requirements, planned savings, financial objectives, and estate goals. Then he can take that personal profile even deeper, reaching into the emotional decisions around the compromises and comfort levels clients are willing to accept throughout their lives.

That data is screened against market analyses and historical performances of various asset classes, and results are illustrated in colorful graphics that are simple to understand. This process helps position Joe's value to his clients by focusing on the elements that he can control, such as asset allocation, instead of analyzing things that are outside of his control, such as market conditions.

"Too many advisors are focusing on the one element that they really can't control—beating the index," Joe says. "We certainly believe in the added value of management, but that's not where the client's focus should be. We'll take care of that for them."

The power of this wealth management process was obvious from the first time he used it. Joe was meeting with a new client who had a substantial portion of his net worth tied up in a concentrated stock position. The stock was rising, and the future looked promising, so the client was reluctant to sell. Using Envision, Joe instantly ran 1,000 Monte Carlo simulations that mapped the client's best-case and worst-case scenarios based on the client's comprehensive financial situation, goals, and objectives. The thousands of separate calculations required to run these complicated projections took just a few seconds, but the picture generated on the computer screen would last a lifetime.

The client's ideal scenario painted a rosy picture. The stock went through the roof, providing him with substantial assets and complete financial piece of mind. The downside was that there was only a 5 percent chance of that actually happening. On the flip side, there was a 12 percent chance that the stock would drop and that the client would encounter a scenario that would be devastating to his long-term plan. By shifting a few things, Joe was able to strike a balance between the client's top priorities and some less important compromises, showing the client an 83 percent probability that he could achieve his long-term goals without taking unnecessary risks with his portfolio to achieve those goals.

Using the program, Joe was able to show the client that, by diversifying away from the concentrated stock position and building a moderate growth portfolio holding 30 percent bonds and 70 percent stock, the client would be comfortable that his lifetime goals would be met. By looking at only one picture, the client had a full understanding of asset allocation and diversification.

"Before I took him though these analyses, it was very difficult to explain to him the benefits of diversifying assets," Joe says. "He took one look at the picture and became very motivated."

With the client's blessing, Joe and his team slowly unwound the single-stock position, using the proceeds to build a diversified portfolio using a variety of asset classes, including equities, fixed income, REITS, hedge funds, and managed futures. Several months later, the company—and the broader markets—hit a major correction, with the stock losing three-quarters of its value. In contrast, the client's portfolio was down marginally in a market that had dropped significantly.

However, it's not the software program that makes the difference, it's how it is used, explains Bill Muth, who works closely with Joe in building wealth management strategies for high net worth clients.

"I think a lot of people might look at it as a tool that tests whether you are going to be successful in meeting your goals, but most high net worth clients are not that concerned about meeting their goals, because they know they have enough money to be successful," Bill says. "With those clients, Envision is a wonderful way to work with them and help them to understand the kinds of risks that are part of the portfolio. This also helps illustrate the portfolio structure and what those structures mean to them personally."

More importantly, this new wealth management system helps clients prioritize their life choices and balance their decisions against market realities. Recently, a client and his wife, both in their early sixties, came to Joe with some pretty extravagant dreams. With $2 million in savings, they wanted to maintain their already affluent lifestyle but leave their son $4 million upon their deaths. The Envision program painted a clear picture of the prospects of achieving that goal.

The simulation showed that the couple had only a 7 percent probability of seeing that ideal situation come to fruition, and the downside could be grisly. Even a compromise choice that showed them leaving their son $3 million required a dramatic cutback in their current lifestyle—a compromise they were unwilling to accept. Finally, they agreed that bequeathing their son $2 million while maintaining their lifestyle was a compromise everyone could live with.

"Now, more than ever, it's a tremendous benefit to be able to work with a client in real time, modeling their future," Joe says. "The high level of service we offer our clients demands that we don't let clients walk away with more questions than they had when they walked in. With our new approach, we never have to leave them hanging for answers."

Once the wealth management plan is in place, Joe and his team monitor each client's progress, rebalancing assets when the markets dictate. The team also stays in regular communication with each client, both over the telephone and in person, making sure that their plan reflects any changes in their personal situations as well.

THE NEXT WAVE IN WEALTH MANAGEMENT

This ability to provide instantaneous and comprehensive wealth analysis for each client is the next wave of financial planning for the high net worth client, Joe says. And it is something that all sophisticated clients—regardless of net worth—will be increasingly demanding from their financial advisors, Joe warns.

"Financial advisors are still spending a great deal of time on asset allocations and helping clients determine their proper risk tolerance level, both of which I agree are indispensable," he says. But that needs to be the beginning of the process, not the end, he insists. The next step is being able to illustrate the potential risks and rewards for a variety of different scenarios and then work closely with them to tailor a plan that meets their unique profile.

"For years, our industry has been diligently finding better ways to profile clients, using methods from simple Q&As to sophisticated psychological tests," he says. "Our system provides a far better way to determine a client's own risk tolerance levels, by working with them as a team."

With that single focus in mind, Joe has built a clientele that ranges from Manhattan's towering centers of finance to California's music industry. The clients' backgrounds couldn't be more diverse, but their goals are essentially the same. Each wants to protect what he or she has and provide for the future. And everyone needs someone who understands his or her individual needs and who can build customized solutions to meet those needs.

It's a tall order, but Joe's consistent ability to deliver has earned him a national reputation—as well as innumerable frequent flyer miles, because he will fly anywhere in the country to meet with people who need the unique service he can deliver. That is what got him on a plane to New York with a team member. A client in New York had referred a friend to him that was in need of special work with trusts. She wanted to put in very specific controls around how and when her heirs could gain access to that trust, and she wanted the same people who set up the trust to manage both the overall trust and the underlying investments.

It was clear to Joe that she needed a dynasty trust, which ensures that assets will be available to her children if they ever need them. If they don't need the money, the assets remain in the trust to provide for future generations. Despite being in the center of one of the world's premier financial markets, she was becoming increasingly frustrated because she couldn't find a financial advisor with the expertise to handle each step of establishing and managing that trust. Joe was able to tap into Wachovia Securities' extensive trust background to build exactly what she was looking for.

"It was hard to believe that we were in the heart of the financial world, and we could build a better mousetrap," Joe laughs.

Maybe it's hard for him to believe, but that's what his clients have come to rely on. By managing both sides of each client's balance sheets, Joe and his team are able to provide guidance on every aspect of a client's financial situation, helping him or her achieve every part of the preferred future—no matter what that future may look like. That is the central element that sets the team apart from its competition.

"What happens if a client wants to buy a beach house?" Joe asks. "Many brokers would only notice that money was being taken out of the account for the down payment."

Not Joe. He helps the client decide how to finance the home and which assets to use where. He then sets up the appropriate mortgage based on the client's income, cash flow, and long-term plans. Joe points to a $20 million client who had his trustee call the team because he wanted to buy a house out West.

"In less than one week, our team arranged the financing," Joe remembers. "Another client called about buying a farm. He had already obtained an attractive rate from the federal farm loan program, but because we could immediately see all of his assets, we were able to obtain a very competitive rate and give him a choice."

That ability to consolidate every aspect of a financial plan into one account is increasingly important to high net worth clients. Joe found out how important when he and his team sent letters to existing client outlining this strategy. The response was overwhelming.

"One client, a CEO of an industrial company, called after he received the letter and told me he loves the idea of having everything in one place, especially the convenience of not having to fill out nine hundred forms," Joe says. He wanted someone from the group to contact him immediately about the tax advantages of taking out a mortgage on his home. Another client immediately transferred all her accounts to the group—including her entire relationship with a Florida bank—because she wanted to consolidate everything, including all her loans.

BRINGING INSTITUTIONAL SERVICES TO INDIVIDUALS

The bottom line is that most high net worth investors have come to understand and appreciate a certain level of financial sophistication in their corporate dealings, and they want the same level of service and the same quality of products in managing their personal finances. Joe has built a team designed to bridge that gap. It's a natural evolution in wealth management, Joe says, but it is one that most advisors can't quite span.

The advisors that can make that transition as smooth as possible for the client, though, create deep—and deeply integrated—relationships that go far beyond investment advice. A perfect illustration is the former CEO of a large medical malpractice insurance firm. Joe was hired in the early 1990s as an institutional consultant to help manage some of the firm's assets. The CEO was so impressed with what Joe was able to bring to the institutional side of the business, that he asked him to handle his personal finances as well.

Taking the same holistic approach with his personal finances as they did with the corporate finances, Joe and his team now handle every aspect of the client's life, from refinancing his mortgage to buying a retirement home in Louisiana (although the client is still far from retiring). When he was tapped to head up one of the largest malpractice insurance companies in the country, the client moved to San Francisco, taking Joe's team with him—both to manage his personal finances and as an institutional consultant to the new company.

And that's not an anomaly. "The individuals behind the institutional accounts have been pleased," says Robin Wilcox with the institutional consulting team. "They want the same institutional-caliber investments and advice for their personal accounts, and we can deliver it. Our experience in working with high net worth individuals gives us the skills to convey information and ideas in ways that make sense."

What the clients see is an in-depth, customized analysis of their finances and an investment plan built around their goals and needs. As a team, the group develops investment policy statements for each account, determining which assets classes they should be invested in based on current holdings, incorporating extensive risk-return analysis. Then the team researches and evaluates outside managers finding the right fit for each client within each specific asset class. Finally, they continue to monitor each outside manager, to make sure they are performing as expected.

From this blueprint, high net worth clients receive the same quarterly report that institutional clients receive. That alone is one of the most important services the team provides because, instead of just providing typical hindsight reporting of what happened in the past, the quarterly reports always look to the future. Along with an analysis of performance, each report includes recommendations designed to improve investment performance or enhance the overall financial plan.

These institutional-style reports are integral to the level of service that ultrahigh net worth clients want and that the Optimal Service Group is committed to delivering, says Bill Muth.

"With Robin's background and what she and T.C. and Bryce do on the institutional side, we are able to leverage those strengths with our bigger retail clients, providing those clients with the types of reports, products, and analysis that most retail clients can't get," Bill says.

THAT'S ENTERTAINMENT

That customized approach to wealth management has attracted a unique group of clients to the firm: entertainers. Musicians and other show business personalities suffer from notoriously unpredictable cash flows. They can be hot for six months or six years, raking in millions of dollars from the popularity and then fall off the face of the earth. Joe's job is to keep their portfolios from crashing when cultural tastes shift.

One client came to Joe via the insurance company CEO. One of that client's friends has a son who was beginning to make it big as a musician, netting a seven-figure income in one year. The client recommended the son meet with Joe, so they got together when the son's group was making a tour stop in the area. Working closely with that client's business manager, Joe had developed a wealth management plan that can withstand the vagaries of pop music.

They landed another account when a business manager tapped Joe to help some of his clients get an apartment in New York. The musician had racked up tons of debt and bad credit while still struggling to make it big, and that history was still following him now that he was on the charts. Joe was able to pull together Wachovia Securities' extensive banking, credit, and investment resources to reestablish the client's credit. They paid off his debt and set him up with a $2 million mortgage. Then they took over managing his assets, setting up a conservative portfolio with a broad allocation into stocks and fixed-income instruments.

"This is a very, very high-risk business, so we try to back-end their financial planning," says Sean Driscoll, who works with Joe on the entertainment side of the business. "We try to figure out where these guys want to be financially after the music stops, and in a number of cases we set up bond accounts to create sort of an income sanctuary."

TIME TO GIVE BACK

The team approach to wealth management not only provides clients with a strong safety net, it allows Joe to focus on two of his top priorities: his family and his community. He and his wife Linda are regulars in the schools and activities of their children, Joseph Jr. and Madeline.

"The team helps me maintain my priorities as they should be," he says. "This allows me greater clarity on what is important. Hopefully, I can bring this perspective to benefit my clients."

Joe dedicates many hours every year to organizations such as William & Mary's Endowment Association. He previously sat on the college's Society of the Alumni and Board of Visitors. Now he sits on the board of the Future of Hampton Roads, The Jamestown Yorktown Foundation Inc., Hampton Roads Academy the Greater

Williamsburg Community Trust, and the Virginia Retirement System's Investment Advisory Committee

"I always try to do what's best for my clients and my community," Joe says. He recommends that all brokers spend time in their community and to try to help others.

"If you help others, you will surely benefit. I receive such fulfillment by being involved," he continues. "I'm a big believer that what goes around, comes around. I've been very fortunate in this business, and I'm thrilled to be so involved in giving back to the community."

The Winner's Circle®
America's Best Financial Advisors

AMERICA'S MOST OUTSTANDING FINANCIAL ADVISORS (2004 LIST)

Name and Firm (Listed Alphabetically)	*Client Types*[2]	*Assets*[3] *(as of 2004)*	*Typical Account Size*[4]	*Typical Client Net Worth*[4]
Alexandra Armstrong Armstrong MacIntyre & Severns, Inc.\FSC Securities Corporation, Washington, DC	IND, HNW, FOU, EN	$650,000,000	$1.75 million	$3 million
Nick M Bapis Morgan Stanley, Salt Lake City, UT	HNW, UHNW	$1,900,000,000	$2 million	$5 million+
Patricia A. Bell Merrill Lynch, Short Hills, NJ	HNW	$485,000,000	$2.5 million	$5–10 million
Shelley Bergman Bear Stearns, New York	IND, HNW, UHNW, FOU, EN, CORP	$700,000,000	$2–5 million+	$5–10 million
Richard M. Blosser Morgan Stanley, Los Angeles, CA	UHNW, FOU, EN	$2,100,000,000	$20–$30 million	$20 million–$1 billion+
Thomas J. Buck (Tom) Merrill Lynch, Carmel, IN	IND, HNW, UHNW, FOU	$750,000,000	$1–20 million	$3–4 million
Ron Carson Carson Wealth Management Group/Linsco/Private Ledger, Omaha, NE	HNW	$878,000,000	$5 million+	$5 million+
Nadia T. Cavner U.S. Bancorp Investments, Inc., Springfield, MO	IND, HNW, UHNW, CORP, FOU, EN	$470,000,000	$250,000	$750,000–$2 million
August Cenname "The Cenname Team," Merrill Lynch, Columbus, OH	UHNW	$3,000,000,000	$10–100 million	$25–500 million
Louis J. Chiavacci Merrill Lynch, Coral Gables, FL	UHNW	$2,500,000,000	$25 million	$60 million
Kim Ciccarelli Kantor Ciccarelli Advisory Services/FSC Securities Corporation, Naples, FL	IND, HNW, CORP	$550,000,000	$1–5 million	$3–10 million
Carrie Coghill DB Root & Co./Commonwealth Financial Network, Pittsburgh, PA	IND, HNW	$508,000,000	$2 million+	$3 million+
Jeffrey S. Cohen Lincoln Sagemark, Terrytown, NY	HNW, UHNW	$560,000,000	$2–5 million+	$10–100 million+
Robert Coleman Morgan Stanley, San Francisco, CA	UHNW, FOU	$2,600,000,000	$2–500 million	$10–1billion+
John Cooke Wachovia Securities, Indianapolis, IN	IND, HNW, FOU, EN	$850,000,000	$1–10 million	$1–25 million
Mark T. Curtis Smith Barney, Palo Alto, CA	HNW, UHNW, EN, FOU, CORP	$6,000,000,000	N/A	N/A
Mary M. Deatherage Smith Barney, Little Falls, NJ	IND, HNW, UHNW, FOU, EN	$525,000,000	$2–10 million	$2–50 million

Donald DeWees Sr. Wachovia Securities, Greenville, DE	HNW, UHNW, FOU, EN	$800,000,000	$3–300 million	$5 million+
Robert Dixon Morgan Stanley, Menlo Park, CA	UHNW, FOU, EN	$2,500,000,000	$15–25 million	$25–$50 million
George Dunn Smith Barney, Washington, DC	IND, HNW, UHNW, CORP, FOU, EN	$2,300,000,000	$1.5–4 million	$5–15 million+
Pete Eckerline Merrill Lynch, Wayzata, MN	IND, HNW, UHNW	$600,000,000	$1–15 million+	$2–15 million+
Ric Edelmann Ric Edelmann/ Royal Alliance Associates, Inc., Washington, DC	IND, HNW, UHNW, CORP, FOU	$2,400,000,000	$150,000–2 million	$500,000–5 million
David Ellis III McDonald Financial Group, Cincinnati, OH	IND, HNW, UHNW, CORP, FOU	$920,000,000	$2–5 million+	$4–6 million+
John F. Erdmann III (Jeff) Merrill Lynch, Greenwich, CT	HNW, UHNW	$2,000,000,000	$10 million+	$15 million+
Todd Feltz Feltz WealthPlan/Linsco/Private Ledger, Omaha, NE	IND, HNW	$500,000,000	$500,000– 750,000	$500,000– 750,000
Harry Ford Legg Mason Wood Walker Inc. , Baltimore, MD	IND, HNW, UHNW, FOU, EN	$600,000,000	$500,000– 5 million	$1–10 million
Robert Fragasso The Fragasso Group/ Linsco/Private Ledger, Pittsburgh, PA	IND, HNW, CORP, FOU, EN	$415,000,000	$250,000– 10 million	$1 million
Anthony Gallea Smith Barney, Pittsford, NY	CORP, HNW, UHNW	$2,600,000,000	$1 million	$10 million
Niall J. Gannon Smith Barney, St. Louis, MO	UHNW	$950,000,000	$25 million+	$50 million+
Thomas B. Gau Oregon Pacific Financial Advisors, Inc., Ashland, OR	IND, HNW	$648,000,000	$1–2 million	$2–5 million
Jeffrey S. Gerson Smith Barney, New York, NY	IND, HNW, UHNW, CORP, EN	$1,080,000,000	$2–7 million+	$2–10 million
Saly Glassman Merrill Lynch, Blue Bell, PA	IND, CORP, EN, FOU	$902,000,000	$2 million	$5 million
Greg Glosser RBC Dain Rauscher, Dallas, TX	IND, HNW, UHNW	$450,000,000	$1–5 million	$1–10 million
Jon Goldstein Smith Barney, Menlo Park, CA	HNW, UHNW	$2,400,000,000	$5 million+	$10 million+
M. Keefe Gorman Merrill Lynch, Ithaca, NY	IND, HNW, CORP	5,400,000,000	$1–5 million	$1–15 million+

Advisor	Clients	Assets	Typical Account	Typical Net Worth
Meg Green Meg Green & Assoc./ Royal Alliance Associates, Inc., North Miami Beach, FL	IND, HNW, UHNW, FOU, EN	$510,000,000	$1–3 million	$2–5 million
Al Guernsey Smith Barney, Chicago, IL	HNW, UHNW, CORP, FOU, EN	$1,200,000,000	$2–10 million	n/a
Bill Gurtin Morgan Stanley, Rancho Santa Fe, CA	UHNW	$3,500,000,000	$5 million+	$10 million+
Martin L. Halbfinger UBS Financial Services, Inc., New York, NY	HNW	$1,200,000	$2–10 million	$5–20 million
Jim Hansberger Smith Barney, Atlanta, GA	HNW, UHNW, FAM	$1,500,000,000	$2–10 million	$20 million+
Steven J. Hefter Morgan Stanley, Chicago, IL	HNW, UHNW, CORP, FOU	$750,000,000	$5–10 million	$10–30 million
Thomas E. Hill Legg Mason Wood Walker Inc., Easton, MD	IND, HNW, UHNW, FOU, EN	$800,000,000	$1 million+	$1 million+
David C. Hou Merrill Lynch, Los Angeles, CA	UHNW, FOU, EN	$2,000,000,000	$10 million+	$20 million
Gregory S. Hurlbrink Legg Mason Wood Walker Inc. , Baltimore, MD	IND, HNW, UHNW, CORP, FOU, EN	$600,000,000	$1 million+	$2 million+
John Kulhavi Merrill Lynch, Farmington Hills, MI	IND, HNW, FOU, EN	$640,000,000	$250,000–3 million	$500,000–3 million
Michael Johnston Smith Barney, Irvine, CA	HNW, UHNW	800,000,000	$5–40 million	$10–100 million
Alan K Jusko Wachovia Securities New York, NY	IND, HNW, CORP, FOU, EN	$600,000,000	$500–40 million	$1 million
Brian J. Kelly Smith Barney, Florham Park, NJ	HNW, UHNW, CORP, EN, IND	$500,000,000	$1–20 million+	$1–20 million+
David W. Knall McDonald Investments Inc., Indianapolis, IN	IND, HNW, UHNW, CORP, FOU, EN	$3,600,000,000	$3 million+	$5 million
Timothy B. Kneen Smith Barney Denver, CO	UHNW, FOU, EN, FOU, EN, HNW	$1,100,000,000	$10–25 million	$15–40 million
Alan R. Leist Strategic Financial Services, LLC, Utica, NY/Palm Beach, FL	IND, HNW, UHNW, FOU, EN	$650,000,000	$100,000–20 million	$250,000–75 million
Charles J. Lewis, Jr. Wells Fargo, Waco, TX	IND, HNW, CORP, FOU, EN	$585,000,000	$1.5–2.5 million	$1.5–4 million

Thomas D. Lips UBS Financial Services, Inc., Hartford, CT	HNW, UHNW, FOU, EN	$700,000,000	$1–10 million	$5–15 million
Malcolm A. Makin Professional Planning Group/Raymond James Financial Services, Westerly, RI	IND, HNW, UHNW, EN	$575,000,000	$500,000–2 million	$1.25–3 million
Roland R. Manarin Manarin Securities Corp., Omaha, NE	IND, CORP	$500,000,000	$1–65 million	$5 million–2 billion+
James D. McCabe Wells Fargo, Beverly Hills, CA	IND, UHNW, FOU, EN	$900,000,000	$5 million+	$5 million+
Michael McGee Smith Barney, San Francisco, CA	HNW, UHNW	$500,000,000	$5–20 million	$5–50 million
Marvin H. McIntyre Legg Mason Wood Walker Inc., Washington, DC	IND, HNW, UHNW, CORP, FOU, EN	$2,000,000,000[1]	$5–10 million	$5–10 million
Hank A. McLarty, Jr. Morgan Stanley Atlanta, GA	HNW, UHNW, FOU, EN	$800,000,000	$2–100 million+	$10 –100 million+
Kirke Meeks JPMorgan, Scottsdale, AZ	HNW, UNHW	$496,000,000	$1–25 million	$5 million
Walter Meranze Wachovia Securities, Washington Crossing, PA	IND, HNW, UHNW, CORP	$1,800,000,000	$2–5 million+	$2–7 million
Frank J. Mirabella, Jr. Merrill Lynch, Galleria, TX	HNW	$500,000,000	$1–3 million	$1–3 million
John Mockovciak III Robert W. Baird & Co., Inc., Dallas, TX	HNW, FAM, FOU	$450,000,000	$1.5–4 million	$1.5–6 million
Joseph W. Montgomery Wachovia Securities, Williamsburg, VA	IND, HNW, UHNW, CORP, FOU, EN	$6,500,000,000	$3–30 million	$5–40 million
Kevin H. Myeroff NCA Financial Planners/ Royal Alliance Associates, Inc., Cleveland, OH	IND, HNW CORP, FOU, EN	$500,000,000	$500,000–5 million	$1–20 million
David A. Novelli Smith Barney, Houston, TX	UHNW, FOU, EN	$1,200,000,000	$3–300 million	$10 million+
Sharon Oberlander Merrill Lynch, Chicago, IL	HNW, FOU	$573,000,000	$2–10 million	$2.5–20 million
John D. Olson Merrill Lynch, New York, NY	HNW, CORP	$1,200,000,000	$2–20 million	$5–30 million
Dan Osborne Banc of America Investment Services, San Francisco, CA	HNW, FOU	$1,500,000,000	$5 million	$10–15 million
Larry Palmer Smith Barney, Los Angeles, CA	HNW, UHNW, CORP	$750,000,000	$1–1.5 million	$3–50 millio
Andrew Perry Deutsche Bank Alex.Brown, New York, NY	HNW, UHNW	$2,500,000,000	$5 million+	$10 million+

Brian Pfeifler Morgan Stanle, New York, NY	UHNW, FOU	$3,000,000,000	$15–250 million	$20 million–$2 billion
Mark Pollard Merrill Lynch, Princeton, NJ	HNW, UHNW, FOU	$1,900,000,000	$2–20 million	$5–25 million
John W. Rafal Essex Financial Services, Inc., Essex, CT	IND, HNW, UHNW, CORP, FOU, EN	$1,300,000,000	$1.7 million	$2–20 million
Gary L. Ran UBS Financial Services, Inc., Farmington Hills, MI	HNW, UHNW	$1,225,000,000	$1–65 million	$1–2 billion
John P. Roe Smith Barney, San Francisco, CA	HNW, UHNW, CORP, FOU, EN	$3,500,000,000	$5 million+	$5 million+
R. Luke Rohrbaugh Wachovia Securities, Lemoyne, PA	HNW, UHNW, CORP FOU, EN	$1,275,400,000	$1–$5 million+	$2–$20 million+
Rebecca S. Rothstein Smith Barney, Los Angeles, CA	HNW , UHNW,	$850,000,000	$2.5–10 million	$10 million+
Richard Saperstein Bear Stearns, New York, NY	HNW, UHNW, CORP	$6,500,000,000	$2–$100 million	$5–$500 million
Phil Scott Merrill Lynch, Bellevue, WA	HNW, UHNW	$700,000,000	$5 million+	$5 million+
Mark Sear Merrill Lynch, Los Angeles, CA	UHNW, EN	$3,000,000,000	$1million–1 billion+	$5 million
Martin Shafiroff Lehman Brothers, New York, NY	HNW, UHNW, EN	$100,000,000,000	$1–100 million+	$1–$5 billion+
Raj Sharma Merrill Lynch, Boston, MA	HNW, UNHW, EN	$2,500,000,000	$5–50 million	$10–100 million
Kay Shirley, Ph.D. Financial Development Corp./Mutual Service Corp., Atlanta, GA	IND	$424,000,000	$100,000+	$1.3 million
Jim Snyder Legg Mason Wood Walker Inc., Bowie, MD	IND, HNW, UHNW, CORP, FOU	$580,000,000	$500,000–10 million	$750,000–12 million
Robert M. Stulberg Merrill Lynch, Bloomfield Hills, MI	HNW, UHNW	$1,000,000,000[1]	$5 million+	$5–100 million+
Scott B. Tiras American Express Financial Advisors, Houston, TX	IND, HNW	$750,000,000	$1–2 million	$3 million
Paul E. Tramontano Smith Barney, New York, NY	UHNW	$2,500,000,000	$5 million+	$20 million+
Dean D. Trindle Merrill Lynch, Cincinnati, OH	HNW, UHNW, IND	$2,000,000,000	$1–10 million	$1–20 million
Kathy Tully Morgan Stanley, Ontario, CA	HNW, EN	$450,000,000	$1–5 million	$2–5 million
Lori A. Van Dusen Smith Barney, Rochester, NY	UHNW, EN, FOU	$2,500,000,000	$10–500 million	$20 million+

Ken Van Wagenen Wells Fargo, Los Angeles, CA	HNW, UHNW, CORP, FOU, EN	$1,100,000,000	$2 million+	$5 million+
Gregory Vaughan Morgan Stanley, Menlo Park, CA	UHNW, FOU, EN	$3,000,000,000	$20–25 million	$50 million+
Ira A. Walker Morgan Stanley, Red Bank, NJ	HNW, UHNW, CORP, FOU, EN	$1,500,000,000[1]	$5 million+	$25 million+
Ron Weiner RDM Financial Group, Inc., Westport, CT	IND, HNW, UHNW, CORP, FOU	n/a	$2–10 million	$2–6 million+
Alan Whitman Morgan Stanley, Pasadena, CA	UHNW, HNW, IND, FOU, EN	$980,000,000	$1–5 million+	$2–5 million+
Pauline F. D. Yore Wells Fargo, San Jose, CA	HNW, UHNW, FOU FOU, EN	$650,000,000	$5–20 million	$35 million
Drew Zager Morgan Stanley, Los Angeles, CA	UHNW, CORP, FOU	$4,400,000,000	$30–100 million+	$100 million+
Charles C. Zhang Zhang & Associates, a financial advisory branch of American Express, Portage, MI	IND, HNW	$500,000,000	$500,000–5 million	$1–6 million
Richard Zinman Smith Barney, New York, NY	UHNW	$2,500,000,000	$10–25 million	$15–35 million

Notes:

[1]Actual number is greater.

[2]Client Types:

IND = Individual (Net worth of $1 million and less, exclusive of primary residence)

HNW = High Net Worth (Greater than $1 million and less than $10 million, exclusive of primary residence)

UHNW = Ultra High Net Worth ($10 million and more, exclusive of primary residence)

[3]Custodied and noncustodied; asset types are considered (e.g., managed money is weighted heavier than restricted stock or institutional assets); prorated share of partnership assets included.

[4]This is core data; actual range may broaden significantly.

[5]Revenue is part of ranking algorithm, but is kept confidential (see Preface).

THE WOMEN'S WINNER'S CIRCLE®—AMERICA'S MOST OUTSTANDING WOMEN FINANCIAL ADVISORS (2004 LIST)

(Listed Alphabetically)

Diane Alecci, Merrill Lynch, Paramus, NJ — $450,000,000
HNW and retail executives, physicians, and women; full wealth management services including comprehensive financial planning and banking services; managed money, portfolio management.

Wanda Austin, Legg Mason, Newport News, VA — $206,000,000
HNW and retail physicians and small business owners; full wealth management services, including trust and estate planning and long-term care; portfolio management, managed money.

Nancy Barrette, Wachovia Securities, Birmingham, MI — n/a
401k's, profit sharing, and defined benefit plans including participants; financial planning, managed money.

Patricia Bell, Merrill Lynch, Short Hills, NJ — $485,000,000
HNW; Comprehensive planning, estate planning; managed money, portfolio management; outsourced family office.

Nadia Cavner, U.S. Bancorp Investments, Inc., Springfield, MO — $470,000,000
Individuals; managed money; comprehensive financial planning; diversification strategies

---

Carrie Coghill, D.B. Root and Company/
Commonwealth Financial Network, Pittsburgh, PA — $508,000,000
HNW and retail; comprehensive financial planning; managed money; estate, tax and insurance planning; retirement planning.

Valery Craane, Merrill Lynch, New York — $894,000,000
HNW and UHNW families, businesses and philanthropies; fee-based financial planning, strategies and borrowing explained and supported in five languages.

Beth Dale, Smith Barney, Atlanta, GA — $600,000,000
HNW and retail executives and single women; financial planning; portfolio management, managed money, options strategies including hedging and covered calls, concentrated stock positions.

Mary Deatherage, Smith Barney, Little Falls, NJ — $525,000,000
HNW, retail; comprehensive financial planning and wealth management services; managed money, insurance, liability management.

Diane Doolin, Smith Barney, Pasadena, CA — $225,000,000
HNW, UHNW, small business corporate foundations; comprehensive wealth management, incl. financial planning, trust and estate planning, philanthropic service, business and family advisory services; managed money.

Saly A. Glassman, Merrill Lynch, Blue Bell, PA — $902,000,000
HNW, UHNW; complete wealth management services including financial planning, credit services and trust and estate planning.

Meg Green, Meg Green and Assoc./Royal Alliance, N. Miami Beach, FL — $510,000,000
HNW families; comprehensive financial planning; managed money, portfolio management.

Nina Hakim, Morgan Stanley, Short Hills, NJ — n/a
HNW families; manage equity and fixed income portfolios, managed money, trust and estate planning.

Trudy Haussmann, Newport Beach, CA, — $325,000,000
Haussmann Financial, Inc./Securities America,Newport Beach, CA
Individuals planning for or already in retirement; financial plans to address long-term care, insurance and estate planning; managed money.

Cynthia Hewitt, Merrill Lynch, Wilmington, DE $460,000,000
Multi generations of HNW families; financial planning, trust and estate planning; portfolio management, managed money.

Barbara Hudock, Hudock, Moyer and Associates/Wachovia Securities,Williamsport, PA $240,000,000
HNW, retail and small businesses; comprehensive financial planning, trust and estate planning, retirement planning; philanthropic services; managed money.

Debbie Jorgensen, Merrill Lynch, San Francisco, CA $475,000,000
Families, corporate executives and businesses. Provide wealth management services including comprehensive financial planning, trust and estate planning, cash-flow projections, concentrated stock strategies, philanthropic services, third-party money management and family offices services.

Susan Kaplan, Kaplan Financial Services/LPL, Newton, MA $400,000,000
HNW and retail families; comprehensive financial planning; portfolio management, mutual funds.

Sheila Keator, Wachovia Securities, Pittsfield, MA $325,000,000
HNW and retail families; comprehensive financial planning; managed money, covered call strategies, portfolio management.

Laurie Kent , Legg Mason, McLean, VA $260,000,000
HNW and retail families; trade associations and not-for-profits; comprehensive financial planning; retirement, education and estate planning; managed money.

Diane B. Kirchner, Bank of America, San Francisco, CA $500,000,000
UHNW, HNW executives and families; single stock diversification strategies, broad portfolio management with sophisticated hedging and asset allocation strategies, alternative investments; managed money.

Dana Orleans Kishter, Morgan Stanley, Washington, D.C. n/a
HNW entrepreneurs, professionals and families; comprehensive personal analyses; portfolio management, managed money.

Rita N.A. Mansour, McDonald Financial Group, Toledo, OH $250,000,000
HNW professionals and business owners, endowments, foundations; comprehensive financial planning, business succession planning, banking/credit needs; trust and estate planning, philanthropic services.

Judith McGee, McGee Financial Strategies/Raymond James Financial Services, Portland, OR $220,000,000
Retail, HNW; comprehensive financial planning; equity income portfolio management, managed money, charitable gifting strategies.

Susan Moseley, Moseley Investment Management/Royal Alliance, Bradenton, FL $300,000,000
Multigenerational HNW families; family wealth management including tax, real estate, and estate planning; managed money, managed portfolios.

Sharon Oberlander, Merrill Lynch, Chicago, IL $573,000,000
Comprehensive financial planning; HNW, entrepreneurs, business owners; portfolio management, managed money; liability management.

Jane Rojas, Rojas Investment Consulting Group, Wachovia Securitie,Tuscon, AZ $252,000,000
HNW individuals, families and businesses; financial planning; asset allocation strategies, fixed-income portfolio management, mutual funds.

Pamela Jo Rosenau, Smith Barney, New York, NY $425,000,000
HNW, corporate execs, professionals, women; financial planning; portfolio management, hedge funds, private equity, asset allocation strategies.

Rebecca Rothstein, Smith Barney, Los Angeles, CA n/a
HNW, UHNW, investment management consulting services; alternative investments; financial planning.

Nan Shertzer, Merrill Lynch, Dallas, TX $493,000,000
HNW entrepreneurs and families; financial planning; full wealth management services; managed money.

Kay Shirley, Ph.D., Financial Development Corp./Mutual Service Corp., Atlanta, GA $424,000,000
Retirement planning for everyone; managed money; asset allocation strategies; comprehensive financial planning.

Sandee Smith, Smith Barney, Kansas City, MO $600,000,000
HNW, corporations, foundations; wealth management services, fixed-income portfolio strategies, asset allocation strategies, investment policy development.

Andrea Soter, Morgan Stanley, Oxnard, CA n/a
HNW and retail retirees and those nearing retirement; financial planning; trust and estate planning; managed money.

Sherri Stephens, Raymond James Financial Services, Flint, MI $250,000,000
HNW, retirement plans; comprehensive financial planning, trust and estate planning; managed money.

Kathy Tully, Morgan Stanley, Ontario, CA $450,000,000
HNW business owners, executives and families; financial planning; estate planning, retirement planning, portfolio management, managed money.

Lori Van Dusen, Smith Barney, Rochester, NY $2,500,000,000
Comprehensive financial planning; investment consulting services, alternative investments; wealth preservation strategies; UHNW, HNW, endowments.

Theresa Ward, Merrill Lynch, Bloomington, MN $1,100,000,000
UHNW corporate executives and individuals, institutions; full wealth management and estate planning services; 10B5-1 plans, hedging and liquidity strategies for concentrated stock positions as well as charitable trusts and foundations.

Lisa Strange Weatherby, Smith Barney, Jacksonville, FL $380,000,000
HNW, UHNW, foundations, endowments, nonprofits; financial and estate planning; investment policy development, managed money, asset allocation strategies, asset/liability studies, performance measurement and attribution, alternative investments and philanthropic services.

Judith L. Werbitt, Merrill Lynch, White Plains, NY $550,000,000
HNW, lines of credit and retirement services for small to medium-sized businesses; full wealth management services, including comprehensive financial planning, trust and estate planning, philanthropic services, credit services; managed money.

Pauline Yore, Wells Fargo, San Jose, CA $650,000,000
UHNW, HNW; full wealth management services, including trust and estate planning, tax planning credit services, and residential and commercial real estate planning; portfolio management, managed money.

Notes:

Client Types:

IND = Individual (net worth of $1 million and less, exclusive of primary residence)

HNW = High Net Worth (greater than $1 million and less than $10 million, exclusive of primary residence)

UHNW = Ultra High Net Worth ($10 million and more, exclusive of primary residence)

Please see Preface for criteria.

CRITERIA

The Winner's Circle is an advocacy organization independent of the firms involved and does not receive compensation from the participating firms or any of its affiliates in exchange for ranking purposes. The organization promotes its missions of best practices and the highest code of ethics, integrity, and professionalism in the industry. The ranking process begins with a survey of approximately 100 securities firms, insurance companies, banks, independent financial advisor practices, and other organizations that employ Series-7 registered financial advisors; each of these firms promotes objective and independent advice with open-architecture access to financial products. These 2004 updated lists, based on prior year's performance measurements, includes financial professionals with a minimum of seven years of financial services experience, and other weighted criteria ranging from acceptable compliance records and wealth management focus to revenue generated and the amount of assets advised by the advisor. The ranking does not consider client portfolio performance. Please see www.winnerscirclenet.com for more information.